Transforming Service

Transforming Service

Reflections of Student Services Professionals
in Theological Education

Edited by
SHONDA R. JONES
and PAMELA R. LIGHTSEY

Afterword by
FRANK M. YAMADA

PICKWICK *Publications* · Eugene, Oregon

TRANSFORMING SERVICE
Reflections of Student Services Professionals in Theological Education

Copyright © 2020 Wipf and Stock Publishers. All rights reserved. Except for brief quotations in critical publications or reviews, no part of this book may be reproduced in any manner without prior written permission from the publisher. Write: Permissions, Wipf and Stock Publishers, 199 W. 8th Ave., Suite 3, Eugene, OR 97401.

Pickwick Publications
An Imprint of Wipf and Stock Publishers
199 W. 8th Ave., Suite 3
Eugene, OR 97401

www.wipfandstock.com

PAPERBACK ISBN: 978-1-5326-9425-7
HARDCOVER ISBN: 978-1-5326-9426-4
EBOOK ISBN: 978-1-5326-9427-1

Cataloguing-in-Publication data:

Names: Jones, Shonda R., editor. | Lightsey, Pamela R., editor. | Yamada, Frank M., 1966–, afterword.

Title: Transforming service : reflections of student services professionals in theological education / edited by Shonda R. Jones and Pamela R. Lightsey ; afterword by Frank Yamada.

Description: Eugene, OR : Pickwick Publications, 2020 | Includes bibliographical references.

Identifiers: ISBN 978-1-5326-9425-7 (paperback) | ISBN 978-1-5326-9426-4 (hardcover) | ISBN 978-1-5326-9427-1 (ebook)

Subjects: LCSH: Theology—Study and teaching.

Classification: BV4020 .T735 2020 (paperback) | BV4020 .T735 (ebook)

Manufactured in the U.S.A.   05/14/20

Contents

Part Two: **Called or Captive?**

Part Three: **Building Institutional Capacity**

Illustrations and Tables

ILLUSTRATIONS

TABLES

Acknowledgments

THIS HAS BEEN A labor of love done within a community of practitioners who are dedicated to students in theological education. We are grateful for the contributions of those who made this publication possible. We are especially thankful for the support and resources of the Association of Theological Schools in the United States and Canada. Particularly of note is the ongoing leadership of Mary H. Young, who provides oversight for the Student Services Personnel Network (SPAN) and who has embraced our vision and provided the needed resources for contributors to put forth their best work. We also acknowledge the work early on of Jo Ann Deasy with SPAN and her continued support of institutional initiatives that enrich our efforts with students. To our student research assistant, Graham Lee, we express our deepest thanks for spending countless hours assisting with this project.

We acknowledge and express sincere gratitude to the many colleagues who submitted proposals and accepted our invitation to be a part of this seminal book in theological education. Many thanks to Wake Forest University School of Divinity and Meadville Lombard Theological School for providing fertile ground for innovative practices and imagination in student affairs and student services.

Finally, we are thankful for students in theological education who make the work of transformation possible in the church and in the communities they serve.

Introduction
Embracing Transformation

STUDENT AFFAIRS AS A profession emerged in higher education as a means to monitor and react to student behaviors. Over the years, student affairs practice (also known as student personnel, student services, and student development) has shifted to focus on the growth and development of students spanning pre-matriculation to graduation and beyond. For our purposes we will more regularly use the term, *student services personnel* though this is considered to be a dated term since the work is far more nuanced than simply providing services. However, the terminology is less essential than how the field and profession has actually progressed. Though the aforementioned shifts in student affairs practice is a reality in higher education institutions, for far too long the voices of student services professionals have been situated on the margins in theological education. Student services professionals in theological education are often absent from theological scholarship and higher education literature. Further, their work and contributions are often considered to be peripheral to the main actors or contributors in theological schools.

As we began this project, we started with the claim that as administrators we are central to the educational task within institutional settings. Situating student services personnel in this way is essential to the work of theological education and legitimizes the profession within higher education. This is a seminal book developed for and by student services professionals. Although our primary audience is student services personnel, we hope this work will resonate with all administrators in theological education and beyond. We recognize that our work is unique and innovative in that it puts the student services professional and their work with divinity students center-stage. Amid the various and serious changes afoot within the church and academy, there is a need for astute and perceptive expertise to assist professionals and institutions in transforming how to reach, serve, and sustain those they wish to enroll—namely students.

This volume, the first of its kind, brings perspectives from experienced administrators on a variety of topics related to student services administrative leadership—from understanding the conceptual models that guide the work and gaining deeper knowledge of institutional contexts, to executing academic and co-curricular goals and recognizing the challenges of doing this work as shown through history. Thus, chapters include original and scholarly research, conceptual papers, and reflective essays. Given the need and desire for theological institutions to create vibrant learning communities, chapters focus on theory and holistic practices, and the various forms of diversity that exist in an ever-changing church and world. It is crucial for administrative leaders in theological education to engage within a community of practice attentive to the needs of diverse students, as well as to thoughtfully reflect on their own vocational identity as student services professionals amid vast changes within the profession. This is an offering designed to establish and sustain conversations among student services professionals in theological schools about the nature of the profession and the students they serve, and to more fully educate those who may not understand the role of student services personnel as theological educator. The aim is to provide a rich combination of useful information, reflective instruction on a host of student and professional leadership issues, and animated narratives on the ways different colleagues address common student affairs practices and challenges in their context.

The book is organized in three major sections. In Part One (chapters 1–5), "Theoretical Frameworks," contributors introduce frames that distinctly guide and ground the work of student affairs professionals. We begin with Shonda R. Jones' "Graduate Theological School Choice: A Case for Multiplicity," in which Jones explores—through the narratives of students of color—ways that racial/ethnic minority masters-level students engage the school choice process in deciding to pursue graduate theological education. Using a comprehensive conceptual model, Jones provides critical information that can help theological schools to reach, cultivate, and serve students of color from the start of their process. With an important shift to the experiences that some students encounter after entering seminary, Anastasia E. B. Kidd then focuses on understanding and constructively grappling with students' crises of faith as an educational frame for student development. In her chapter, "Supporting Seminarians Through Crises of Faith as a Means of Transformative Learning," Kidd uses transformative learning theory to suggest best practices for supporting students having crises of faith and how institutions can develop methods that are explicit to the curricula to address and further understand these crises. Following this, Yvette D. Wilson-Barnes provides sharp focus on burnout with student affairs administrators and student services practitioners in "So that you can Endure: Pastoral and Prophetic Insights as Competencies for Graduate Theological Student Services." Adding specific and essential professional competencies, Wilson-Barnes provides administrators with ways to be personally sustained and continuously successful in the profession. Drawing on Applied Critical Leadership Theory, Joanne Solis-Walker demonstrates a possible path for institutions to be culturally responsive communities utilizing transformative leadership approaches in order to better serve Latinx students. Here, it is argued that cultural responsiveness includes critical pedagogy that is linked to the everydayness of life for students. Donna Foley's chapter proposes an integral ecology of vocation. In "Home with Movement," Foley provides a poetic frame in which both students and student services professionals are encouraged to take seriously movement, location (home), and vocation as essential to formation and spirituality. Each of these chapters provide important theoretical frames and concepts that can be valuable in transformative service to students.

In an intentional and provocative way, Part Two, "Called or Captive?" (chapters 6–10), provides space for practitioners to think deeply and theologically on their vocational tasks, the rhythms of work, and the institutional and environmental conditions emerging. Posed as a question, this section is an inquiry for professionals gifted for administrative ministry and also for those who may be confined by traditional, rather than transformative, ways of doing theological education. To lead this section, in "The Lord Requires *What* of me?" C. Mark Batten and Shelly E. Hart reflect on the vocational call of student services administrators and the ways in which their work and the work of colleagues in the profession is ministry. Using a case study approach through the lens of the reflective practitioner, Graham McKeague and Ashley VanBemmelen examine various enrollment practices in theological education. Specifically, the backdrop is a particular setting in which enrollment professionals are affirmed as unique contributors to institutional contexts as they have the potential to articulate the unfolding narratives of prospective students, the institution, and larger narrative of the Gospel. In "Bureaucratic Grace," Vince McGlothin-Eller provides an overview of the role of the registrar and the qualities and competencies that are crucial. Similarly focused on a particular role within the seminary context, in Adam J. Poluzzi's chapter, he considers how culture is communicated by way of the admissions officer. Through a qualitative study, Poluzzi unpacks how admissions officers have communicated culture to prospective students and their perception of effective methods for such communication. Rounding out this part of the book, Pamela R. Lightsey is attentive to how campuses and administrators respond to twenty-first-century era student outcries and protests. Lightsey challenges us to move beyond using conciliatory crisis management and to consider other campus crisis management approaches, especially in light of issues of racism and other -isms. By raising questions, engaging deep reflection and praxis, and offering new perspectives of practices, this section offers student services personnel tools to embrace notions of calling and consider ways to be free to do creative and transformative work.

Building institutional capacity is the emphasis of Part Three (chapters 11–16). This section is attentive to how student services administrative leadership can be transformative within the context of theological education. This last and final part is concerned with learnings and practices that build our capacity toward a brighter and more informed future as theological educators. Thus, it includes a reflection, "Staff Leadership: Forming Collaborative Teams and Hospitable Academic Communities," by Alexandria Hofmann Macias on building effective teams between staff and faculty with keen insight on the leadership capacity of staff. Next, Katherine H. Smith and Amy E. Steele offer wisdom about their own theological school setting as a means of sharing resources for student services personnel and institutions interested in enhancing their practices in radical hospitality with LGBTQ+ seminary students in their chapter on "Radical Hospitality." Recognizing the changing demographics in theological education, Jo Ann Sharkey Reinowski draws attention to the need to transform academic advising in order to have better student success outcomes in her chapter, "[Degree] Planning Ahead." Naming an important shift in capacity building, Reid A. Kisling notes the changing nature of theological education, particularly, with student development. Here, Kisling argues that there has been a change from traditional student growth models to emphasis on learning outcomes. Further, in his chapter "In Service of Character Formation," Kisling posits that character formation is part of the task of student development in theological education, and thus, offers ways to consider the development of character as a part of our shared work. In the last two chapters of this section, Lillian Hallstrand Lammers offers guidance on vocational discernment and career planning in "A Lamp unto Their Feet." Here, Hallstrand Lammers emphasizes how institutions must partner with their students to support discernment and career planning efforts. Kris Bentley, Charisse L. Gillett, and Windy Kidd identifies the clear theological and financial challenges that seminary students face. They offer suggested practices and policies that can make a difference to students and institutions in the final chapter entitled, "Transforming Economic Challenges."

The book is organized in this way to usher readers through foundational material that introduces theory and then provides ample space for readers to learn about how this is embodied in particular practices across various administrative roles and tasks for the student services professional. Understanding that the voices and work of student services professionals are essential to theological education is an initial step in embracing transformation for the work ahead.

PART ONE

Theoretical Frameworks

CHAPTER 1

Graduate Theological School Choice
A Case for Multiplicity

SHONDA R. JONES

AMID ALL THE CHANGE occurring within graduate theological education, the student profile of those attending theology schools has shifted dramatically with more racial/ethnic minority students seeking graduate ministry degrees. Reflecting on this hallmark shift in what historically has been a space that has been white and male-centered, theological institutions must adapt strategies and service models to attract, retain, and educate students of color. Thus, the work before us is to deeply examine the potential pool of candidates attending seminaries and understand more fully the students of color in our midst. Unfortunately, assumptions are often made about who these students are, their motivations for seeking graduate ministry degrees, and what they need to excel in theological education. Oftentimes there is the inexplicable notion that these are monolithic communities or that there are not important differences that require attention and distinct pedagogical strategies needed inside and outside the classroom. As theological educators and student services professionals, it is essential that we consider the layered realities and multiplicity of students of color in order to cultivate a meaningful and sustained culture in which these students can thrive. It is this backdrop that motivated me to make this the focus of my research and subsequent dissertation work.[1]

---

1. Jones, "Graduate Theology School Choice," 6. Much of this chapter originally appeared in the author's dissertation, which is available in full online through ProQuest.

This chapter, using data that emerged from my doctoral research, examines particularly how the school choice process unfolds for US racial/ethnic students enrolled in the Master of Divinity (MDiv) degree program at Wake Forest University School of Divinity. That is to say, I will focus attention on how students in a particular divinity school describe their decision-making as they considered graduate theological education. This discovery takes place as a result of twenty-seven students of color being interviewed and sharing individual stories of their lives, family context, educational background, aspirations, and vocational goals. Further, each student of color talked specifically about their graduate theology school choice process. These students are African-American, Biracial, Latinx, and Multiracial students enrolled in the MDiv degree program in an ecumenical university-related divinity school. Those interviewed represent a diverse group of students with different backgrounds. While the mode age is twenty-three years old, ages of the student participants ranged from twenty-three years old to sixty years old, with an average age of thirty years old. Though there are commonalities in some cases, no single story is exactly the same. As each individual is unique, so is their narrative. Racial/ethnic minority students are not uniform and offer distinctive and personal accounts of their aims, opinions, beliefs, motivations, and values. The narratives of these students represent the weaving together of stories that highlight the individuality of persons (habitus—their system of values and beliefs that shape their views and interpretations[2]), while also holding in tension the structural contexts that make up the material and economic realities of not only persons, but communities of peoples. Thus, the process of *how* racial/ethnic students choose the MDiv program has not been completely clear. This is what I would hope to uncover by centering the narratives of students of color.

Let me briefly summarize the relevance of examining students of color and why their choice process is crucial to theological schools. Graduate theological education in America and Canada has recently demonstrated enrollment stability after years of a dramatic decrease in student enrollment in theological schools accredited by the Association of Theological Schools (ATS). However, pressure remains in what has traditionally been considered the gold standard degree—the Master of Divinity. The number of students enrolled in the MDiv went from about 29,300 in 1998 to 28,400 in fall 2017.[3] It is important to note that the MDiv reached its peak enrollment at nearly 35,000 student headcount in 2006. Recently, the overall numbers are encouraging with 50 percent of all ATS schools having enrollment increases

---

2. See chapters 2–3 in Bourdieu, *Outline of a Theory of Practice.*

3. Meinzer, "Master's Enrollment," 1.

in overall enrollment, and 45 percent of all ATS schools had enrollment increases in the MDiv.[4] Much of the gains are evident for evangelical Protestant theological schools, with at least half of the schools having experienced enrollment increases in every degree category from 2016 to 2018. The reality is a bit different for mainline Protestant theological schools where only 40 percent of the schools experienced enrollment increases in the MDiv. However, 60 percent of all ATS schools showed enrollment increases in the professional MA category.[5] While there is obvious growth in professional MA degree enrollment, there also appears to be growth potential in the MDiv with racial/ethnic students. Racial/ethnic minority students enrolled in graduate theological education grew from 13 percent in 1990 to 41 percent in 2017, according to ATS data. Looking at these numbers, I would argue that after a decade of decline, enrollment stabilization has occurred, in part, due to the influx of students of color to graduate theological education. The shifts in the religious environment and those attracted to theology schools will have lasting consequences on theological institutions of the future. The changing trends in graduate theological education have implications for student recruitment, enrollment, and retention, as well as how the school choice process unfolds for particular students considering vocations where theological education is important.

Drawing on data collected through interviews with students of color enrolled in a MDiv program, I examine how their habitus and other social and cultural capital shapes the process of choosing divinity school. I do so by employing Perna's conceptual model[6] of student college choice as a theoretical frame with a focus on (1) the individual's habitus; (2) school and community context; (3) the higher education context; and (4) the broader social, economic, and policy context (see figure 1). Drawing on a conceptual model that integrates both economic and sociological perspectives, I assumed that students' graduate school decisions are determined, at least in part, by their habitus. Thus, this chapter focuses on the students' habitus, or the system of values and beliefs that shape their views and interpretations. Similarly, I listened for the structural and cultural factors, or organizational habitus, experienced within the undergraduate and other institutional contexts from which racial/ethnic MDiv students emerge. Measures of social and cultural capital that include race, financial resources, and academic preparation and achievement, play an important role in explaining the educational decisions of racial/ethnic students. By exploring these influences, I

4. Meinzer, "Closer Look at Enrollment," 1.
5. Meinzer, "Closer Look at Enrooment," 1.
6. Perna, "Studying College Access and Choice," 99–149.

hope to offer insights into the graduate theology school choice of racial/ethnic MDiv students.

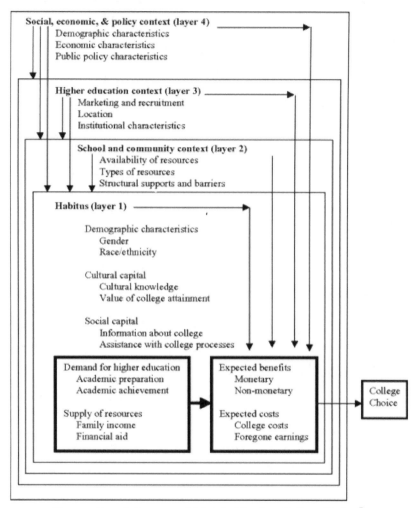

Social, economic, & policy context (layer 4)
    Demographic characteristics
    Economic characteristics
    Public policy characteristics

Higher education context (layer 3)
    Marketing and recruitment
    Location
    Institutional characteristics

School and community context (layer 2)
    Availability of resources
    Types of resources
    Structural supports and barriers

Habitus (layer 1)

    Demographic characteristics
      Gender
      Race/ethnicity

    Cultural capital
      Cultural knowledge
      Value of college attainment

    Social capital
      Information about college
      Assistance with college processes

Demand for higher education
    Academic preparation
    Academic achievement

Supply of resources
    Family income
    Financial aid

Expected benefits
    Monetary
    Non-monetary

Expected costs
    College costs
    Foregone earnings

College Choice

Figure 1. Perna's Conceptual Model of Student College Choice.[7]

Though Perna's model specifically examines choice as students move from high school to college, her model can serve as a useful framing of choice as students move from undergraduate studies to post-baccalaureate education—specifically, graduate theological education. While all layers of this model aids in a deeper and nuanced understanding of the school choice

7. Adapted from Perna, "Studying College Access and Choice," 117.

process, I am most interested in magnifying the first layer of Perna's model. Habitus can be linked to one's embedded social and cultural capital and represents a series of internalized dispositions that individuals use to form perceptions, decisions, and choices.[8] My interest is not so much in *why* racial/ethnic students choose a particular theology school, but in *how* these students engaged the school choice process. How is it that these racial/ethnic students decided to enroll in the MDiv program? What does the choice process for this group look like? What internalized messages were front of mind for these students as they decided to pursue their theological degree? Discoveries from these questions can inform student affairs practice and institutional praxis in theological schools, seminaries, and divinity schools.

UNDERSTANDING SCHOOL CHOICE

A number of studies examine undergraduate college choice.[9] Among the most commonly cited model related to college choice is Hossler and Gallagher's[10] three-stage model of *predisposition, search,* and *choice.* The initial stage outlined in Hossler and Gallager's model is *predisposition,* which typically occurs between seventh and tenth grades in high school. In this stage, students develop aspirations and interest toward attending college. The second or *search* stage is when students begin their college search by gathering information about colleges. According to Hossler and Gallagher, it is at this stage that students determine an initial group of colleges and universities that they will consider applying to and proceed to gather information about the institutions. Students also develop preferences among institutions and consider an ability to pay, along with considering criteria for admissions. Likewise, students develop expectations and perceptions about the institution. *Search,* at the undergraduate level, typically is during the tenth and twelfth grade, while the third stage, also known as *choice,* occurs in the eleventh and twelfth grades when students select an institution and decide to enroll to a particular college or university.[11] According to Perna, little is known about the timing of the three-stage model for nontraditional enrollment for those who do not attend college immediately after high school. Further, there is limited information about graduate school choice

8. Winkle-Wagner, "Foundations of Educational Inequality," 1–21.

9. See Litten, "Different Strokes in the Applicant Pool"; Manski and Wise, *College Choice in America*; McDonough, *Choosing Colleges*; Perna, "Studying College Access and Choice."

10. Hossler and Gallagher, "Studying College Choice," 207–221.

11. Cabrera and La Nasa, *Understanding the College Choice.*

processes. Graduate-level decision process has been described as complex. The complexities of graduate student school choice are multidimensional concerns of ability, income, costs, and return on investment.[12] There remain a relatively small number of studies that examine the college choice decisions of graduate and professional students.[13] Even a smaller number of studies include findings specific to racial/ethnic graduate student choice issues. In recent years, several researchers have adapted or applied Perna's conceptual model to graduate school choice processes.[14]

What is known about MDiv students is that over 55 percent considered graduate theology school before or during college, while 27 percent first considered the MDiv after some type of work experience.[15] Most first-year students enrolled in the MDiv most likely learned about their degree program from a friend, graduate, or pastor/religious superior. It should be noted that the school's website is among the top five ways that a student first learned about their school and was the top method for gaining more information about the school, followed by communication with the school's staff[16] Further, entering students in theological education ranked the following as the most important factors in the decision to pursue theological education and the MDiv in particular: (1) experienced a call from God; (2) desire to serve others; (3) opportunity to study and growth; (4) desire to make a difference in the life of the church; and (5) intellectual interest in religious/theological questions[17] Additionally, entering MDiv students who completed the ATS Entering Student Questionnaire also indicated that the primary factors in their decision to attend their institution was quality of the faculty, curriculum, academic reputation, and comfort with the school's theological perspective. These data specify how these responses differ between male and female students, however, they do not specify information about the school choice process for students of color. Also, quantitative data of this sort only tell part of the story. The current milieu in theological education provides the opportunity to examine more closely how shifts in culture, religious leadership, and demographics influence racial/ethnic minority students who seek to hold religious positions, engage ministry vocations, and their decision-making to attend divinity schools.

12. Olson and King, "Preliminary Analysis," 304–315.

13. See Perna, "Racial and Ethnic Group Differences"; Zhang, "Advance to Graduate Education."

14. See English, "Graduate School Choice."

15. ATS, "Total School Profile."

16. ATS, "Total School Profile."

17. ATS, "Total School Profile."

As we explore more fully the school choice process for students of color in an MDiv program, using Perna's conceptual model of school choice is the most appropriate framework. Unlike other theoretical approaches, Perna integrates aspects of sociological and economic approaches.[18] Ultimately, Perna's model is based on the comparison of the benefits of college enrollment versus the cost of enrollment, but the model is not just influenced by supply and demand or one's ability to pay. This integrated model is also influenced by an individual's habitus, by school and community, the higher education context, and social, economic, and policy context. The conceptual model provides the opportunity to examine more closely issues of school choice in graduate theological education. The inclusion of both economic and sociological approaches to understanding student choice is compelling and serves as an excellent theoretical source for developing a model for graduate theological education.[19] Perna's model in figure 1 is used as a starting point in probing the narratives of students and is useful in framing the layered context by which graduate theology school choice occurs.

HABITUS—TELLING THEIR STORIES

To better understand the students' narratives in the context of graduate theology school choice, in addition to using Perna's conceptual model as a theoretical frame, narrative inquiry is used as a technique in order to engage in sense-making of their stories. As I present the narratives of racial/ethnic minority students, I use a hermeneutic lens of habitus that focuses on the biographical and psychological aspect of storytelling. Because I am concerned about factors like race/ethnicity, family origin, life events, and persons of influence in their life, a biographical approach to narrative analysis is highlighted. Similarly, I am interested in learning more about the thoughts and motivations of students of color, including their contextual knowledge, and the psychological aspect of their stories. For our purposes, the hermeneutic or interpreting lens is that of habitus as outlined in Perna's first contextual layer. The focus here is on the student's narratives and how they articulate the factors that influence their decision-making and school choice for divinity school. Using narrative inquiry, an interdisciplinary method, themes and groupings emerged that informed the overall narratives of these students of color enrolled in the MDiv degree program. In order to maintain confidentiality of the students interviewed, pseudo-names are used throughout.

---

18. Perna, "Studying College Access and Choice," 115.
19. Perna, "Studying College Access and Choice," 115.

Demographic Characteristics

Many students expressed expectations of being in the racial minority in divinity school. Often their sentiment stemmed from their previous contexts and was influential in their graduate theological school choice. Marcus grew up in a small town and was often the only person of color in his Honors or AP classes. Thus, he had not fully considered what it would mean for him to attend a predominately white institution for graduate theology school. He recalls typically being the only African-American in a class of at least twenty students from Kindergarten to college. Marcus reflectively proclaimed:

> So this entire time, this entire time until my first year in divinity school I never identified myself mentally as a black male. I knew I was black; I was in black organizations, I was in NAACP, all this stuff. I knew I was black, I knew "Lift Every Voice" better than anybody that's singing in harmony. But I had never grasped it and made it my own and didn't realize what this skin meant until first year of divinity school. (Marcus, first-year MDiv)

A few participants articulated being keenly aware of their race/ethnicity and were cognizant of enrolling in a predominantly white institution. Gilberto is in his final year in the MDiv program and was, at the time of the interview, the only Latino male in the program. He stated:

> I kind of like felt that—in other work that I've done in ministry, too, I'm not afraid of going to a place and knowing that you're going to be the only one. Because I kind of see it as an opportunity to be like the trailblazer, in a way. Somebody's got to be there. Otherwise, no one's going to be there. So yes, I was conscious of that and I thought in optimistic terms that maybe I could help in bringing the Latino perspective to the students— To bring my voice, my perspective, into the discussions. So, I saw that as a positive thing. (Gilberto, third-year MDiv)

Andrew articulated the importance of diversity generally but shared that regardless of the demographic composition of the student body that if he was accepted into the program, he would simply make the best of the situation. After reflecting more on race and his graduate theology school choice process, Andrew acknowledges feeling like being at his theological institution would equip him to not only exist in his context in terms of the African-American church but would also prepare him for leadership in any context and any religious community.

Having attended a Historically Black College and University (HBCU) for her undergraduate experience, Janay conveyed similar sentiments since she was the only African-American woman invited to scholarship weekend for the school where the most prestigious scholarships are offered to applicants. Janay said:

> I was already under the impression that I would be one of a few, even on the [scholarship] visit, I was the only black female so in my mind, I felt like I had already created an expectation of what I was gonna walk into. I expected to be the only one. (Janay, second-year MDiv)

Some students who expressed the importance of race in their consideration of a graduate theology program reflected on this demographic component in how they saw race/ethnicity represented by the institution. For instance, there were some thoughts that emerged regarding a visible person of color in the admissions office. Marcus admits that he had limited information about the divinity school but was motivated to apply after meeting an African-American woman on the admissions staff when he visited campus. He recalled his amazement when he learned that the woman was the dean of admissions. The visible representation of a person of color in a position of power had such a profound influence on Marcus that he reported this to his mother immediately following his visit to the school.

For several of the students of color interviewed, there was minimal consideration of matters related to race in their decision to apply to divinity school. Malika expressed that for her, race was not much of an influence on her decision to attend a particular divinity school. Rather, she discussed being extremely self-aware of being a black woman and how that fueled her desire to be highly educated. Her perception was that because of her race, she was all the more motivated to personally excel. While socioeconomic status was not heavily emphasized by students, many referred to their socioeconomic status with interrelatedness to their racial identity. In other words, for some students their drive to achieve was connected to their desire to have more and to be more.

Racial diversity and other forms of diversity was extremely important and influenced the graduate theological school choice for many students. For Regina racial diversity was essential, thus, in her search for an MDiv program, she also looked for other forms of diversity. Regina articulated, "I wanted some place that was diverse not necessarily racially, but just in other areas as well." She went on to expound on her thoughts in this area after reflecting on the school's mission and vision:

> I just didn't want a school that was cookie cutter; everyone's the same kind of mentality. And I definitely saw that and really

> what [the divinity school] stood for which was mind, body, and spirit—really growth of the whole person. When I saw the "whole person," I was like yep, that's where I need to be. (Regina, second-year MDiv)

Minerva, whose racial identity is biracial with a Mexican and white racial background, also indicated a desire for diversity beyond just race. She explains one of the reasons she decided to attend Wake Forest University School of Divinity:

> I'm not just interested in racial diversity, but also LGBTQ and various theologies. Well, all the professors come from different faith traditions, that's really important. It's just that [the divinity school] is more open in accepting of like—not just like LGBTQ or different races. It's accepting of different theologies, and I feel like I'm not being boxed in by a particular tradition. (Minerva, first-year MDiv)

Cultural Capital

For students of color interviewed, cultural capital included their cultural knowledge, their parent's education and expectations, perceptions about higher education, and funds of knowledge. Parental expectations were a central part of the narratives of most participants. Parental encouragement and family variables are an important predictor in the predisposition phase of the college choice process.[20] These were not important factors, however, for students of color discerning whether to attend divinity school. Most of the younger students expressed general support from their parents, but not necessarily in the form of encouragement for them to pursue a graduate theological education. There were many stories of parents who offered little to no encouragement for students to attend graduate theology school. Ben, a second-year MDiv student, knew from an early age that he would attend college and was steered toward a particular large public university in his home state. His mother and stepfather are both college-educated. Ben's mother has a Master's in Social Work, while his biological father has a high school education. Ben's stepfather, who has been in his life since age fourteen, has the Doctor of Medicine (MD) degree. As Ben explored the option of attending divinity school, his mother was not encouraging. Since Ben majored in Public Policy and African-American Studies, his parents

20. Perna and Titus, "Relationship Between Parental Involvement," 485–518.

encouraged him to go to law school. Though his parents were influential in his life, he explained:

> I was studying for the LSAT one night and I realized that it didn't matter to me. . . . And I realized that I needed to make sense of my life and the lives of those around me. And if I was going to believe that it was God that was controlling it all, that's fine. If I wanted to believe that there was no God, that's fine. But I had to figure out what I believe for me. (Ben, second-year MDiv)

Ben's stepfather was also discouraging of his interest in the MDiv. "My stepdad still doesn't tell people I'm going to divinity school." According to Ben, his stepfather is concerned about the financial investment of pursuing the MDiv and the perceived limited return on investment. He also reported that other family members think this degree is just a stepping stone to where he will ultimately go—law school or a PhD program. Additionally, most students revealed no expectation from parents for them to attend graduate theology school. Minerva, a first-year MDiv student, has parents who have always valued higher education. Her father, a business owner in the US, has a master's degree from Mexico. Her parents met in Mexico when her mother was working on her master's degree. Minerva grew up in a middle-class family that was bicultural and bilingual with English and Spanish spoken in her home. As Minerva recounted expectations from her parents, she stated, "It's just expected. I mean, both my parents have master's degrees. However, there was not a similar expectation for Minerva to attend graduate school for theology. Nonetheless, Minerva shared "they are supportive. My dad doesn't really get. He just doesn't get it. He thinks I'm spending a bunch of money to become poor."

The limited cultural knowledge or "funds of knowledge" that students and their families have about graduate theological education was a theme demonstrated consistently. Kiyama defines funds of knowledge as the "historically accumulated and culturally developed bodies of knowledge and skills essential for household or individual functioning and well-being."[21] For students of color, among the themes that emerged throughout this project was the sense that family members did not quite understand theological education or what they were doing as a graduate student. Toni, a first-generation college student and first-year MDiv student, mentioned that her husband and children are supportive but not knowledgeable about what she is doing. "I think there's a positive response, but they don't understand because nobody really has ever done it." In the same way, Felecia who is also a first-generation college student reported "they haven't really said anything

---

21. Kiyama, "College Aspirations and Limitations," 133.

about me being in seminary. I don't think they fully understand what it is and what I'm actually doing."

The lack of knowledge or cultural capital is often detrimental to the college-going process,[22] but not ultimately a barrier for students of color deciding to attend graduate theology school. Though there was limited cultural capital as it relates to graduate theological education, students were not deterred in their pursuit of the MDiv. However, a lack of guidance and basic knowledge from support systems can limit the decision-making process and slow processes.[23]

Social Capital

Social capital generally focuses on relations between people that provide productive benefits. Thus, social capital includes expectations spoken and unspoken, information channels between people, and norms between community members. Social capital frameworks help identify how, and which resources and networks are crucial in the college choice process for racial/ethnic minority students.[24] In this way social capital conveys norms and standards through various relationships—parental involvement, social and support networks that include family, friends, peers, mentors, pastors, and other influential relationships. These connections often provide information about graduate school and provide assistance with processes.

For many students of color under the age of thirty, parental involvement was a key part to their college choice process. Parental involvement in the graduate theology school process, though sometimes limited, was still present for some students. In some cases, parents were explicitly supportive, like Rachel, who described her mother's support by saying, "She was right across from me and said I've known you were going to go into ministry since you were four, I was wondering how long it was going to take you to figure it out." While older student Bridgette said, "There's still a little, I think, resentment that I am taking so much time to be a part of this contemplative world and that, sort of ivory tower view of school by working class people." Parental or family support ranged from enthusiastically supportive to concern about ministry not being a financially lucrative field.

The theme of peer support was important for all students of color interviewed. Several students referenced a shifting from parental involvement

22. Kiyama, "College Aspirations and Limitations," 133.

23. McDonough, *Choosing Colleges.*

24. Pérez and McDonough, "Understanding Latina and Latino College Choice," 249–65.

to experiencing more peer support. For instance, a friend was instrumental in introducing Marcus to the idea of graduate theology school. During his senior year in college, Marcus recalls meeting a new friend on his undergraduate campus. He engaged his friend who was also a senior and inquired what he would do after graduation. Marcus's friend replied, "I'm going to divinity school." Marcus curiously responded, "What's divinity school?" Marcus went on to learn that his friend was considering several different options for graduate theology school and invited him to sign up for a student of color day at a divinity school. "They're having a Student of Color Day. You should go check it out," Marcus remembered his friend saying. Marcus went to visit for the special day at the suggestion of his friend. Shortly after the visit, Marcus felt led to consider divinity schools. Although he did not matriculate at that initial school of inquiry, his search started and progressed to Wake Forest due to peer interactions. Peer mentoring was an important aspect of the search and choice stage for several students. As Ashley's call to ministry became evident, she depended on a group of friends in her undergraduate community for peer mentoring. Ashley was a leader in the gospel choir in college and had a close-knit group of peers who provided support for one another. Ashley struggled to decide about which graduate theology school she would attend. She was accepted at two university-related divinity schools, received comparable scholarship offers from both, and similar opportunities for student employment. Ashley remembers relying on her friends for prayer and discernment.

Findings in the research confirmed that other relationships like that of professors, spiritual mentors, pastors, and religious leaders were instrumental in the graduate theology school process. For some students support during their graduate theology school choice process was located in their religious communities. Christine was born and raised in the Black Baptist tradition. Her mother is an educator who has a master's in education and her father went to vocational school. Christine's support network includes her mother, pastor, and the first lady of her church. Though Christine's father and brother do not believe that women should be leaders in ministry, Christine has found support and affirmation among others. Additionally, Christine described the importance of her relationship with Pastor Scott. He was a professor at her college, who also was a bi-vocational pastor, so students referred to him as Pastor Scott. It was Pastor Scott who first encouraged Christine to go to divinity school. "He always told us to get a degree, go get a secondary degree, so I said 'Okay, I'm gonna do divinity school.'" Christine expressed comfort in knowing that her support network was there to encourage her. "These people were surrounding me and telling me that I could, when I felt like I couldn't," explains Christine. Christine also discussed her relationship with Pastor Ayers, a female pastor who encouraged her to specifically explore the MDiv program she selected. Just the suggestion of Pastor Ayers to look into this particular divinity school, had tremendous influence on Christine—"A mentor of mine, Pastor Ayers, she told me to look into [Wake Forest School of Divinity], and I looked into [the school] without visiting it, but I just knew this is where I was supposed to be."

Yet for other participants, professors and mentors were instrumental in their graduate theology school choice. Chantrell was immersed in a graduate program in communications when she realized that the MDiv was a better fit for her vocational goals. In college, her support network included an African-American female professor. Chantrell attended a large public state university and recalls that her experience with her professor was the first time she was taught by someone who looked like her in a higher educational setting. Chantrell identifies this professor as a mentor and a significant part of her support network. Recognizing that she had a call to ministry, Chantrell attributes the encouragement of this professor, as well as her father, for helping her start down the path of graduate theological education.

Demand for Graduate Theological Education

Embedded in the idea of habitus is the perceived demand for graduate education which is pivotal to comprehending graduate theological school choice. In addition to reflecting on an individual's demographic characteristics and cultural and social capital, there are other elements that are also components of habitus. The perceived demand that graduate theological school choice for students of color included discovery of their passions, how they view the need for an educated clergy, perceptions about how academically prepared they were for graduate school, how they viewed the reputation of the theological school, as well as whether they felt a sense of community and belonging.

Self-Awareness of Passions

An important theme in the graduate theology school choice process for *all* students was a growing awareness of what makes them come alive or their passions. Felecia majored in Health Science at a small Historically Black College/University (HBCU). It was her pastor who first mentioned divinity school to her as a possibility. Felecia's pastor has a PhD and encouraged her to consider that the next step in her responding to her call would be to attend seminary. Felecia's response to this idea was, "I was thinking of all I would learn, and I was thinking about my own passions. Like, my passion is the Bible, my passion is God, so if I wanted a career then I was going to have to go to a school where I could learn the necessary skills that I needed in order to pursue a career in that." Connecting one's passions to theological education was an important refrain for students. Karen completed her undergraduate degree at age thirty-one at a liberal arts women's college. Karen immigrated to the United States and grew up in a household with the ideals that to gain knowledge is to gain power. She realized that she likes discussing theology. Further, Karen believes that faith issues and spirituality are important to every aspect of our lives. "It affects our ethics, it affects how we think about people, it affects how we think about human dignity and human worth," she passionately stated. Having felt a sense of call at the age of sixteen, Karen expressed wanting to change the world and believing the MDiv will equip her for the task:

> There is the thought in the back of my mind that I don't always give a voice to—Like wanting to start a non-profit organization. A faith-based, non-profit organization that helps people who are in a food or economic crises that moves them from dependency to independent sustainability. I can change the world with what I do here and what I learn here. I can make connections with other people. (Karen, first-year MDiv)

Karen's graduate school choice was directly related to connecting her passions with the institution's mission and resources. "[The School of Divinity] talks about social justice issues. And not very many theological [schools] or seminaries talk about social justice, not just within the context of church, but outside the walls of church." Karen's interests go beyond serving in a church setting. She is fervent about talking about racial issues, social justice issues, and economic equality and discussed how the MDiv program at the divinity school aligns with her interests.

Malcolm thought of attending a Bible College at some point in his undergraduate studies. He opted to attend a graduate theological program upon completing his Business and Finance degree because he thought it would offer him more. He explained, "I believe divinity school offers more exposure to theological and different philosophies and I feel like when I get out of here, I'll be able to navigate through any environment." Malcolm has a passion for business and has started a process of imagining how he can mix his interest in ministry with business. As Malcolm dreamed about the possibilities in our discussion, he mentioned entrepreneurship as a means of providing a flow of resources to ministries that need them the most.

Some students started exploring their passions and that eventually led them to making a choice for graduate theology school. Evelyn came to graduate theological education not because she was clear on a particular vocational path. Rather, she came with her questions and wanted space to explore these questions. "And so, I had questions that are still not answered because in seminary you have more questions than you have answers by the time you finish." Evelyn discussed the desire of being in an open environment where she could explore her interest as she explained, "I had questions that I wanted to wrestle with, and I wanted to be in an environment in which I could do that. And that was driving me towards coming to theology school."

Others had considered what made them come alive for some time and knew that theological education was the next step. Kirk, a native of South Carolina, first thought of pursuing a call to ministry his sophomore year of college. He was raised in a middle-class religious family who values education. Though his father wanted him to pursue dual degree options like the MDiv and the JD so that he could earn a more substantial salary, he was only interested in the MDiv. Nonetheless, Kirk applied to law schools to appease his father but was not accepted. Kirk demonstrated clarity about wanting to become a pastor in a congregational setting. Given the sense of call to be a pastor, Kirk expressed that being an educated clergy was essential. He explained, "All the pastors who I began to look at whether it was inside South Carolina or outside South Carolina, all of them had MDivs."

Academic Preparation

Several students expressed a concern about being academically prepared for graduate theology school. Their concerns ranged from feeling inadequate, not knowing what to expect, worry about having a low undergraduate grade point average, to perceptions about the academic reputation of the institution. These types of perceptions can influence decision-making related to school choice and cause students to exclude themselves based on their sense of belonging.[25] "I guess that was the biggest concern—that I would not be prepared for a situation like this, especially from what a lot of people would assume coming from a historically black college," replied Andrew when asked if he was academically prepared for graduate theology school. Andrew reported that his undergraduate transcript was inconsistent.

25. McDonough, *Choosing Colleges.*

Despite his inconsistent academic history, once Andrew was accepted into the MDiv program he reflected upon how he now feels the need to prove that he actually belongs here. His perceptions of his level of academic preparedness and connection to how he views the institution became clearer when Andrew explained: "This is an esteemed university. One of the best private institutions in the country and, and in my opinion it's kind of, it's kind of like that place on the hill where you have to deserve the right to go there." Other students also expressed a concern about being academically prepared for graduate theology school. DeWan, a vocal performance major, attended a rigorous high school and was in the International Baccalaureate (IB) Program. Most of his peers went on to college. DeWan went on to enroll in a college strictly for the arts. He expressed deep regrets about choosing such a narrow undergraduate path. As he considered his choices for a graduate theology school program, he said, "So I considered all of the big names and immediately crossed a lot of them off the list for economic reasons, for my sense of feeling like I'm not prepared. . . . When asked if he was academically prepared for graduate theology school, he responded, "No, I felt like my high school program prepared me for graduate school." DeWan clarified that because of his participation in the IB program, he was doing college level coursework that required a lot of writing each week. Although DeWan graduated from his undergraduate program with a high GPA, it was in the IB program that he learned time management "and actually taking ownership of an academic vocabulary and lexicon came at that time, not in undergrad." Further he asserted:

> The divinity school process was actually a lot more complicated because my undergraduate degree did not give me tools to jump into an academic environment that was in any way related to what I was doing while I was there. We were not an academically focused school at all. It was all about your art and that took precedence over the academic thing. (DeWan, first-year MDiv)

Some students reported concerns about their academic preparedness because of having been out of school for a long period of time. Bridgette, having been out of school for twenty years, had no idea what to expect in graduate theology school. Bridgette started her time in college in community college prior to joining the military. After several challenging experiences, Bridgette was encouraged to complete her degree by a close network of mentors and friends. Her undergraduate career in Recreation, Parks, and Tourism Sciences was not challenging but she worked three jobs while completing the degree. Nonetheless, Bridgette graduated with at least a 3.0 grade point average (GPA). "I've been through Air Force basic training, I've been in war zones, I've seen horrible crime scenes, I've done law enforcement, I grew up in a violent home, and the hardest thing I ever did was my first semester at div school." Bridgette already has a master's in education but feels called to chaplaincy. Though she expressed having confidence and a good intellect, she discussed struggling with more technical items related to academic success like doing citations properly. Janay described the idea of pursuing the MDiv as uncomfortable. She had transitioned to divinity school from working a few years in the banking industry. She was unfulfilled in her career but discovered her passion to work with young girls and became invigorated spiritually. "I think I was academically prepared, but I don't think I've been trained to operate within this context academically. I've never experienced it. Did I have academic capacity upon coming? Yes. The academic capabilities, yes but had I ever done this before? No." Yet, some students were confident in how academically prepared they were coming into the MDiv degree program. Regina attended a highly selective Ivy League school and said, "I was definitely prepared socially and then even through skills of learning how to study, how to read, all these things that I always tweaked and learned added things on to." Minerva also attended a highly selective university and recalls that she had an exceptional GPA in her undergraduate program and emphasized having good study habits.

Institutional Reputation and Perceptions

The reputation of the institution and perceived quality of the theological education was an emerging theme. The reputation factors named about a graduate theology school were not only academic reputation. Rather, the students' narratives spoke about institutional reputation related to matters of diversity: racial, sexual identities, denominations, multi-faith, etc. Additionally, perceptions related to institutional resources, offerings, and inclusiveness influenced the choices of many students. For instance, Lisa only considered university-related divinity schools. As she reflected on why that was the case, she recounts her undergraduate faculty advisor encouraging her to apply to specific places. She was admitted to two of the three schools. When discussing why she made the choices she made, Lisa explained, "The Div School, is smaller. It's newer. And I would say that even though [others] have programs that talk about diversity, it wasn't a lot of diversity." Lisa admits to not knowing much about divinity school options. Having only applied to university-related theology schools—all of which are not affiliated with a denomination—was a demonstration of Lisa's desire not to attend a school where she would "get shoved into a doctrine that I did not understand or believe."

Many students mentioned that earning the MDiv was motivated by the need or desire to have credibility. Ben said proudly, "I was looking for schools that had institutional clout that would open doors." Marcus wanted to attend a reputable theology school that was accredited. His denominational seminary in his hometown is not accredited and is primarily designed for those without a college education. Since he would be relocating for divinity school, it was important to Marcus to have the resources to make his education possible. He recalls having a potential job on campus, housing, and a scholarship all lined-up. Chantrell did not visit campus prior to applying to the school. She indicated that the prestige of the institution was important, and she wanted a place that valued diversity. Doing all of her research about divinity schools via the Internet, Chantrell reported she could sense the diverse community and affirmation of all people.

Campus Environment and Location

For students of color, graduate theology school choice was also influenced by the campus climate, level of faculty/student engagement, and proximity to home. Research of racial/ethnic graduate students, more generally, indicates that reputation of school and faculty, proximity to home or work, financial considerations, preferred academic program, and campus environment were influential factors for graduate students when choosing a graduate school.[26] The visit to campus was a critical part of the decision-making process for some students. "When I was touring the campus, people were asking me about what I was interested in doing, and they actually sounded interested and they were telling me classes that I might want to take or people I should talk to," recalls Ben. He took this personal and relational approach to heart during his graduate theology school choice process. Ben shared that he appreciated the strong sense of community, the accessibility of faculty, and the presence of African-American professors. Ben also felt assured in his graduate theology school choice once he imagined how he could be a contributor to school. He explains, "And I thought that at [the School of Divinity] I could actually have a voice and be a part of the—be a part of who [the school] is and what [the school] becomes." Ben limited his graduate theology school search to his home state. As a native of the state, he said "I didn't want it [theology school] to be far away and feel like I was on my own for three years." As he narrowed in on a decision about which

26. Strayhorn et al., "Sex Differences in Graduate School Choice," 174–88.

institution to attend, Ben carefully explained, "I got to the place of where would I feel most comfortable at, and [this divinity school] kind of won out. And so that means that when I went on tours, I saw people that looked like me." Regina's experience upon visiting campus was positive. She shared, "I felt the sense of calm and warmth and peace and I felt similar to how when I found my undergrad school. Further, those she met made an impression on her. "I loved the faculty that I met, and I loved just the piece that got me about [the school]—that you focus so much on vocation."

For a few students, location or proximity to home was a driving force in their school choice process. Most of these students were older and considered less mobile due to family expectations or obligations. Rosalyn is among the oldest students in the program. She was keenly aware that she wanted to attend a graduate program near her current residence. Proximity to home was also important to Gilberto. He researched online options for the MDiv, but Gilberto decided he wanted a more structured place-based program. He felt that a residential educational environment would help him. He explained, "I wanted to make a full commitment to doing this kind of academic work." Recognizing that moving out of state was not an option for his wife and small children, proximity to his home was a significant factor.

Supply of Resources

This project revealed that both economic and sociocultural factors influence graduate theology school enrollment for racial/ethnic minority MDiv students. The supply of resources to pay the costs associated with enrollment in the MDiv plays an important role in graduate theology school choice. For graduate theology students there was typically no mention of family income related to their parents. Rather, students only considered their individual circumstances or, if married/partnered, their immediate family situation. As students reflected about their socioeconomic status (SES), they typically reverted to the SES growing up and not as a reference to their individual or current circumstance. For some students, scholarship and financial aid was essential to their choice process. Michael, a second-year MDiv student, was among a select group of applicants invited to participate in the scholarship weekend. As a prospective student, Michael presented a strong application for admission and was considered for some of the school's most distinguished scholarships. As Michael reflected back on his application process to multiple theology programs, he said, "Well, according to my advisor, she said if I could get a 3.5 [GPA] with my black male status, you're golden anywhere you want to go." Michael continued on to explain how he consciously understood his status as a black male with high academic achievement and his expectation that institutions would provide resources for this education. Similarly, the availability of scholarships was among the top three reasons Minerva cited for attending her divinity school. Minerva graduated with a GPA of 3.9 out of 4.0 from her undergraduate institution. Minerva expressed that she appreciated that the school offers practical skills for vocations inside and outside the church. She explained her reasons for being in divinity school in the following way: "God wanted me to, . . . because you guys offer a touch of the secular I wanted, . . . you guys are paying me to go here, and that's a third reason." Felecia agreed that having the resources to pay for school was significant for her. She indicated that her primary motivation for coming to the divinity school "was my pastor encouraging me to come and also . . . the ministry and to answer this call." She clarified, "first of all [the school] was giving me a scholarship—a full scholarship, so I was thinking about that. But I was also thinking about the fact that I was feeling a pull, type, thing to [the school]." Felecia shared this information as she reflected on the many African-Americans in her social and support network encouraging her to attend a black theology school.

Many students reported that their ultimate decision was not driven by financial aid or ability to pay through their own resources. Wanting to respond to her call faithfully, Lisa proclaimed to God, "I'll do what you want me to do, but you know I can't afford it. Whatever you want me to do, you'll make a way." For Ashley, who reported that she grew up in a lower middle-class family, she was elated to have received a scholarship and to be provided federal aid. However, the scholarship was not a factor in her decision to attend any particular divinity school. Regina receives a good scholarship, but still has loans. She said, "So it wasn't necessarily fully the money, that helped, but I still have a lot of loans, so it was just a sense that nope this is where I'm supposed to go." Though the supply of resources is generally deemed important, for many students of color, the ability to pay was not mentioned as *the* motivating factor in the decision-making process. In fact, several students only mentioned financial resources when directly asked about how they were paying for school. Only 22 percent of students (six out of twenty-seven) proactively mentioned the role scholarships or financial aid played in their graduate theology school choice.

Expected Benefits and Costs

According to Perna, college choice is ultimately based on a comparison of the benefits and costs.[27] However, she argues, and I concur, that the assessments of the benefits and costs are not only shaped by the demand of higher education and the supply of resources, but also by an individual's habitus. Students of color in this study articulated their reasons for enrolling in the MDiv degree program and expressed the benefits in terms of gaining the knowledge and professional skills needed for various vocations in ministry. The costs associated with the degree were secondary, at best, for most students. Consideration of the benefits was at the forefront of their stories while cost was in the distant background. Several students expressed the benefits of seeking the MDiv as they reflected on the skills they would gain for professional ministry. Jimmy, a first-year MDiv student, is married and has two small children. They are supportive of him coming to divinity school to respond to God's calling in his life. Jimmy explained what he hopes to get out of his theological education:

> I wanted to increase my vocabulary. It's one thing to just talk about the Bible, and know about the Bible, and to understand how vast this world of God, of theology really is. You cannot know all of it. I figure it would be an advantage to come to a place where it will give me a start, for example. (Jimmy, first-year MDiv)

Many students mentioned the desire to become more knowledgeable about the Bible and theology in order to better serve people. Toni is active in her church and as a result of going to a series of Bible classes led by her pastor, she became interested in learning more about theology and the Bible. "I want to be the best qualified minister or preacher that you can be because people are hurting, and they have things that you don't want to pass or minister incorrect information." Toni believes that by attending theology school she is positioning herself to be the best she can be. Further, she articulated that the MDiv is preparing her for her future work and is professionally formative. "So you want to know why I came to divinity school? Okay. I guess just to be the best that I can be to serve God's people, that's it. And I think also you get connections, too." The benefit of a theological education affords her the opportunity to expose herself to new things and higher learning. Michael said he decided to attend seminary "to get a broader theological understanding beyond some of the garbage I was getting preached from the pulpit." In addition to the MDiv being required in his denomination,

27. Perna, "Studying College Access and Choice," 99–149.

he expressed a deep desire to use rhetoric in a meaningful way. Michael believes the church is in trouble, and he is concerned about the direction of the church. Thus, Michael expressed that a graduate theological education is essential to the church. "An educated clergy is able to better administrate, better educate, and better inform," Michael asserted. Some students expressed the benefits of enrolling in the MDiv degree program beyond just gaining biblical knowledge. Bridgette is seeking to gain more knowledge for her vocation as an ordained minister who will likely go into chaplaincy. Bridgette also believes the benefit of seminary is about formation or polishing. She explained the benefit in the following way:

> In seminary we basically learn a foreign language. All these ideas, and values, and theologies that I hold I've had for a while and they're being validated. Some are being shifted. I've not been changed dramatically, but I'm able to articulate now and will continue to learn how to articulate God in a way that people can understand. And while the Bible is one source of relationship with God, it for me, is the lesser source and that ministers who have not navigated divinity school, don't have access to other sources is—I think, the real reason the church is on decline. (Bridgette, second-year MDiv)

Further, many students articulated the need to be prepared to provide leadership in a complex world. Andrew said, "So I thought that if I want to be the most productive in what I want to do then seminary is definitely a non-negotiable tool that I need." Andrew did not consider graduate theology school as an optional exercise. Rather, he felt it was essential. "I think for me, in the twenty-first century, where you have to answer a number of questions . . . concerning sexuality and gender, you can't just operate on the Holy Spirit or whatever you call it. You need stepping stones and academic education," Andrew boldly proclaimed. Though financial resources and an ability to pay for school was not the most influential factor for Andrew in deciding to attend divinity school, he understood the benefit of good academic name and that it would cost something.

For racial/ethnic minority students the path to the MDiv program varies. There are various, and sometimes complex reasons that these students embark on an educational and vocational trajectory that are often marred with uncertainty, limitations, and shortcomings. Yet, the journey is accompanied with faith, a sense of hope, and anticipation. Thus, understanding more about the embodied habitus of racial/ethnic minority MDiv students, both individual agency and integrally linked structural conditions, offer insight into this matter. Specifically, understanding the span of decision-making from undergraduate choice processes to graduate school choice processes is necessary if there is to be greater examination of the narratives and choice processes of racial/ethnic MDiv students. This is especially significant in examining the ways that structure influences agency and vice versa in racial/ethnic student populations, and to what extent is school choice really *a choice* for certain agents in lower social hierarchies. Using Perna's conceptual model as a catalyst to deeply examine the habitus of the students interviewed, a new thematic model of graduate theological choice emerged (see figure 2).

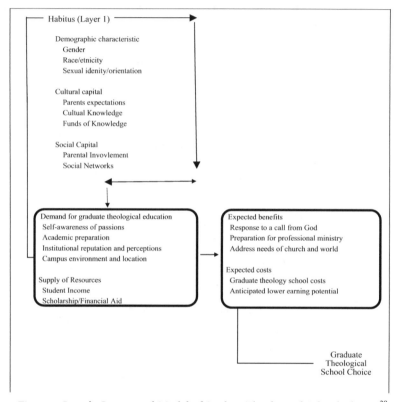

Figure 2. Jones's Conceptual Model of Student Theological School Choice.[28]

Not only did students of color express something about how they see themselves, but they also said just as much about how they experience God in their lives. "I think I'm supposed to go to greater platforms than just what I have now. I think fear has limited my vision to see what actually God has in store," said Yolanda, a third-year MDiv, who has a desire to work in ministry

28. Adapted from Perna, "Studying College Access and Choice."

with young people. Some stories demonstrate a sense of release into God's will and God's desire, even amid great uncertainty about pursuing the degree and the participant's professional future. Janay, a twenty-six year old African-American woman who had been in the workforce for three years prior to applying to graduate theology school indicated, "This is it and it's not even so much about it being easy because it wasn't an easy decision for me to leave the security of being in banking, a very profitable industry, to leave a salary where I could be at the top of a corporate ladder."

A sense of God's calling was articulated by all students, and was often recalled from an earlier age:

> Well, I've had a calling to the ministry dating back to March of my eleventh-grade year of high school. So I knew that at some point this would be on the career trajectory. And so after getting the calling and finally saying yes, then I knew it was a done deal. (Michael, second-year MDiv)

Michael's sense of his call goes back to a specific period in high school. Not only is he able to recall the specific time, but he also acknowledges a surrendering to the call. He further articulated that his tradition in the African Methodist Episcopal Church requires the MDiv as a necessary step for ordination. Zoe, a first-year student, recalls conversations with her mother about ministry:

> My mom asked me what I was going to do when I grew up and then I was probably like nine years old, and I was like, well, I want to be a preacher. God called me to be a preacher. I'm going to be a preacher. (Zoe, first-year MDiv)

Amid the call stories, often the narratives included expressions of giving up one's own desires to answer God's call. For example, Rosalyn explicitly states, "God called me against my will like most people, and I feel like if I'm going to do this, I represent [God] and I have to be the best. And the best means I have to know what I'm talking about." Other expressions were also explicit in describing how the call may have deterred other plans:

> I was called like everybody else. I didn't want to come to divinity school. At first, I wanted to go to law school, but it just seemed like everything was kind of pushing me towards this. And that was it. And I just said, you know, God, I'll do what you want me to do, but you know I can't afford it. Whatever you want me to do, you'll make a way. (Lisa, second-year MDiv)

This sense of call or pursuit toward vocational ministry is a framing narrative for most and informs decisions related to the graduate theology school choice process. The many stories shared suggest that an individual's call story is a significant and pivotal part of the overall narrative expressed by the students. Whether a call from early in life or one that requires relinquishing some things, one's call story is formative and generative in nature and informs decisions related to graduate theology school choice.

Another benefit expectation that emerged was around notions of diversity. For example, Rachel's previous experiences compelled her to want similar encounters in graduate theological education. Rachel is a candidate for ordination in order to be a pastor in the Lutheran Church. Being a part of a diverse setting is crucial to her and where she thrives. Rachel attended a small, yet very diverse college in terms of racial and sexual identity. She is also a member of a theologically diverse church. Similarly, several students perceived the institution to be diverse and open in multiple ways. The range of diversity was expressed well by Rosalyn when she stated:

> I wanted a program where I could learn and be who I am and not have to worry about being ridiculed for my beliefs. You had different religious affiliations, different denominational affiliations. And I wanted to be able to meet people who could add to me and help me kind of grow and stretch personally, but more than anything spiritually. (Rosalyn, first-year MDiv)

Rosalyn considered attending a Bible College since her older brother had attended a local Bible College. Since she plans to seek a PhD in biblical languages, she was interested in attending a well-respected university. Rosalyn was also concerned about receiving a theological education that would prepare her for a variety of vocations—not just for pastoral ministry. Many students also expressed how crucial it was for them to enroll in an MDiv program that was denominationally diverse. For Jimmy, attending a graduate theology school that was ecumenical was a significant factor. "I came to [the School of Divinity] as opposed to some denominational school that would want me to be a denominational guy." Gilberto also expressed that even though there would not be very many Latinos at the school, he liked that the school was ecumenical. Minerva also emphasized how essential a diverse graduate school environment was to her. She not only noted that an ecumenical and racially diverse environment was important, but she also discussed curricular requirements that suggested preparation for serving in diverse contexts. For Minerva, who is concerned about global relationships, this type of requirement helped form an impression of the type of institution she would consider. Minerva stated, "You guys offer the dual degree, and you guys offer good financial aid, and you're just like where seminaries need to be going generally." She went on to explain, "Like theologically, you're with the modern times. You know what I mean? I feel like seminaries especially are way behind."

CONSIDERATIONS FOR PRACTICE

This chapter illustrates the ways that racial/ethnic minority MDiv students engage the graduate theology school process. Perna's conceptual model and my adaptation of that model provide a comprehensive approach to understanding the graduate theology school choice of students of color. The racial/ethnic minority MDiv students interviewed for the study demonstrated that individual habitus, one's embedded social and cultural capital and a series of internalized dispositions, is used to form decisions and choices. As noted in Perna's model, the economic context is also important, accounting for the demand for graduate theological education, supply of resources, and expected benefits and costs. All are weighted as these students make decisions about enrollment. By building on this conceptual model of student college choice, with a particular focus on habitus (layer 1) of the theoretical frame—demographic characteristics, cultural capital, and social capital, there is greater clarity in understanding the theology school choice process for students of color. Whether directly or indirectly influenced by cultural or social capital operating in their lives, the narratives that were shared provided a greater understanding of the aims and motivations of the student's graduate theology school choice. As participants recount their call stories, they highlight how influential their professors, pastors, mentors, and friends have been in propelling them toward graduate theology school. Support networks provide these students with valuable social capital that aids in negotiating their graduate theology school choice. Though many of those in their family have limited knowledge about theological education, participants demonstrated determination to seek knowledge, skills, and credentials that would help them in being responsive to God's call to professional ministry.

The realities facing religious communities and theological institutions are sobering. The demographic factors affecting undergraduate higher education, and thus, graduate theological education is well documented. As the US is becoming less white, institutions of higher learning must adapt to emerging realities. The shift in the number of racial/ethnic minorities in the US population will also impact communities of faith and the pipeline of leaders who will serve them. Given the recent history of decline and tacit stability through new degree programs and modes of delivery coupled with the realization that a major area of enrollment growth is with racial/ethnic minorities, theological schools must understand the choice processes of these students. Theological schools must learn how to reach, cultivate, and serve racial/ethnic minority students if they are going to continue to remain solvent, competitive, and relevant. For some theological institutions, they will need to devise long-term strategies to recruit and retain racial/ethnic minority students if they are going to survive and thrive into the future.

One of the most significant findings in the study is how essential the notion of multiplicity is during the graduate theology choice process. Students in the study clearly identified that among the drivers to their school choice was seeing or experiencing a multitude of diversity. They not only discussed racial diversity as pivotal, but they were interested in an environment where other types of diversity were held as an institutional value. Thus, creating and sustaining a theological academic environment that values multiple voices and multiple ways of being is crucial to attracting and nurturing racial/ethnic minority students. For some institutions, this will require a cultural shift in which long-term strategies will need to include recruiting faculty and staff that represent various forms of multiplicity. An institution's legacy of inclusion or exclusion can influence how the campus climate is perceived. Thus, theological institutions must take steps to ensure diversity, inclusion, and equity are more central educational values and are an institutional priority.

Any institution that seeks to make multiplicity a central value of their educational enterprise, must recognized that this is an embodied effort. Students of color often privilege the relational characteristics of communities for which they are a part. Influencers or those in their support network are an example of how relationships can influence decision-making. Living out and communicating a student-centered/community-focused ethos to prospective racial/ethnic minorities and to those that influence them is a critical tactic that should be explored by theological institutions. Any communication must be authentic to the contextual reality of the institution. Further, there can be no ambiguity in the role of theological institutions in the socialization process of racial/ethnic minority students. Socialization, however, cannot be an exercise in assimilation. Rather, it has to be deliberate action by the institution to ensure all students are able to be functioning and contributing members of the community. The more institutions tend to this reality, the more sense of community will exist for all students. Theological institutions should consider developing strategic educational programs that are curricular and co-curricular to not only help community members discuss race differences, but also the notion of multiplicity which includes theological perspectives, sexual identities/orientations, plurality of denominations, multiple generations, and various faith traditions. Theological institutions have much to gain from listening to the narratives of racial/ethnic minority students. Giving attention to how the school choice process takes shape for these students is crucial to recruit, enroll, and serve this growing population, and to educate them (and others) to serve a diverse church and world.

BIBLIOGRAPHY

Association of Theological Schools (ATS). "Total School Profile: Entering Student Questionnaire 2017–2018." December 12, 2017. Online. http://www.ats.edu/uploads/resources/student-data/documents/total-school-profiles/esq-total-school-profile-2017-2018.pdf.

Bourdieu, Pierre. *Outline of a Theory of Practice.* Translated by Richard Nice. Cambridge: Cambridge University Press, 1977.

Cabrera, Alberto F., and Steven M. La Nasa. *Understanding the College Choice of Disadvantaged Students.* New Directions for Institutional Research 107. San Francisco: Jossey-Bass, 2000.

English, David J. "Graduate School Choice: An Examination of Individual and Institutional Effects." PhD diss., North Carolina State University, 2012.

Hossler, Don, and Karen Symms Gallagher. "Studying College Choice: A Three-phase Model and the Implications for Policy-makers." *College and University* 62.3 (1987) 207–221.

Jones, Shonda R. "Graduate Theology School Choice: An Examination of Racial/Ethnic Minority Master of Divinity Students." EdD diss., University of Alabama, 2014.

Kiyama, Judy Marquez. "College Aspirations and Limitations: The Role of Educational Ideologies and Funds of Knowledge in Mexican American Families." *American Educational Research Journal* 47.2 (2010) 330–56.

Litten, Larry H. "Different Strokes in the Applicant Pool: Some Refinements in a Model of Student College Choice." *Journal of Higher Education* 53.4 (1982) 383–402.

Manski, Charles F., and David A. Wise. *College Choice in America.* Cambridge: Harvard University Press, 1983.

McDonough, Patricia M. *Choosing Colleges: How Social Class and Schools Structure Opportunity.* Albany: State University of New York Press, 1997.

Meinzer, Chris. "A Closer Look at Enrollment." *Colloquy Online* (January 2018). https://www.ats.edu/uploads/resources/publications-presentations/colloquy-online/a-closer-look-at-enrollment.pdf.

———. "Master's Enrollment—A Changing Landscape." *Colloquy Online*, April 2018. Online. http://masters-enrollment-in-ats-member-schools.pdf.

Olson, Carol, and Milton A. King. "A Preliminary Analysis of the Decision Process of Graduate Students in College Choice." *College and University* 60 (1985) 304–315.

Pérez, Patricia A., and Patricia M. McDonough. "Understanding Latina and Latino College Choice: A Social Capital and Chain Migration Analysis." *Journal of Hispanic Higher Education* 7.3 (2008) 249–65.

Perna, Laura W. "Racial and Ethnic Group Differences in College Enrollment Decisions." New Directions for Institutional Research 107 (2000) 65.

————. "Studying College Access and Choice: A Proposed Conceptual Model." In vol. 21 of Higher Education: Handbook of Theory and Research, edited by J. C. Smart, 99–149. Amsterdam: Springer, 2006.

Perna, Laura W., and Marvin A. Titus. "The Relationship between Parental Involvement as Social Capital and College Enrollment: An Examination of Racial/Ethnic Group Differences." The Journal of Higher Education 76.5 (2005) 485–518.

Strayhorn, Terrell L., et al. "Sex Differences in Graduate School Choice for Black HBCU Bachelor's Degree Recipients: A National Analysis." Journal of African American Studies 17.2 (2013) 174–88.

Winkle-Wagner, Rachelle. "Foundations of Educational Inequality: Cultural Capital and Social Reproduction." ASHE Higher Education Report 36.1 (2010) 1–21.

Zhang, Liang. "Advance to Graduate Education: The Effect of College Quality and Undergraduate Majors." The Review of Higher Education 28.3 (2005) 313–38.

CHAPTER 2

Supporting Seminarians through Crises of Faith as a Means of Transformative Learning

ANASTASIA E. B. KIDD

INTRODUCTION[1]

I HAVE SERVED OVER a decade in the Admissions Office of the same seminary where I earned my own degrees. My role has been to help incoming students discern their first steps into theological higher education. With regularity, I have noticed a few students returning to my office in tears, typically a few months into classes each fall, often threatening to leave the seminary. Citing a variety of personal reasons, they fear they have made a mistake entering theological education. Listening to these students over the years, I began to hear patterns within their stories. I also noticed how these patterns mirrored my own movement through seminary.

Attending an urban university far away from my home in the rural South, my first semester of seminary was a wash of new experiences: riding (and often getting lost) on public transportation, paying an exorbitant price for a 300-square-foot studio apartment without laundry or air conditioning,

---

1. Much of this chapter appeared first in the author's Doctor of Ministry dissertation, which is available fully online through ProQuest. See Kidd, "Beyond It Gets Better."

and making new friends from a wider diversity of people and theological viewpoints than I had previously known existed, given my rather homogenous upbringing. To top it off, the entire country was reeling from its experience of 9/11, which happened during my first week of seminary coursework. I had no time or energy to consider the cumulative effect of these many changes on my psyche since graduate theological education was rigorously academic and assignments preoccupied every waking moment. I was new to the field, and each of my courses that semester—Introductions to Hebrew Bible, Church History, and Philosophical Theology—offered readings that confounded my understanding of my Christian heritage. Scriptures I had considered holy writ became filled with contradictions I had previously glossed over with eyes of the faithful.

I was at a Chili's restaurant when I hit my existential breaking point, tearfully asking my patient husband, "So, what if none of this is real? If there are all these problems and inconsistencies, who's to say there's even a God?" We had a much longer conversation than the waitress likely wanted us to have, but nothing was resolved. Nor would it be for years as I wrestled with questions of faith and doubt alongside my studies. With time, continued reading, and lots of conversations with others, my crisis of faith receded into a belief system that looks much different than that of my childhood, but is a solid platform from which to minister. However, some of my peers, who I learned were going through similar existential crises, left seminary for other vocations or reconciled their doubts by eschewing religion altogether. Despite all these cases, I knew that my seminary's goal was not to undermine its students' faith, but rather to challenge them to look critically at it so that they might be prepared to face a complex and ambiguous world as a religious leader.

I wondered if such "crises of faith" happened elsewhere, or were they a function of only my own institution? Looking into this question, I was unable to find consistent mention of student existential crisis in the literature on theological higher education, and virtually nothing on how to support students in the midst of one. Unsatisfied, I constructed a definition of "crisis of faith" borne of the common characteristics found in the stories of students I had encountered over the years. I then used this definition to survey several administrative peers at other mainline seminaries (n=44). The definition is as follows:

A crisis of faith is a season of theological limbo when previously-held truths are deeply questioned and no longer satisfy a person's current uncertainties, yet at the same time new truths have not been found, resulting in a feeling of being untethered. Some people navigate such turning points without crisis, but for others this is a disturbing and emotional experience. Many crises of faith result in a profound sense of confusion, fear, loss, anger, apathy toward studies or one's spiritual life, depression, and even physical or mental pain. Additionally, one can experience feelings of isolation from one's God, faith community, family, friends, or wider world. Crises of faith can be sudden or prolonged, and they happen to people of every faith tradition. They also arise frequently in the context of seminary education, where varieties of beliefs are introduced and challenged with regularity both within and outside of the classroom.

The survey found that nearly all of the non-faculty administrators (93 percent) had comparable stories from among their students. A common lament was that they did not know how to address student crises of faith systemically as an institution beyond "open door" policies and plenteous tissues at the ready. I undertook a simultaneous study of millennial-aged seminarians[2] in the Master of Divinity program of my institution (n=30), using the same definition above. This survey found that 76 percent of students reported having had an existential crisis themselves. Taken together, the results of the two surveys suggested that crises of faith are more than just an anecdotal occurrence at my own institution, but rather a common issue in theological higher education.[3]

CRISES OF FAITH: PART OF THE EXPLICIT, IMPLICIT, OR NULL CURRICULUM?

If crises of faith are frequently part of theological education, how are seminaries addressing them? Elliot Eisner, in a popular curricular theory, asserts that every educational institution teaches in three distinct ways. The "explicit curriculum" publicly shows up on course syllabi.[4] The implicit, or "hidden curriculum," is everything taught beyond the syllabi by the values portrayed by the institution and its rules, teacher preferences, the pedagogy of the courses, or even the setup of the building itself.[5] For example, a teach-

2. For the purpose of the survey, "millennial-aged students" were defined as anyone at the seminary who had been born after 1980. The goal of studying only one age group was to protect against generational and age-based confounding of the data, since stages of faith have been shown to develop over the course of a person's lifecycle. For more information on the stages of faith development, see Fowler, *Stages of Faith*. Additionally, at the time of the study, millennial-aged Master of Divinity students were the largest single group of students of all those enrolled in institutions accredited by the Association of Theological Schools. See ATS, "2016–2017 Annual Data Tables."

3. For full results of these surveys, see Kidd, "Beyond it Gets Better."

4. Eisner, *Educational Imagination*, 87–88.

5. Eisner, *Educational Imagination*, 88–93.

er's tendency to choose male voices to answer questions in the classroom would be "hidden curriculum" teaching that men are more valued in their opinions than people of other genders. But there is a third curriculum in Eisner's model, the "null curriculum," or what is not taught at all within the school.[6] Eisner offers, "It is my thesis that what schools do not teach may be as important as what they do teach."[7]

In many seminaries students' crises of faith are relegated to either the implicit curriculum or the null curriculum, and rarely are they treated as a central part of students' theological education. Crises of faith have broad-ranging implications for students' personal religious lives, spiritual formation, and vocational discernment. If crises of faith are only addressed peripherally or not at all within the seminary curricula, students who experience crises of faith do so in the vacuum of their own minds, supported only in so much as they are willing to reach out for help. Moreover, if a student finds their existential questions about God or religion troubling or shameful, they may be less likely to seek help even from those close to them.

While crises of faith are overlooked by those within the theological academy, there certainly exists an external narrative about them. The idea that people lose their faith in seminary has become a cliché—one that entire books have been written about,[8] as well as numerous blogs and online journals.[9] This argument has been used by those opposed to theological education to validate anti-intellectualism within churches and their leadership.[10] Seminaries should address student crises of faith directly, both through the explicit, classroom curricula and in implicit, co-curricular ways. This will help refute external claims that theological education is spiritually damaging and, most importantly, help students navigate their existential crises openly, with institutional support and care.

CRISES OF FAITH ARE A VALUABLE LEARNING TOOL

Research within psychology and educational theory suggests that crises of faith are helpful to human development and learning. Veronica Ton

6. Eisner, *Educational Imagination*, 97.

7. Eisner, *Educational Imagination*, 97.

8. See Roscher, *Keeping the Faith in Seminary*; Mathis and Parnell, *How to Stay Christian in Seminary*.

9. Many blogs and online journals recount individuals' feelings and personal experiences on this subject. For example, see Highland, "Seminary or Cemetery?"; Dreher, "How Seminary Ruins One's Faith."

10. Wheeler, "General Trends and Emerging Models," 664.

explored crises of faith in religious people from a psychological point of view. She mentions that faith crises often arise in early adulthood and offers, "Psychologically, as the ego expands, its demands to embrace polarities become greater."[11] Ton then lists a number of psychologists, Carl Jung the most recognized among them, who all credit crises of faith and their resultant psychic struggle as fundamentally important to a person's psychological growth.[12]

Daniel Aleshire, former Director of the Association of Theological Schools (ATS), recalled in a conference speech directed toward newly-appointed seminary faculty that it is their role to help students encounter new and potentially foundation-shaking ideas. He says, "You invite students across the divide between the naïve faith that most of them bring to seminary and the critically informed faith that will provide the foundation for their future work in ministry."[13] Yet this process of a seminary education that develops a critically-informed faith is by necessity more holistic than just cognitive learning.

The Carnegie Foundation's seminal *Educating Clergy* study named three different formational factors vital to successful religious training and leadership: cognitive (intellectual), practical (skill-based), and normative (personal and spiritual identity formation).[14] While seminary courses and contextual field education placements cover these first two factors, normative formation is shaped by students' coursework as well as by their own personal religious backgrounds and wider life experiences. The Association of Theological Schools' degree program standards require seminaries to have a cohesive educational mission that engages all three of these factors, with "normative" formation being depicted by ATS as "growth in spiritual depth and moral integrity."[15]

While it is true that seminary faculty are primarily, and rightfully, at the helm of seminarians' cognitive and practical formation, normative formation occurs in a variety of settings, and mostly outside of actual coursework. The *Educating Clergy* study found that spiritual formation practices offered by seminaries often take place beyond the classroom.[16] This is reinforced by a study at Fuller, which discovered that students' conversations around

11. Ton, "Crisis of Faith," 203.

12. Ton, "Crisis of Faith," 35–46.

13. Aleshire, "Work of Faculty."

14. Foster et al., *Educating Clergy*, 6–13.

15. ATS, "Degree Program Standards," 1.

16. Foster et al., *Educating Clergy*, 274.

real-world issues regularly moved from the classroom into the school's community life.[17]

Those who are training to be twenty-first-century religious leaders face questions like climate change, the complications of technology-fueled globalism, religiously-motivated terrorism and violence, and upticks in xenophobia and nationalism endangering longstanding cooperative political enterprises like the European Union and United Nations. They will face these global problems along with the local concerns of their communities, such as poverty and homelessness, racism and homophobia, pastoral care and mental illness, not to mention all the administrative minutiae that pester pastoral leaders. (A minister friend once quipped that he can sit by the hospital beds of dying parishioners and never doubt God as much as he does in church business meetings.) With all of these pressures and "big questions" to address, it is right for theological education to make students wrestle with ontological reality and existential meaning as part of their training so they will know how to wrestle with it authentically and faithfully as a religious leader.

USING TRANSFORMATIVE LEARNING THEORY TO UNDERSTAND CRISES OF FAITH

Classroom learning occasionally conflicts with a student's faith traditions, political viewpoints, or moral compass. In some ways, this is what education is meant at its core to do—to introduce a student to new and mind-expanding ideas, and to help them wrestle with their meaning and application in the world. This happens both within theological higher education and in secular educational settings, as well.

Crises of faith are talked about frequently in the context of secular learning theory, albeit by different names. For example, the work of educational theorist Jack Mezirow on Transformative Learning Theory (TLT) provides an excellent model for understanding how crises of faith function pedagogically. TLT also offers a language—disorienting dilemmas, changing assumptions, perspective transformation—that helps structure the seemingly-chaotic crisis of faith experience. TLT is well-known in the field of secular educational theory, but it is hard to find Mezirow or his intellectual progeny in research on specifically theological higher education.[18]

17. Lee et al., "Theological Education," 93.

18. There seems to be rather extensive research on TLT in fields such as medicine, communications, and business, but there is very little within the field of theological education. Even *Religious Education*, the primary journal of those in the field of religious

TLT's goal is to help students examine their assumptions, which often leads them to a shift in perspective.[19] Mezirow starts with the fundamental understanding that each adult learner brings to the classroom their own point of view, or "habits of mind," which has been shaped by both cognitive and tangible experiences in their life to date.[20] Some of these habits of mind may be individual beliefs unique to that person, influenced by one's culture and family of origin. However, a student's habits of mind often include paradigms shared collectively by many people,[21] for example, the religious doctrines espoused by the church of their youth or a certain political party.

Transformative learning begins when the student encounters a "disorienting dilemma," or something that does not fit with their current worldview, and they seek to reconcile it. This process has four major movements: the student's initial experience of a "disorienting dilemma," a time of internal critical reflection, engagement in external relational discourse, and responsive action.[22] I found that this four-fold process described by TLT was mirrored in the experiences of the Master of Divinity students I surveyed at my own institution.

BEST PRACTICES FOR SUPPORTING SEMINARIANS HAVING CRISES OF FAITH

Among the students surveyed, those who had reconciled their crises of faith reported three primary means of support that helped them through: persistent academic study, faith formation, and personal supportive guidance. Using each of these as subheadings, and drawing upon the TLT literature, below are some practical ways seminary faculty, staff, and administrators can collaborate with one another to support students through their crises of faith.

---

education and pedagogy, shows only a handful of articles (fifteen at last count in April 2018) that cite Mezirow's work anywhere, and only about half of those go into much detail on the theory itself. It seems that TLT is simply not fully on the radar within the field of theological education. Interestingly, Parker Palmer, whose work shares much in common with the basic principles of TLT, is extensively cited (almost four thousand times) within *Religious Education*. I believe that understanding the TLT model can enhance the discussion of crises of faith in seminary education among staff, faculty, and administrators alike.

19. Mezirow, *Learning as Transformation*, 296–97.

20. Mezirow, *Learning as Transformation*, 20.

21. Mezirow, *Learning as Transformation,* 20.

22. Cradit and Hunsaker, "Leveraging Transformative Learning Theory."

Persistent Academic Study

1. *Address crises of faith as part of the explicit curriculum of the seminary by helping students think of them as a "rite of passage" through theological education.*

Psychotherapist and educator Larry Green helpfully describes the movement between a disorienting dilemma and transformation (time that can be understood as a "crisis of faith") as a "liminal zone."[23] He believes this is an existential moment of choice: "Do I make the leap of faith [to transformation] or stay with what has served me up to this point?"[24] Green suggests that excellent mentoring and teaching is an important part of helping students make the decision to move forward rather than backward. He likens this "liminal zone" to the rites of passage in traditional and aboriginal cultures,[25] which make a path through which their people navigate challenging transitions. He says:

> These rites communicate: "Others have been here before you and others will follow." Moreover, there is a communal aspect to those rites that reassure the transforming individual that their community continues to support them and will recognize and affirm their new way of being. With these supports, the individual is more likely to experience the confidence to exercise their agency and see the process all the way through.[26]

So, even when crises arise within them, the person undergoing a rite of passage feels supported in their movement forward toward transformation. This is an excellent metaphor for crises of faith in theological education. Seminaries could use it both in terms of preparing students to experience crises of faith as part of their learning, and to prepare those around them (educators, as well as friends, family, and ecclesial leaders) to support them. This concept could be developed, for example, through Orientation programming and in first-year classes, as well as in robust student mentoring via faculty, administrators, or alumni networks.

23. Green, "Liminal Zone," 210–13.

24. Green, "Liminal Zone," 213.

25. One should be sensitive to cultural appropriation when imagining crises of faith within theological education as a rite of passage. The motifs of initiation, progression, and transformation can be useful descriptions of the process by which someone experiences a crisis of faith, as can the resources of a mentor/guide to "journey" alongside the person in crisis. However, non-indigenous people should not try to appropriate actual historical rituals to which they do not belong culturally. Here I am using "rite of passage" language metaphorically.

26. Green, "Liminal Zone," 214.

2. *Notice and address students' emotions, providing ample discussion time beyond the classroom to work through jarring academic concepts.*

When students' emotions arise in the context of the classroom or in the community life of the school, this experience can be distressing for teachers as well as fellow students.[27] Often the impulse is to attempt to quell those emotions as quickly as possible to return to the quiet of conventional academic decorum. Today, most research on TLT agrees that schools should take notice when students' emotions arise, as these are cues to their experience of learning.[28] Transformative learning is "messy," and demands that educators provide means by which student emotions can be expressed, whether as part of the curriculum or co-curriculum. John Dirkx has explored in his writings the emotional dimensions of adult transformative learning[29] and offers, "We have a ways to go before educators recognize emotions in adult learning, especially so-called negative emotions, as something other than a barrier or challenge to effective learning experiences, something to get off one's chest before real learning can occur."[30]

Dirkx goes on to discuss the role of emotions in helping adult learners work with one another in authentic dialogue across difference. Educators may perceive classroom outbursts, community disturbances, and heated online arguments between students as incidents to quash for the sake of institutional harmony. However, this distaste for emotion within the educational environment, Dirkx suggests, suppresses the learning potential inherent in these episodes.[31]

Parker Palmer similarly invites educators to employ integrative pedagogical practices that move beyond pure lecture-style teaching and provide classroom space for honest and open, even emotional conversations.[32] Recognizing not every teacher will want to, have time to, or be prepared to do this integrative work, another option is to develop regular personal reflection groups, staffed by non-faculty (ex. doctoral students, staff members, alumni, or area religious leaders), to further discuss academic concepts that upend students' emotions.

27. Dirkx, "Meaning and Role of Emotions," 8.

28. Clark and Dirkx, "Emotional Self," 90–91.

29. For examples, see Dirkx, *Adult Learning and the Emotional Self*; "Power of Feelings," 63–72; "Engaging Emotions in Adult Learning," 15–26.

30. Clark and Dirkx, "Emotional Self," 91.

31. Dirkx, "Meaning and Role of Emotions," 11–15.

32. Palmer and Zajonc, *Heart of Higher Education*, 6–15. This book calls on educators to consider the holistic formation of each student by helping them integrate their cognitive lives with how they engage the world, thus "integrative" education.

3. *Offer lifelong learning opportunities.*

Transformative learning is a cyclical process. Transformation is never completed "once and for always" in a person's life. Seminary graduates may encounter new information and experiences that shake their faith even as professional religious leaders or ordained clergy. Indeed, crises of faith can occur at any age or stage of theological development. For this reason, seminaries do well to create a robust network of alumni opportunities for lifelong learning. Options might include allowing alumni to participate in coursework at a reduced cost, offering "webinars" or conferences on controversial yet timely topics, or simply providing online space for thoughtful conversations between alumni, perhaps mediated by faculty or non-faculty student support staff.

Faith Formation

1. *Provide incoming students ample information about area faith communities, including times of services and contact information of other students who attend them.*

Students who travel to new locations for seminary may have left their faith communities behind. Others may begin to prioritize time for study over time spent in regular worship or faith development. Having a faith community beyond the seminary helps students experiencing a crisis of faith remain engaged in spiritual practice.

2. *Offer spiritual enrichment opportunities through the seminary and encourage student participation.*

Most seminaries provide some sort of regularly-scheduled community worship service.[33] At some schools, the liturgy is well-attended, central to community life, and integrated with the classroom experience; while worship other places is described by the Carnegie study as "almost tangential," with low attendance and no apparent link to the community's culture or curricula.[34] For this reason seminary worship may or may not be a central source of support for students having crises of faith. Beyond worship services, seminaries can encourage students' co-curricular spiritual formation by offering enrichment opportunities such as student retreats and programming that models various spiritual practices.

---

33. Van Driel, "Online Theological Education," 73–74.

34. Foster et al., *Educating Clergy*, 274.

3. *Create a culture where faculty, staff, and administrators model speaking about faith and doubt honestly.*

Since most institutions have a weekly chapel service, integrating personal testimony that affirms the difficulty of wrestling with crises of faith may open dialogue in other settings, as well. Normalizing crises of faith as something those in leadership have also gone through will assure students that they, too, will be able to navigate them successfully.

Personal Supportive Guidance

1. *Establish peer or alumni/ae mentoring networks.*

No one understands the experience of a crisis of faith more than those who have had one themselves. Seminaries can identify leaders from among their upper-level current student body or alumni/ae to pair with incoming students from similar regions, denominations, or areas of study. Residential seminaries may want to further encourage dialogue between students and their mentors by providing an opening reception where they can meet in-person. Mentors should be invited at some point in their relationship with the students to share briefly their own stories of wrestling with doubts, mentioning that this might occur acutely during seminary study. If and when it does, the student will have this person as a resource for further discussion.

2. *Provide students information on confidential counseling services or spiritual direction outside of the seminary community.*

The study of millennial-age Master of Divinity students at my institution showed that a third of them cited issues of personal identity as precipitating their crises of faith, not just classroom learning. The students who listed personal identity issues as a trigger to their crisis of faith described experiences such as coming to terms with their own sexuality or gender-identity, reconciling their LGBTQIA status with their Christian upbringing, experiencing lapses in mental health, or being a woman called to ordained ministry in a denomination that discourages female leadership. These "disorienting dilemmas" may feel too personal to share with anyone in the seminary administration. Unfortunately, it is also true that not all theological schools are places where issues such as sexual identity or mental health can be discussed by students without fear of stigma, or even ecclesial reprisal in cases of those seeking ordination. As such, seminary leaders should remember the importance of facilitating students' therapeutic relationships with outside professionals bound by confidentiality.

3. *Utilize non-faculty administrators and staff in personal student support.*

Students having crises of faith benefit from speaking with others about their experience, particularly those who can empathize with them. The survey I undertook of non-faculty seminary professionals (n=44) found that a vast majority (84 percent) held at least one theological degree. More than two-thirds of respondents (69 percent) had received the Master of Divinity, and were thus formed for professional religious leadership as part of their theological education. Unfortunately, there is not a comprehensive survey of non-faculty seminary professionals to which one could point to say whether these numbers are indicative of a norm. (This would be an excellent study for the ATS to undertake.) However, it could be that many institutions already have a population of seminary-trained religious leaders available to support their students' co-curricular needs within their own staff.

This theory is backed by the decades' worth of research that has occurred in secular higher education's Student Affairs field. Student Affairs has become a specialized discipline with professional membership organizations, peer-reviewed journals, and national conferences. To provide "academic support" is secular Student Affairs' primary professional goal.[35] Either this research from the secular Student Affairs discipline has not been on the radar of most theological educators, or it has been ignored. As such, it is likely that in many seminaries, non-faculty student services staff are neither held to the professional development standards of training and expertise that their secular counterparts are, nor are they thought of as viable partners for co-curricular academic programming in consultation with faculty. There is an opportunity for seminary non-faculty staff to be professionalized in the same way that this career cohort has been within secular higher education. Doing so could build upon existing Student Affairs research but grow the field with particular attention to the unique formational needs of students within theological education. Addressing seminarians' crises of faith would be an excellent starting point toward this collaborative partnership between institutions' academic and student services departments.

CONCLUSION

Seminaries that move student crises of faith into their institutions' explicit curricula will normalize them as an important step in the faith formation of twenty-first-century religious leaders. Understanding crises of faith as transformative learning in the model of Mezirow will help seminary faculty and non-faculty administrators develop methods of addressing them within and beyond the classroom. Such plans should provide resources for

35. See ACPA, "Student Learning Imperative"; "Trends and Issues."

persistent academic study, faith formation, and personal supportive guidance, as these have been shown to aid in students' reconciliation of crises of faith.

BIBLIOGRAPHY

Aleshire, Daniel. "The Work of Faculty and the Educational Goals of Theological Schools." Paper presented at the ATS Seminar for Newly Appointed Faculty in Theological Education, Pittsburgh, PA, October 2010. Online. http://www.ats. edu/uploads/resources/publications-presentations/documents/work-of-faculty-and-the-educational-goals-of-theological-education.pdf.

American College Personnel Association—College Student Educators International (ACPA). "Student Learning Imperative: Implications for Student Affairs." September 10, 2008. Online. http://www.myacpa.org/sites/default/files/ ACPA%27s%20Student%20Learning%20Imperative.pdf.

———. "Trends and Issues in Academic Support: 2016–2017." Commission for Academic Support Monograph. 2017. Online. https://www.myacpa.org/sites/ default/files/ACPA%20CASHE%20Monograph%20FINAL.PDF.

Association of Theological Schools (ATS). "2016–2017 Annual Data Tables." Online. https://www.ats.edu/uploads/resources/institutional-data/annual-data-tables/2016–2017-annual-data-tables.pdf.

———. "Degree Program Standards." January 21, 2015. Online. https://www.ats.edu/ uploads/accrediting/documents/degree-program-standards.pdf.

Clark, M. Carolyn, and John M. Dirkx. "The Emotional Self in Adult Learning." *New Directions for Adult and Continuing Education* 120 (2008) 89–96.

Cradit, Nate, and Marc Hunsaker. "Leveraging Transformative Learning Theory to Promote Student Development in Times of Campus Crisis." Paper presented at NASPA: Student Affairs Professionals in Higher Education, Indianapolis, IN, March 12–16, 2016. Online. https://www.slideshare.net/NateCradit/leveraging-transformative-learning-theory-to-promote-student-development-in-times-of-campus-crisis.

Dirkx, John M., ed. *Adult Learning and the Emotional Self.* San Francisco: Jossey-Bass, 2008.

———. "Engaging Emotions in Adult Learning: A Jungian Perspective on Emotion and Transformative Learning." *New Directions in Adult and Continuing Education* 2006.109 (2006) 15–26.

———. "The Meaning and Role of Emotions in Adult Learning." *New Directions for Adult and Continuing Education* 2008.120 (2008) 7–18.

———. "The Power of Feelings: Emotion, Imagination, and the Construction of Meaning in Adult Learning." *New Directions for Adult and Continuing Education* 2001.89 (2001) 63–72.

Dreher, Rod. "How Seminary Ruins One's Faith." *Beliefnet* (blog), May 2010. Online. http://www.beliefnet.com/columnists/roddreher/2010/05/how-seminary-ruins-ones-faith.html.

Eisner, Elliot. *The Educational Imagination: On the Design and Evaluation of School Program.* 3rd ed. New York: Macmillan, 1994.

Foster, Charles R., et al. *Educating Clergy.* San Francisco: Jossey-Bass, 2006.

Fowler, James W. *Stages of Faith: The Psychology of Human Development and the Quest for Meaning*. San Francisco: HarperOne, 1995.

Green, Larry. "Transformative Learning: A Passage Through the Liminal Zone." In *Psychoanalysis and Education: Minding a Gap*, edited by Alan Bainbridge and Linden West, 199–216. London: Karnac, 2012.

Highland, Chris. "Seminary or Cemetery?" *Patheos* (blog), July 21, 2014. Online. http://www.patheos.com/blogs/rationaldoubt/2014/07/seminary-or-cemetery.

Kidd, Anastasia E. B. "Beyond It Gets Better: Utilizing Seminary Student Affairs Professionals to Support Millennial Students Through Crises of Faith." DMin diss., Boston University, 2018.

Lee, Cameron, et al. "Theological Education in a Multicultural Environment: Empowerment or Disempowerment?" *Theological Education* 43.2 (2008) 93–105.

Mathis, David, and Jonathan Parnell. *How to Stay Christian in Seminary*. Wheaton, IL: Crossway, 2014.

Mezirow, Jack, ed. *Learning as Transformation: Critical Perspectives on a Theory in Progress*. San Francisco: Jossey-Bass, 2000.

Palmer, Parker, and Arthur Zajonc. *The Heart of Higher Education, A Call to Renewal: Transforming the Academy Through Collegial Conversations*. San Francisco: Jossey-Bass, 2010.

Roscher, Ellie, ed. *Keeping the Faith in Seminary*. Minneapolis, MN: Avenida, 2012.

Ton, Veronica. "Crisis of Faith and Reconciliation: A Psychological Exploration of Religion." PhD diss., Wright Institute, 1993.

Van Driel, Edwin Chr. "Online Theological Education: Three Undertheorized Issues." *Theological Education* 50.1 (2015) 69–79.

Wheeler, Barbara. "General Trends and Emerging Models Across Christian Denominations." In *Religious Leadership: A Reference Handbook*, edited by Sharon Henderson Callahan, 661–68. Los Angeles: Sage, 2013.

CHAPTER 3

So That You Can Endure

Pastoral Care and Prophetic Insights as Competencies for Graduate Theological Student Services

Yvette D. Wilson-Barnes

God will also provide a way out so that you can endure it.

—1 Corinthians 10:13 (NIV)

THE MINISTRY AND THE GAP

The work of student affairs practitioners, in general, can be extremely demanding and challenging—leading to burnout. For those called to the ministry of graduate theological student services, even more so. To provide student affairs practitioners with a framework to do the work, the College Student Educators International (ACPA) and the Student Affairs Administrators in Higher Education (NASPA) established professional competencies. These competencies are benchmarks for measuring degrees of field-based knowledge and proficiency. Although helpful in cultivating professional development in the field, there is a need for competencies that speak to the spiritual and theological dimensions of graduate theological student services. Adding pastoral care approaches and prophetic insights as professional competencies for graduate theological student services will address this gap. These competencies will lead graduate theological student services practitioners to take prophetic action that responds thoughtfully and powerfully to the needs of students and to endure the work.

COMPETENCIES GUIDE THE WORK

It is reassuring to know what is expected in the daily activities of any profession. In the field of student services, a student affairs practitioner needs to understand and live into the competencies of the role to successfully assist students on their academic journey. ACPA and NASPA spent years fine-tuning these competencies as blueprints to guide the work regardless of the student affairs practitioners' specialization. The ten competencies in total, intersect with each other, and are as follows:

1. Personal and Ethical Foundations

2. Values, Philosophy, and History

3. Assessment, Evaluation, and Research

4. Law, Policy, and Governance

5. Organizational and Human Resources

6. Leadership

7. Social Justice and Inclusion

8. Student Learning and Development

9. Technology

10. Advising and Supporting

They begin with the competency of personal and ethical foundations which calls the student affairs practitioner to establish and adhere to a moral and ethical compass that informs professional behavior.[1] The second, focused on values, philosophy, and history, describes the way the profession of student affairs has evolved and is trending, allowing the practitioner to envision new approaches to the practice of administering student services.[2] The third, centered around assessment, evaluation, and research, highlights the need for student affairs practitioners to determine a methodology for

1. ACPA and NAPSA, "Professional Competency Areas," 16–17.
2. ACPA and NAPSA, "Professional Competency Areas," 18–19.

measuring student learning, program impact and service delivery outcomes.[3] The fourth requires an understanding of how law, policy, and governance supports equity and due processes, mitigates any thoughts of rendering arbitrary and capricious administrative decisions as well as helps with minimizing institutional risk.[4] The fifth interacts with organizational and human resources as a way of supporting professional development, facilitating the prevention of conflicts or interceding to resolve existing ones, and advocating for resources needed to effectively do the work of student affairs.[5] The sixth is about leadership; the way decisions are made, the way stakeholders are engaged; the way teams are built; and the way authority is embodied and lived out to effect change, develop other leaders, and foster a spirit of consensus and collaboration.[6] The seventh warrants the facilitation of social justice and inclusion to educate and bring awareness to how power can be abused, privilege can be misused, and oppressive tactics and practices create barriers to access and opportunities.[7] All of which need to be dismantled. The eighth states the importance of cultivating student learning and development by understanding the intersectionality of diversities across the student community and how it informs learning, feelings of inclusivity, and belonging.[8] The ninth engages technology—inviting a better understanding of how digital resources can enhance student learning outcomes.[9] And the tenth and final competency speaks to the impact of advising and supporting students' academic progress, social interactions, emotional well-being and development, and vocational discernment and aspirations.[10]

Although ACPA and NASPA captured competencies relevant to the work of student affairs in general within higher education, the competencies also inform the knowledge and skill sets needed to enhance the theological, academic, spiritual, and emotional well-being of students obtaining a graduate theological education. These competencies speak to the technical nature of the work, not how to withstand the challenges of the work for the long-haul—how to endure.

3. ACPA and NAPSA, "Professional Competency Areas," 20–21.

4. ACPA and NAPSA, "Professional Competency Areas," 22–23.

5. ACPA and NAPSA, "Professional Competency Areas," 24–26.

6. ACPA and NAPSA, "Professional Competency Areas," 27–29.

7. ACPA and NAPSA, "Professional Competency Areas," 30–31.

8. ACPA and NAPSA, "Professional Competency Areas," 32.

9. ACPA and NAPSA, "Professional Competency Areas," 33–35.

10. ACPA and NAPSA, "Professional Competency Areas," 36–37.

ENDURING FOR SUCH A TIME

Endurance is the fuel needed to keep us going. Its' spiritual dimension gives strength when we are weak, tired, and feel like giving up. Endurance is needed not just to survive but to feed our thriving and passion for this student affairs ministry I have been a part of for more than eight years.

Endurance is resiliency. The authors of *Resilient: How To Grow An Unshakable Core of Calm, Strength, and Happiness* define it as the ability "to cope with adversity and push through challenges in the pursuit of opportunities."[11] They also show a direct correlation between resilience and well-being.[12] In *Exceptional Senior Student Affairs Administrators' Leadership: Strategies and Competencies for Success*, Eileen Hulme highlights the important relationship between well-being and hope.[13] Hulme wrote, "It is easy to let discouragement seep into your work. . . . Each day presents countless issues to address and problems to solve."[14] Then Hulme posed a question important for all student affairs practitioners to reflect on and answer, "How can leaders maintain a hopeful mindset in the midst of these demands?"[15] I propose seeing the power and impact of integrating pastoral care approaches and prophetic insights as invaluable competencies to endure the ministerial work of student services.

PASTORAL CARE APPROACHES IN THE MINISTRY OF STUDENT SERVICES

Burnout is a reality for student affairs practitioners. It hit home quickly upon assuming the role of Associate Dean for Student Life and Assistant Director of Recruitment at Union Theological Seminary (Union) in the City of New York on February 1, 2010.

As I engaged and settled in to my new role it became clear immediately that traveling for admissions recruitment and managing the day-to-day operations of the Office of Student Life and responding to the needs of students would be challenging. My work as a recruiter pulled me away from focusing primarily on student matters. I worked diligently and intentionally over a three-year period with the administration to have the recruitment responsibilities within my portfolio evaluated, with a recommendation to have

11. Hanson and Hanson, *Resilient*, 2.

12. Hanson and Hanson, *Resilient*, 2.

13. Hulme, "Leader as an Agent of Hope," 253–66.

14. Hulme, "Leader as an Agent of Hope," 263.

15. Hulme, "Leader as an Agent of Hope," 263.

recruiting removed from my job description to focus solely on student life. With this shift, my title changed to Associate Dean for Student Affairs and the office name changed to the Office of Student Affairs (hereinafter, Office). The emphasis was to support the highest quality education for students and ensure compliance with internal and external regulations, while facilitating building a student culture of ownership, leadership, and engagement in collaboration with students, staff, and faculty. In addition, the position provides visionary administrative leadership and strategic management of the office to create, foster, and sustain a safe, healthy, and supportive atmosphere and community that synchronizes the academic, theological, spiritual, intellectual, physical, social, and emotional development, orientation, retention, and graduation of students dedicated to addressing the most complex social justice and faith issues of this era. All of this is done with limited full-time staff which includes myself and an administrative assistant, and a few part-time student workers as I oversee disability services; international student services; student health insurance enrollment/waiver processes; referral processes for students to obtain services, as needed, from Columbia University's counseling and psychological services, medical services, and sexual violence response center support; new student orientation; spiritual formation and spirit care resources; career development and job placement resources in conjunction with the Office of Integrative and Field-Based Education; academic advocacy and support; extra-curricular programming, events, and workshops; the provision of Title IX support; and much more.

How do I endure this ministerial work? First, by praying, for myself and being prayed for and praying for the student body, faculty, and staff/administration. Second, by creating a team with other colleagues where our work intersects. One example is collaborating with the Director of Housing and Campus Services who although is a part of a different department, shares a common vision of facilitating the building of intentional community between students, staff, and faculty. This occurs with the efforts of the student caucus leaders and the assistance of two Student Life Assistants (SLA) hired every academic year. Third, by having an Executive Coach (EC) to facilitate an annual SLA team retreat. The EC also checks in with the SLA team at least three times per semester. This is to facilitate reflecting on our accomplishments and growing edges and to reground us to continue the work.

It is at the SLA retreat that we identify the pastoral care approaches needed to do the ministry of student services for the upcoming academic year. But it is not without first taking time to assess the prior year. The work of student services cannot be done alone, it must be a team effort. Even if you do not have a team, you can create one.

Throughout the retreat we take the time to reflect on and answer the following general questions: What worked? What did not work? What was needed for us to be and do a better job of providing student services? How did we grow, communicate effectively and support each other as a team or not? Did the student demographic change and if so, were we prepared and equipped to meet the needs of the changing student population? What systemic student issues from the prior academic year can we anticipate will reemerge in the upcoming academic year? How should we approach addressing these issues differently than the prior year? These are a few questions to reflect on and inform a retreat agenda.

At one of the SLA team retreats we engaged questions such as, how do we:

1. Negotiate with the faculty and administration on matters students are against?

2. Hold onto our integrity when we are not in alignment with an institutional decision we must help facilitate as a part of our job responsibilities?

3. Establish a strong relationship with each other?

4. Slow down, so others can catch up?

5. Bring the vision of hope to others?

6. Foster better communication across the institution?

7. Build and sustain a solid team?

Before we attempted to answer these questions, we decided that it was important to determine what the spirit of our team needed to be. As we began to name who we needed to be, it became clear that what we named for ourselves, which is not an exhaustive list, is what we want and need to foster in our campus community. So, the answers to our questions were the catalyst for what we needed to embody personally and collectively:

Table 1. Naming Exercise

• Oneness/Unity	• Inspiration	• Alignment with the Divine
• Trustworthiness	• The capacity to share one's feelings; encourage vulnerability	• Love and Kindness
• Better Communication	• Respect	• Diversity, Justice, and Equity
• Openness to receiving the Spirit	• Authenticity	• Solidarity
• Healthy ways to deal with conflict	• Accountability	• Gratitude
• Courage	• Strength/Power	• Joy

It was a profound revelation to name what gives us as a team the ability to endure this important ministry. Rick Hanson and Forrest Hanson talk about the benefits of positive emotions in supporting physical health and recovery from loss and trauma and in allowing us to see the bigger picture of life and the opportunities they bring to connect people to each other.[16]

After the team named who we needed to be to understand what we need to help inspire on our campus, we engaged in a case study on how to address the needs of community members and a returning student from medical leave. The student, prior to being placed on leave, exhibited behavior that triggered fear and trauma within the community. The student, however, received the mental health-related support warranted and had met all the requirements of their return plan including medical clearance from their health provider.

Identifying some of the needs of the student and campus community, as a team, provided us with an action plan that can be used as a guide to address similar scenarios in the future with calm, resolve, caution, compassion, and understanding.

16. Hanson and Hanson, *Resilient*, 2.

Table 2. Response to Student's Return to Campus
and Community's Triggers/Traumas

Response to Student's Return to Campus and Community's Triggers/Traumas	
Student Needs	**Community Needs**
• Prayer	• Prayer
• Regular check-ins	• Space to adjust to student's return and to provide assurance of safety
• To feel part of the community	• To communicate at different levels (i.e., classroom and dorm peers)
• To not directly feel all eyes are on them	• Check-in's with some returning students and other community members
• To determine who they can trust and talk to when they feel triggered	• To manage gossip and panic
• Space to settle-in	• To foster understanding of the varied dimensions of mental health issues and triggers, and the intersectionality of race, gender and bias
• To understand the community's needs and concerns related to triggering the community	• To address student's right to return and right to privacy and confidentiality
• To address feeling lonely, isolated, and targeted by members of the community	
• To address students right to return and right to privacy and confidentiality	

Darby Dickerson's chapter on "Legal Issues for Campus Administrators, Faculty, and Staff" in *College Student Mental Health: Effective Services and Strategies Across Campus* outlines how extremely important it is to find a balance between the confidentiality of a student experiencing a mental health crisis and the safety of the campus.[17] Dickerson provides steps that should be considered such as:[18]

• Ensuring the institution's policies and procedures are in alignment with state and federal laws and that faculty and key administrators protect student's confidential information

17. Dickerson, "Legal Issues," 35–101.
18. Dickerson, "Legal Issues," 59–60.

- Providing campus safety training to community members recognizing that the health and safety concerns can override rules of privacy

- Helping students understand what is non-private versus private information that can be released, and the high levels of confidentiality health providers are subjected to

- Determining whether the institution is governed by the Health Insurance Portability and Accountability Act (HIPAA) and consult with an attorney to ensure compliance

Another part of our retreat exercise is to identify other issues we need to anticipate addressing in any given academic year and beyond. For example, addressing the impact of the deaths of professors and scholars who significantly influenced the campus community (i.e., Rev. Dr. James Cone and Rev. Dr. Katie Cannon). We discussed class dynamics regarding race, religion, gender, age, sexuality, and ableism, etc. We reflected on the impact we felt mid-term elections would have on the society's political and spiritual psyche and on campus life. We considered the cultural shock and adjustment of new students including international students to campus. We brainstormed support for students struggling with addictions and/or maintaining their recovery. We discussed how to support students with suicidal ideations, trauma from domestic violence, sexual harassment, assault, and misconduct. And we contemplated the fears of students with existing and accumulating debt and their concerns about finding employment post-graduation that aligns with their vocational calling. We pondered students' heartfelt concerns about police brutality in this country and therefore, police presence on campus for non-emergency situations. And then we needed to consider the power dynamic and differential between the administration, faculty, and students and how it informs who, how, and when there is trust. The issues are considerable, extending to how students will adjust to new academic programs and requirements as well as students feeling not enough safe spaces exist in and outside the classroom, to be heard. We even thought about departments with limited staff and classroom spaces to serve an increasing student population. And thought through the support needed for student bereavements and those trying to understand who the seminary will be in an ever-changing and evolving complex world. These important facets and opportunities within student affairs beckon us to always be prepared for a crisis to emerge depending on how community members react to how these topics are addressed.[19] In *Masters of Disaster: The Ten Commandments of Damage Control,* authors Christopher Lehane, Mark Fabiani,

19. Lehane et al., *Masters of Disaster*, 9–17.

and Bill Guttentag claim there is an art to handling crises that are guided by three principles.[20] The first principle is to do no harm.[21] The second is to take a disciplined approach.[22] The third is to preserve credibility.[23]

The three principles are also important in pastoral caring. Howard Clinebell in the *Basic Types of Pastoral Care & Counseling*, defines pastoral care as an inclusive ministry of healing and growth that a community mutually agrees to be a part of.[24] Clinebell states that when people are not able to move forward in life because of a crisis, pastoral counseling as a therapeutic method helps repair a person's ability to function.[25] Certainly, in the instance where a student is in crisis, such as in the case study discussed earlier, the role of the student affairs practitioner is to refer the student to a service that will provide the student with the support they need. It is also critical to help facilitate the student getting there. Clinebell believes that pastoral care must infuse psychological and theological insights that foster a holistic, liberative, and growth centered approach.[26] In order for this approach to work, the pastoral care provider, in this context, the student affairs practitioner, must be committed to self-reflection and personal growth.[27] Clinebell poignantly states, "To be an enlivener, we must stay alive. To enable healing, we must be vulnerable enough to face and accept our own continuing need for healing."[28]

Kevin Cashman in *Leadership From The Inside Out* calls this growth, personal mastery.[29] It is about being aware of our total selves; embracing our gifts and strengths; and confronting our blind-spots and growing edges.[30] Cashman discusses eight principles to follow on the path to personal mastery for the manifestation of leadership that is authentically courageous.[31]

- Principle 1: Take Total Responsibility—Fully commit to the process of mastery.

20. Lehane et al., *Masters of Disaster*, 18.
21. Lehane et al., *Masters of Disaster*, 18.
22. Lehane et al., *Masters of Disaster*, 18.
23. Lehane et al., *Masters of Disaster*, 18.
24. Clinebell, *Basic Types of Pastoral Care*, 26.
25. Clinebell, *Basic Types of Pastoral Care*, 26.
26. Clinebell, *Basic Types of Pastoral Care*, 25–45.
27. Clinebell *Basic Types of Pastoral Care*, 28.
28. Clinebell, *Basic Types of Pastoral Care*, 28.
29. Cashman, *Leadership from the Inside Out*, 15.
30. Cashman, *Leadership from the Inside Out*, 15.
31. Cashman, *Leadership from the Inside Out*, 13–42.

- Principle 2: Bring Beliefs to Conscious Awareness—Reflect on and challenge beliefs and how those beliefs determine how others are impacted by those beliefs.

- Principle 3: Develop Awareness of Character and Coping—Know character changes situations and increases vitality and coping reacts to circumstances and expends vigor.

- Principle 4: Practice Personal Mastery with Others—Take the risk to be vulnerable with others. Connecting with others allows personal blind spots to surface to be assessed and addressed.

- Principle 5: Listen to Feedback—Receive input and learn from others for lifelong learning.

- Principle 6: Consider Finding a Coach—Accept professional support to accelerate leadership development.

- Principle 7: Avoid Confusing Self-Delusion with Self-Awareness—Use validated assessment tools to help identify the areas of growth in need of work.

- Principle 8: Be Agile—Be flexible. What worked in the past may not work in the future.

These methods are powerful tools for supporting personal growth and professional leadership development. When student affairs practitioners within graduate theological education commit to this important self-work, the pastoral care approaches they provide will be beneficial to students. This self-work will also help us as leaders power through with prophetic insight and action to endure this good work and inspire hope.

POWERING THROUGH WITH PROPHETIC INSIGHT AND ACTION

It is a divine gift and the generosity of spirit that enables anyone to power through with prophetic insight and action. My definition of prophetic insight and action is the ability to discern or understand what happened in the past and what is happening in the present as a predictor of what could happen in the future. The understanding of the past and present helps with the discernment of what next steps could and should take place. Insightful action as a result becomes fuel for enduring what is to come. This is because future issues have already been identified to mitigate their escalation through the development of an action plan that is intentional and strategic.

The goal is always to address them with thoughtfulness for a short—or—long term solution.

In *Success Under Stress: Powerful Tools for Staying Calm, Confident, and Productive When the Pressure's On*, Sharon Melnick states that "Stress is not necessarily the result of the workload, the lack of response, the interruptions, or the "traffic jam" of unfinished projects and overextended commitments. It occurs when the demands of a situation exceed your perceived ability to control them. The key is that the more you perceive you can control, the lower your stress, and vice versa."[32] This perceiving discussed by Melnick, is the prophetic insight I am referring to which follows by taking action that is manageable because short-term solutions for long-term results has been identified.[33]

In recent years Union made the decision to sell a section of its campus' air rights to developers of condominiums which will include housing Union's faculty and some administrative offices. Additionally, one of the residential halls was sold. And furthermore, the seminary's campus renewal project to improve accessibility, enhance student housing, and improve classrooms and office spaces, has been an important strategic planning commitment. News about the development of condominiums on Union's campus alarmed some constituents of the seminary who feel the project goes against the seminary's mission and commitment to social justice as they think about gentrification, displacement and lack of affordable housing in the city of New York. Like many seminaries around the country Union is faced with the question of sustainability and survival, considering its aging infrastructure and exorbitant maintenance costs. As the seminary embarks on this project, the Office of Student Affairs (Office) is one of several departments that anticipates and weighs all student concerns as the project unfolds and students face changes that will impact their lives and the entire campus community. While there are many who will grapple with what kind of seminary Union will be post-campus renewal and condominium development, the role of the student affairs practitioner and the Office in this moment is to help facilitate conversations between the students and the administration that supports students being heard as they think about how construction noise and debris as well as space limitations will impact their studying, learning, and living conditions and situations. Ellen Heffernan, a contributing author to *Exceptional Senior Student Affairs Administrators' Leadership* is clear that, "Successful student affairs leaders understand that it is not about "advocating for students," instead, it is about being able to

32. Melnick, *Success Under Stress*, 19.

33. Melnick, *Success Under Stress*, 19–30.

articulate student issues and concerns and identifying, for the president and the board, how a decision will impact the ability of students to successfully graduate."[34] This speaks to our gift as student affairs practitioners to hold tensions, articulate concerns and facilitate bridge building. It is a delicate line to walk when organizational change is occurring.

In *Understanding and Facilitating Organizational Change in the Twenty-First Century,* author Adrianna J. Kezar explains that external factors alone do not contribute to change.[35] In fact, Kezar details that an institution's culture affects the type of change occurring and the way change occurs, suggesting that the best way to monitor change is to commission a committee to do so.[36]

This change management committee is most effective with the student affairs practitioner on it. Being a part of such a committee at Union has given me the opportunity to share with its members the impact of the project on students. It also allows me to make recommendations for solutions to address the impact. Student affairs practitioners get to be agents of change in seasons of change when change is not easy to accept and feels more like a crisis. According to Kezar the savviest change agents have knowledge of who has campus influence, what alliances should be established, when informal processes can be most effective, what conflicts are arising, and what is motivating the change.[37] When change feels like a crisis, the student affairs practitioner should be a haven for students to share their questions, concerns, and feedback.[38] Details matter when responding to the questions and any attempt to marginalize information magnifies the lack of it, creating mistrust.[39] Increase trustworthiness by minimizing discrepancies.[40]

Student leaders in collaboration with the student affairs practitioner are an important constituent to engage the administration in seasons of change. They can play a crucial role in communicating with their peers, brainstorming solutions, and negotiating with the administration for the best possible outcome.[41] It has been extremely productive at Union for the Student Life Assistants and Caucus leaders to exist in that role, particularly regarding the projects. How the seminary adequately prepares for the

34. Heffernan, "Competencies," 118.

35. Kezar, *Understanding and Facilitating Organizational Change,* 115.

36. Kezar, *Understanding and Facilitating Organizational Change,* 115.

37. Kezar, *Understanding and Facilitating Organizational Change,* 115–16.

38. Lehane et al., *Masters of Disaster,* 154.

39. Lehane et al., *Masters of Disaster,* 111.

40. Lehane et al., *Masters of Disaster,* 111.

41. Miser and Cherrey, "Responding to Campus Crisis," 611.

projects and who the seminary decides to be during them, will help determine who the seminary will be when the projects are done.

THE CALL IS TOO IMPORTANT TO IGNORE

Student affairs practitioners are called to discern mitigating factors to help assess the impact a situation or a decision can have on a campus community. Student affairs practitioners are forerunners. We are a gift to any institution, particularly to graduate theological schools who are committed to preparing students to be faith leaders in the academy, church, or society. To be of service to students and tackle the myriad of issues and concerns they bring to our attention, calls for a pastoral approach that is prophetically insightful and action-oriented towards making the student experience in seminary meaningful and the ministry of service enduring.

BIBLIOGRAPHY

American College Personnel Association—College Student Educators International (ACPA), and Student Affairs Administrators in Higher Education (NAPSA). "Professional Competency Areas for Student Affairs Educators." 2015. Online. https://www.naspa.org/images/uploads/main/ACPA_NASPA_Professional_Competencies_.pdf.

Cashman, Kevin. *Leadership from the Inside Out: Becoming a Leader for Life.* 3rd ed. Oakland, CA: Berrett-Koehler, 2017.

Clinebell, Howard. *Basic Types of Pastoral Care & Counseling: Resources for the Ministry of Healing & Growth.* Nashville, TN: Abingdon, 1984.

Dickerson, Darby. "Legal Issues for Campus Administrators, Faculty, and Staff." In *College Student Mental Health: Effective Services and Strategies Across Campus,* edited by Sheryl A. Benton and Stephen L. Benton, 35–101. Washington, DC: NASPA, 2006.

Hanson, Rick, and Forrest Hanson. *Resilient: How to Grow an Unshakable Core of Calm, Strength, and Happiness.* New York: Harmony, 2018.

Heffernan, Ellen T. "Competencies for the Seasoned Senior Student Affairs Officer: View from The Top." In *Exceptional Senior Student Affairs Administrators' Leadership: Strategies and Competencies for Success,* edited by Gwendolyn Jordan Dungy and Shannon E. Ellis, 117–52. Washington, DC: NASPA, 2011.

Hulme, Eileen. "The Leader as an Agent of Hope." In *Exceptional Senior Student Affairs Administrators' Leadership: Strategies and Competencies for Success,* edited by Gwendolyn Jordan Dungy and Shannon E. Ellis, 253–66. Washington, DC: NASPA, 2011.

Kezar, Adrianna J. *Understanding and Facilitating Organizational Change in the Twenty-First Century: Recent Research and Conceptualizations.* Vol. 28. San Francisco: Jossey-Bass, 2001.

Lehane, Christopher, et al. *Masters of Disaster: The Ten Commandments of Damage Control.* New York: St. Martin's Griffin, 2014.

Melnick, Sharon. *Success Under Stress: Powerful Tools for Staying Calm, Confident, and Productive When the Pressure's On.* New York: AMACOM, 2013.

Miser, Keith M., and Cynthia Cherrey. "Responding To Campus Crisis." In *The Handbook of Student Affairs Administration*, edited by George S. McClellan and Jeremy Stringer, 647–70. 3rd ed. Hoboken, NJ: John Wiley & Sons, 2009.

CHAPTER 4

Developing Culturally Responsive Student Services for Latinx

Joanne Solis-Walker

Although the educational mission of a university may not change drastically over time, it is now clear that universities must evolve to remain relevant and successful in fulfilling their mission.

—David Hodge and Bobby Gempesaw[1]

There are academic institutions within the Association of Theological Schools (ATS) that have served for many years Latinx[2] students from different cultural backgrounds. These seminaries are credited with creating pathways of educational opportunities for Hispanics. Over two decades ago, they ventured into marketing and recruiting Latinx students when others remained hesitant and on the sidelines. The pace was slow and work was done with limited resources. Some translated curriculums, hired Spanish-speaking adjuncts, and brought onboard a bilingual faculty member, administrator and/or a staff affairs practitioner who could serve both Spanish- and

---

1. Hodge and Gempesaw, *Academic Leadership in Higher Education*, 32

2. The terms Latinx and Hispanic are used interchangeably for parsimonious reasons but with caution. The term Latin@ is used when citing directly from a published resource.

English-speaking students. These are important steps we celebrate but there were also significant challenges that hindered these seminaries from offering culturally responsive theological education.

In 2017, the Latino/a Education Peer Group[3] assembled by ATS participated in the Educational Models and Practices project. After assessing various Hispanic programs (See Appendix A), the group identified three crucial issues to improve theological education for Latinx: (a) programming and assessment, (b) finances (cost of education/scholarship opportunities), and (c) cultural competence of the institution. This chapter addresses the third issue of cultural competence by proposing a framework for increasing the cultural responsiveness of ATS member schools.

THE NUMBERS

The Hispanic population in the United States is over fifty-eight million and is projected to be 25 percent of the total population by 2045.[4] It is the largest minority group in the United States (US) and "nearly half of US-born Latinos are younger than eighteen"[5] and "six-in-ten Hispanics are millennials or younger."[6] In 2014, there were seventeen states where one out of every four kindergartener was Hispanic[7] and 94 percent of Latinx under the age of eighteen are US citizens.[8] The Hispanic Church is strong and rapidly expanding but needs help keeping up with the overall growth of Hispanics in the US. This creates a service opportunity for seminaries.

There are approximately 238 US-based schools listed on the official membership list of the ATS.[9] None are Hispanic institutions based in the United States mainland.[10] About eight seminaries offer programs or tracks

---

3. The seminaries from the Association of Theological Schools that participated in the peer group were Barry University, Calvin Theological Seminary, Denver Seminary, Oblate School of Theology, Wesley Seminary at Indiana Wesleyan University, and Western Seminary. For a full copy of the report, see ATS, "Educational Models and Practices."

4. US Census Bureau, "Hispanic Heritage Month 2018."

5. Patten, "Nation's Latino Population."

6. Patten, "Nation's Latino Population."

7. Krogstad, "View of the Future."

8. Moreno, "Study."

9. ATS, "2018–2019 Annual Data Tables," 4

10. Mainland US is used to refer to the 50 states, not including Puerto Rico. Seminaries accredited by ATS in Puerto Rico were not included even though Puerto Rico is a commonwealth of the United States.

in Spanish or for Latinx[11] and out of 72,828 there are 5,209 Latinx students enrolled at ATS-accredited institutions in the US,[12] while the number of Hispanic faculty is under 4 percent.[13]

Based on the disparity of these statistics it is not surprising the number of Latinx enrolled in theological education remains low[14] and the need remains significant. While there has been progress this information underscores the need for seminaries to change the cultural landscape of their institutions.

It can be said with confidence that most theological schools serving Hispanics have the right intentions. Concurrently, many are holding tightly to organizational structures created decades ago for a primarily white student body and leadership.[15] Is it possible to adequately respond to the needs of Latinx students in the twenty-first century using a framework that was not crafted for such diversity? Theological schools committed to training and equipping culturally diverse ecclesial leaders must shift from serving a mono-cultural body of students to serve multi-ethnic students.

These are not the only alarming factors. Many Latinx students, staff, faculty and administrators wrestle with the embedded organizational culture that pressures them to "check their *Latinidad* at the door"[16] pushing them to succumb to the ways of the majority culture.[17] Succeeding academically or advancing professionally often comes at the "expense of their cultural and psychosocial well-being."[18]

CHECKING LATINIDAD AT THE DOOR

Imagine a student walking into orientation and picking up his nametag only to find his name is misspelled and the hyphen eliminated. He mentions it to a staff leader who apologizes and attempts to correct the spelling. The staff leader asks him to slowly pronounce each letter of his name but when done, his nametag is still incorrect. The frustrated staff member gives him a

---

11. Solis-Walker, "Does Applied Critical Leadership Theory Really Apply?," 108.

12. ATS, "2018–2019 Annual Data Tables," 38.

13. ATS, "2015–2016 Annual Data Tables," 3. Composition of Faculty and Compensation of Personnel.

14. Hernández et al., "What Can Seminaries Do?"

15. Gusa, "White Institutional Presence."

16. Solis-Walker, "Latinidad and Leadership."

17. Camacho Liu, "Investing in Higher Education for Latinos."

18. Ladson-Billing, *Culturally Relevant Pedagogy,* 475.

sharpie and tells him to write his own name and the new student walks away embarrassed and confused.

This story is a simple illustration of an exchange that happens on a continual basis. If this interaction turns out to be an isolated issue, the student will most likely set it aside and move on. However, picture that same student in class and the professor asking, "What would be the English version of your Spanish name? Can we call you that name instead?" A few weeks later this same student goes online to apply for a scholarship but receives an error in the field of 'last name' because the hyphen is not an acceptable symbol and there are too many characters. When the student calls to inform the financial aid office, the staff member apologizes for not being able to understand clearly over the phone due to the strong accent and politely asks the student to come to the office. The student leaves work early in order to arrive before the finance office closes. He explains the situation and the staff leader instructs him to pick one of the two last names and resubmit the form. That evening the student goes online and follows the directions, but it is rejected again because the student ID number does not match either of the individual last names.

The student returns to the financial aid office the following week and informs someone different about the problem. The staff member apologizes and consults someone higher up only to get another apology and no solution. The staff leader informs the student, "We'll need to figure out what we can do. Please come back in a few days." The student who is emotionally exhausted responds cordially but recognizes it is a futile attempt. The Latinx student leaves the finance office and steps into the classroom where he is now expected to respond to another name. His professor is white. His classmates are white, and the books were written from the perspective of the dominant culture by white authors. An internal dialogue is triggered and the student who once felt called to seminary starts to question what went wrong. What he is learning is not applicable to his cultural or ecclesial contexts, and he no longer believes it is worth sacrificing his cultural identity. Shortly after, the scholarship deadline expires. The student does not return, and the student affairs practitioners are concerned but unable to respond.

The above scenario produces the kind of results no one wants. The recruiting efforts end with the student dropping out of the program. Systems and processes were not contextualized and the student services professionals and faculty were not equipped with the cultural competencies needed to serve Latinx students. It resulted in an unfortunate loss for the student, and it also diminished the cultural enrichment of the institution.

CULTURAL RESPONSIVENESS

As theological education continues to grow, increasing the cultural responsiveness within ATS member schools must be a priority. Cultural responsiveness is the "ability to learn from and relate respectfully with people of your own culture as well as those from other cultures."[19] This includes being in tune with one's personal cultural identity and having an awareness of strengths as well as cultural biases.

Cultural responsive education "refers to a multi-dimensional, student-centered approach that promotes equitable excellence and serves to validate and affirm the experiences and contributions of students from all cultures and backgrounds."[20] This applies to curriculum design and course development as well as the intentionality of making sure that the systems, processes, and policies intended to serve all students are actually serving all students.

Starting Point: Assessing Cultural Responsiveness

Creating a culturally responsive community begins with gaining a sense of what is already in motion and accessible within the institution. What is the Office of Diversity and / or Intercultural Programs already doing? Collaborate to hear the voices of students, especially students of color. Planning for a listening tour is an essential first step that will require creating sacred spaces for transparent conversations.

Taxonomy of Cultural Responsiveness as an Assessment Resource

This chapter will draw from the Taxonomy of Cultural Responsiveness (figure 1) as a tool used to determine the climate (from Compliance to Responsiveness) in three domains: (a) institutional, (b) individual, and (c) instructional.[21] The *Institutional* domain represents policies, processes, and structures that are part of the organizational culture of an institution. The *Individual* domain refers to a single person like the student affairs practitioner or the entire student services office. The *Instructional* domain is concerned with the curricular requirements and focuses on areas such as curriculum, learning outcomes, and course materials.

---

19. NCCRESt, "Culturally Responsive Pedagogy and Practice."
20. Samuels et al., "Examining Perceptions," 51.
21. See Richards et al., "Addressing Diversity in Schools."

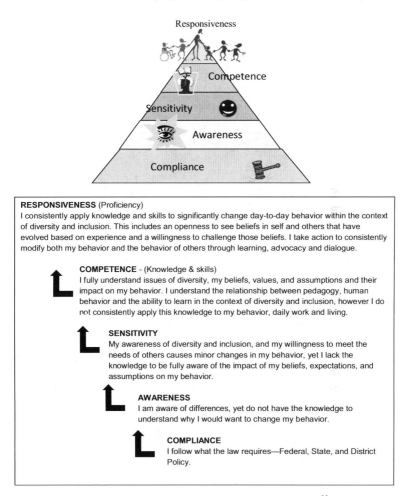

Figure 3. Taxonomy of Cultural Responsiveness[22]

To utilize the Taxonomy of Cultural Responsiveness, gather an assessing team, which should consist of culturally diverse members, who can provide both individual and group feedback. The team's role is to collaboratively determine where each of the seminary's domains (institutional, individual, and instructional) exists on the spectrum from Compliance to Responsiveness. Once the cultural responsiveness level for each domain is determined, develop a plan to increase the cultural capacity of the seminary, its leaders, and the curriculum. The goal is to move towards cultural responsiveness.

22. Used with Permission by Dr. Lena Crouso. See CEE, "Taxonomy."

In order to facilitate this progression, Applied Critical Leadership theory serves as a framework that helps define the plan.

APPLIED CRITICAL LEADERSHIP THEORY AS A CULTURALLY RESPONSIVE FRAMEWORK

Applied Critical Leadership Theory (ACL) is the "emancipatory practice of choosing to address educational issues and challenges using a critical race perspective to enact context-specific change in response to power, domination, access and achievement imbalances resulting in improved academic achievement at every academic level of institutions schooling in the US."[23] In other words there are educational issues and challenges limiting the academic success of students of color. These have to do with imbalances related to power, domination, educational access and academic achievements. As a result leaders within academic institutions have to address the challenges that contribute to inequity with the purpose of bringing freedom and change to the systems.

ACL Theory and Cultural Responsiveness: Putting Them Together

ACL theory correlates to Cultural Responsiveness given that the three tenants of ACL Theory (see table 3) correspond to the three domains (institutional, individual, and instructional) of the Taxonomy of Cultural Responsiveness. As a result, ACL Theory then provides a focused approach to growing cultural responsiveness in each of the domains.

---

23. Santamaría and Santamaría, *Applied Critical Leadership.* Leaders and practitioners are seeing the increasing need for practical transformative models and theories to address academic, cultural, and socio-economic gaps separating learners at all levels of the educational system. *Applied Critical Leadership in Education* proposes a shift in leadership and a need to transform status quo educational practices. This book explores a leadership model arising from critical theory and critical pedagogy traditions and provides examples of applied critical leadership, ultimately expanding ways to think about current leadership models. The authors examine qualitative case studies featuring critical leaders in early childhood education, elementary school, middle school, high school, district level, and higher education and follow with analysis, discussion, and application questions for readers to address. The cases are followed by critical questions for readers, suggestions for readers to begin conversations around issues of social justice and equity, and brief profiles of other critical leaders engaged in leadership for change around the country. This timely book explores an exciting new leadership model in a time of urgency for critical leadership and sustainable change.

Table 3. Taxonomy of Cultural Responsiveness
and Applied Critical Leadership Theory

Applied Critical Leadership Theory	Domains: Taxonomy of Cultural Responsiveness
1. Transformative Leadership: 4-fold Critical Approach	Institutional
2. Applied Critical Leader: 9 characteristics	Individual
3. Critical Pedagogy	Instructional

Transformative Leadership and Institutional Cultural Responsiveness

Transformative leadership exists as a stand-alone educational theory, but it is central to ACL theory because it is concerned with the systems that limit the academic success of students. The four-fold critical approach of transformative leadership[24] is a tool used to evaluate the systems within the institution and implement the type of change that leads to cultural responsiveness. The approach requires critical awareness, critical reflection, critical analysis, and critical action.

Critical awareness or *conscientization* "begins with awareness—of the strengths, weaknesses, and challenges of our society and of our school system."[25] Some key questions to ask: How is systemic racism embedded in our culture and seminary? When were our systems and policies created and have they been revised to address needs of Latinx students? What is the seminary's policy on immigration, and how is it communicated internally and externally? What are the expectations upon faculty and staff, and does

---

24. Shields, *Good Intentions Are Not Enough*, 11. *Transformative leadership* (not to be confused with transformational leadership) is a critical approach to leadership grounded in Freire's (1970) fourfold call for critical awareness or *conscientization*, followed by critical reflection, critical analysis, and finally for activism or critical action against the injustices of which one has become aware. Hence, it begins with awareness—of the strengths, weaknesses, and challenges of our society and of our school system. It requires critical reflection of for whom the system is working and for whom it is failing, of who is advantaged, privileged, and always included and who is marginalized and excluded. Once problem areas of inequity are identified, transformative leadership calls for critical analysis of beliefs, values, practices, and policies that need to be changed in order to promote equity. Finally, transformative leadership calls for action—action to redress wrongs and to ensure that every child who enters into an educational institution has an equal opportunity to participate fully, to be treated with respect, and to develop his or her capabilities.

25. Shields, *Good Intentions Are Not Enough*, 11.

each department in the seminary have the infrastructure to support Latinx students? How does the human resource office recruit, hire, and onboard Hispanic employees?

Critical reflection inquires "for whom the system is working and for whom it is failing, who is advantaged, privileged, and always included and who is marginalized and excluded."[26] Do our policies protect Latinx students, staff, and faculty from the effects of institutional racism? What do our systems do or not do for Latinx students? Do the immigration policy and communication practices convey to Deferred Action for Childhood Arrivals (DACA) students that they are welcomed and valued? Are there services available to the general student population that Latinx students cannot access? Is it necessary for Hispanic staff to provide support services outside their area of responsibility? Are the hiring practices and professional development opportunities advancing Hispanic faculty?

The third step is focused on critical analysis. It establishes that "once problem areas of inequity are identified, transformative leadership calls for critical analysis of beliefs, values, practices, and policies that need to be changed in order to promote equity."[27] What belief systems are embedded in our institution that propagate systemic racism? What policies and processes need to be created or contextualized to address deficiencies in service to Latinx students and promote diversity, inclusion, and equity? What needs to change in our belief and value system concerning the equitable treatment of DACA students? What must change in our beliefs concerning the professional advancement[28] of Hispanic faculty who provide support outside their area of responsibility?

The last step "calls for action—action to redress wrongs and to ensure that every child [and adult] who enters into an educational institution has an equal opportunity to participate fully, to be treated with respect, and to develop his or her capabilities."[29] The types of questions in this step are solution-focused. What training do we offer to change the mediating narrative and address the cultural biases? Who will revise our belief statements to ensure equity and inclusion, and how will we utilize these statements to implement change in the seminary? Who will oversee policy contextualization, and what training will be made available to empower the ongoing creation of equitable policies? How will we adjust cultural norms to accommodate

26. Shields, *Good Intentions Are Not Enough*, 11.

27. Shields, *Good Intentions Are Not Enough*, 11.

28. Professional advancement includes faculty ranking, tenure-ship, salary, promotion, and professional development.

29. Shields, *Good Intentions Are Not Enough*, 11.

DACA and other Latinx students? How do we advance Latinx faculty members who have been shouldering the invisible workload of translating and contextualizing courses and mentoring Hispanic students and employees?

Nine Characteristics of an Applied Critical Leader and Individual Cultural Responsiveness

At the core of the ACL theory is the applied critical leader who is a catalyst that "create(s) the environment and engage(s) in the conversations necessary in order to provoke change."[30] There are nine characteristics[31] this leader uses to address systemic issues (see table 4) that can assist the leader to move towards Responsiveness.

Within ACL theory there are two types of applied critical leaders: (a) those who identify with marginalization as a lived experience, and (b) leaders that chose regardless of their ethnic background to practice social justice and educational equity.[32] ACL theory calls on non-Latinx leaders to make use of their privilege and engage in the nine characteristics on behalf of Latinx who may not have the same platform. This approach contributes to the retention of Latinx and is an equitable alternative to the "token" model of diversity, which hires one leader to help the school change and reach Latinx students without appropriate support and financial resources. ATS seminaries should utilize the nine characteristics to grow individuals and teams and also to develop training for all constituents and target new hires to strengthen the team in each area.

Table 4. Nine Characteristics of ACL

Item	Characteristic	Description
1	Critical conversations	Initiates and engages in conversations pertaining to educational issues and challenges such as race and gender
2	Critical Race Theory (CRT) lens	Four elements: (a) Racism is normal; (b) there is value in storytelling; (c) critical of liberalism; and (d) aware of interest convergence
3	Consensus building	Considered to be the preferred decision-making Strategy

30. Solis-Walker, "Does Applied Critical Leadership Theory Really Apply?"
31. Santamaría, "Transformative Critical Leadership in Action."
32. Santamaría, "Applied Critical Leadership through Latino/a Lenses," 6

4	Stereotype threats	Conscious of the threats related to fulfilling negative stereotypes associated with a perceived racial, ethnic, or linguistic group
5	Academic discourse	Make empirical contributions and add to the research-based literature regarding underserved groups
6	Honors constituents	Seek to honor all members including staff, student family, community members, and stakeholders
7	Leads by example	Gives back to meet the unresolved educational needs or challenges
8	Trust with mainstream	Trust is built in the process of working with mainstream constituents or partners who do not share an affinity toward issues related to educational equity
9	Servant leadership	Driven by a sense of calling to lead, often referred to as led by the spirit

Critical Pedagogy and Instructional Cultural Responsiveness

Critical pedagogy,[33] which is central to the mission of theological education, is the tenet within ACL theory that relates to the *Instructional* domain of the Taxonomy of Cultural Responsiveness. At its core, critical pedagogy (CP) views education as an "emancipatory act that grants oppressed people the freedom to make decisions that contributes to the well-being of all people."[34]

One of the ways to apply critical pedagogy to the Instructional domain is through the contextualization of the curriculum. CP aims to teach students how to identify and respond "to oppressive and inequitable social relations and belief patterns ingrained within institutions and social structures of power."[35] This is why it does not suffice to translate curriculums from English to Spanish. Without contextualization Hispanic pastors are trained in seminaries to lead white churches while pastoring Hispanic congregations.

CP can also increase cultural responsiveness by its problem-posing approach to education versus the banking model of education. Banking

33. In 1968, Paulo Freire introduced critical pedagogy as a philosophy of adult education. Freire was convinced that education was power that added dignity to fieldworkers who were not viewed as equal due to illiteracy. He believed that educating people contributed to empowering them to experience freedom from oppressive systems that limited the quality of living.

34. Santamaría and Santamaría, *Applied Critical Leadership*.

35. Burbules and Berk, "Critical Thinking and Critical Pedagogy."

education places the instructor in the center where the professor has all the knowledge and students have nothing to contribute. In this model students do not develop critical thinking abilities. The professor's teaching is disconnected from what is relevant to the students and within society. In problem-posing pedagogy the student is at the center and is expected to engage their communities in order to develop critical consciousness and contribute towards a solution. This is why theological education "should occur in an environment connected to everyday life encouraging discussions conducted within the language and knowledge of the students."[36]

WRAPPING IT UP

If seminaries are seeking to equip Hispanic ecclesial leaders they must strive to become culturally responsive communities. In order to effectively make this shift they must assess their institutional processes, their individual leaders, and the instructional pieces. Because student affairs professionals are charged with the responsibility of providing services that contribute to the academic success of all students, this chapter offered ACL theory as a framework to assess and implement changes. ACL Theory draws from transformative leadership's four-fold critical approach to confront policies and systems, the nine characteristics of an applied critical leader to grow leaders, and critical pedagogy to impact the instructional portion. This holistic approach offers ATS seminaries a culturally responsive framework to move past heartfelt efforts to serve Latinx students well and empower them to thrive in their education and beyond, without checking their *Latinidad* at the door.

36. Aliakbari and Faraji, "Basic Principles of Critical Pedagogy."

APPENDIX A

Table 5. Theological Education Models (TE) of Schools Participating in the
Latino/a Peer Group

	1	2	3
Education	"Standard" theological education provides a standard curriculum without any adaptation to Latino/a cultural or educational needs	"Standard" theological education with: Support from Latino/a and Spanish speaking faculty Occasional courses given in Spanish Some undergrad pre-reqs. available in Spanish Students able to write in Spanish Spanish resources available in syllabi Student advising conducted in Spanish	Culturally adapted "standard" theological education available: Taught by Latino/a and Spanish speaking faculty Courses (more than 50 percent) taught in Spanish or bilingually Undergrad pre-reqs available in Spanish Resources (text books, library resources) in both Spanish and English Student advising conducted in Spanish
Recruitment	Standard recruitment practices applied to all Occasional bilingual staff	Standard recruitment practices applied to all Written material available in Spanish Electronic media available in Spanish Registrar and recruitment staff are bilingual	Standard recruitment practices plus: Written material available in Spanish Electronic media available in Spanish Targeted opportunities for face-to-face interaction with Latino/a serving congregations, parishes, associations Registrar and recruitment staff are bilingual

| Institutional Support | No institutional support articulated by school mission statement or administration Institutional support for Latino/a students is the same as those given to others, in the areas of finances. This could range from scholarship and grant programs, to assistance from the student's congregation or religious affiliation Outreach to provide TE to Latino/a students, not an explicit goal, assumed to be implicit in the school's mission statement | Institutional support articulated by school mission statement and/or administration Institutional support for Latino/a students is the same as those given to others, in the areas of finances. This could range from scholarship and grant programs, to assistance from the student's congregation or religious affiliation Reduced tuition Outreach to provide TE to Latino/a students, explicit goal for a particular department OR: Outreach to provide TE to Latino/a students, explicit goal in institution's mission statement | Institutional support articulated by school mission statement and administration Institutional support for Latino/a students is the same as those given to others, in the areas of finances. This could range from scholarship and grant programs, to assistance from the student's congregation or religious affiliation Agreements with Latin American institutions allow schools to offer reduced tuition Outreach to provide TE to Latino/a students, explicit goal for a particular department OR: Outreach to provide TE to Latino/a students, explicit goal in institution's mission statement |

BIBLIOGRAPHY

Association of Theological Schools (ATS). "2007–2008 Annual Data Tables." Online. https://www.ats.edu/uploads/resources/institutional-data/annual-data-tables/2007-2008-annual-data-tables.pdf.

———. "2015–2016 Annual Data Tables." Online. https://www.ats.edu/uploads/resources/institutional-data/annual-data-tables/2015-2016-annual-data-tables.pdf.

———. "2018–2019 Annual Data Tables." Online. https://www.ats.edu/uploads/resources/institutional-data/annual-data-tables/2018-2019-annual-data-tables.pdf.

———. "Educational Models and Practices in Theological Education: Formation in Online Contexts Final Peer Group Report." Online. https://www.ats.edu/uploads/resources/current-initiatives/educational-models/publications-and-presentations/peer-group-final-reports/peer-group-final-report-book.pdf.

Aliakbari, Mohammad, and Elham Faraji. "Basic Principles of Critical Pedagogy." *International Proceedings of Economics Development and Research* 17 (2011) 77–85. Online. http://www.ipedr.com/vol17/14-CHHSS 2011-H00057.pdf.

Burbules, Nicholas C., and Rupert Berk. "Critical Thinking and Critical Pedagogy: Relations, Differences, and Limits." In *Critical Theories in Education: Changing Terrains of Knowledge and Politics,* edited by Thomas S. Popkewitz and Lynn Fendler, 100–108. New York: Routledge, 1999.

Camacho Liu, Michelle. "Investing in Higher Education for Latinos Trends in Latino College Access and Success National Conference of State Legislatures." *National Conference of State Legislators* (July 2011). Online. http://www.ncsl.org/documents/educ/trendsinlatinosuccess.pdf.

Center for Educational Effectiveness (CEE). "Taxonomy of Culturally Responsive Teaching and Learning." Online. https://static1.squarespace.com/static/57cf1310197aea734bbebfec/t/5aa1794c0d9297d31d2 5c892/1520531789973/CEE+Taxonomy+of+Cultural+Responsiveness-Brief_Final.pdf.

Gusa, Diane Lynn. "White Institutional Presence: The Impact of Whiteness on Campus Climate." *Harvard Educational Review* 80.4 (2010). Online. http://www.oregoncampuscompact.org/uploads/1/3/0/4/13042698/gusa_white_institutional_presence.pdf.

Hernández, Edwin I., et al. "What Can Seminaries Do to Prepare Their Students for Ministry in the Latino Community?" *Latino Research at Notre Dame* 5.3 (2008) 1–8.

Krogstad, Jens Manuel. "A View of the Future through Kindergarten Demographics." *Pew Research Center,* July 31, 2014. Online. https://www.pewresearch.org/fact-tank/2014/07/08/a-view-of-the-future-through-kindergarten-demographics.

Moreno, Eric. "Study: 1 in 4 Latino Kids Come from a Home with Undocumented Parents." *Salud America!* (blog), October 26, 2017. Online. https://salud-america.org/study-1-4-latino-children-undocumented-immigrant-parent.

National Center for Culturally Responsive Educational Systems (NCCRESt). "Culturally Responsive Pedagogy and Practice." 2018. Online. https://www.nccrest.org/professional/culturally_responsive_pedagogy-and.html.

Patten, Eileen. "The Nation's Latino Population Is Defined by Its Youth." *Pew Research Center,* April 20, 2016. Online. https://www.pewresearch.org/hispanic/2016/04/20/the-nations-latino-population-is-defined-by-its-youth.

Richards, Heraldo V., et al. "Addressing Diversity in Schools: Culturally Responsive Pedagogy." *Teaching Exceptional Children* 39.3 (2007) 64–68. Online. https://bcpskenwoodhs.pbworks.com/w/file/fetch/59216594/addressingrdiversity.pdf.

Samuels, Amy J., et al. "Examining Perceptions of Culturally Responsive Pedagogy in Teacher Preparation and Teacher Leadership Candidates." *SRATE* 26.2 (2017) 50–60.

Santamaría, Lorri. "Transformative Critical Leadership in Action: Re-Visioning an Equity Agenda to Address the Community College Achievement Gap." *Journal of Transformative Leadership and Policy Studies* 2.1 (2012) 15–25.

Santamaría, Lorri, and Andres P. Santamaría. *Applied Critical Leadership in Education: Choosing Change.* New York: Routledge, 2014.

———. "Applied Critical Leadership through Latino/a Lenses: An Alternative Approach to Educational Leadership." *The International Journal of Education for Social Justice* 3.2 (2014) 1–36.

Shields, Carolyn M. *Good Intentions Are Not Enough: Transformative Leadership for Communities of Difference*. Lanham, MD: Scarecrow, 2003.

Solis-Walker, Joanne. "Does Applied Critical Leadership Theory Really Apply? The Formation of Hispanic Latin@ Ecclesial Leaders at Seminaries Accredited by the Association of Theological Schools: A Historical-Critical Analysis of the Progress and Challenges." PhD diss., Regent University, 2016.

———. "Latinidad and Leadership: Cultura Does Matter in Organizational Culture." *HTI Open Plaza* (blog), February 27, 2020. Online. https://www.htiopenplaza.org.

US Census Bureau. "Hispanic Heritage Month 2018." *Census.gov—Newsroom*, September 13, 2018. Online. https://www.census.gov/newsroom/facts-for-features/2018/hispanic-heritage-month.html.

CHAPTER 5

At Home with Movement

An Integral Ecology of Vocational Development

DONNA FOLEY

INTRODUCTION

> Learning should foster, in addition to the acquisition of knowl-
> edge, the capacity to understand and assess one's tradition and
> identity and to integrate materials from various theological dis-
> ciplines and modes of instructional engagement in ways that en-
> hance ministry and cultivate emotional and spiritual maturity.[1]

ECOLOGY MATTERS, AND MATTERS of ecology shape a spirituality of vocational development. In citing current institutional and program standards given by the Association of Theological Schools' Commission on
Accreditation, I would like to propose that ministerial programs which treat
ecology as a contemporary cultural and social issue will help foster students'
capacity for self-understanding, enhance ministry, and cultivate emotional
and spiritual maturity. Academic and co-curricular programs for ministry
students should account for the impact of movement and displacement,

1. ATS, "Standards of Accreditation," 6. "The program shall provide opportunities
to develop a critical understanding of and creative engagement with the cultural realities and structures within which the church lives and carries out its mission" (ATS,
"Degree Program Standards," 2). Whatever revision occurs, something of the spirit of
these standards is likely to remain.

along with the influence of natural and human-made spaces on those ministers-in-formation. I also propose that attention to the concept of "integral ecology" in vocation will help student service professionals themselves to thrive. I use this term as it appears in current Catholic Christian discourse, especially as used in the 2015 papal encyclical *Laudato si'*.[2] As they assist students in their vocational discernment, administrators of all stripes must tend to their own development with what Seattle University's Michael R. Trice calls an "entrepreneurial spirit."[3]

In juxtaposing the terms "ecology," "students," and "professionals," I am not indicating "campus environment" in the sense often employed within the field of student services.[4] Rather, the approach taken here stresses the effects of individual relationships with the natural world or, as many Christian traditions name it, creation. In this it is also distinct from, but related to, important recent work in the social sciences around human ecology theory and social network theory.[5] My choice to address the vocational implications of concrete location and physical movement was born out of two considerations: promulgation of the papal encyclical *Laudato si'* in 2015, and my own work in student services at the Franciscan School of Theology in Southern California. Not surprisingly, that physical and spiritual location will color this offering in brown Franciscan tones, yet my hope is that others will find something in the texture and hue to complement their own settings.

Scripture, examples from human studies, and the academic field of spirituality will be used to describe the significance of physical location and dislocation in vocational development. This is done with an eye towards the formation of those graduate students who wish to serve in diverse capacities within and outside church settings. Included in this gaze are also student services professionals themselves, at a time when serving in theological education can feel, as one colleague put it, "like perpetual whitewater." In this discussion of movement, location, and vocation, the terms "place," "home," and "ecology" will all be used. Additionally, as it is a Christian tradition

2. See Francis, *Laudato si'* para. 15, 137, 141.

3. Trice, "Dawning of the Faculty-Administrator," 53.

4. As in, for example, Becker and Drum, "Essential Counseling Knowledge and Skills," 201–8. The authors use "ecology" and "environment" as the terms are often employed in the behavioral sciences to describe the ways systems and procedures impact the social, cultural, and interpersonal world of students, faculty, and staff.

5. For an illuminating example of this approach, see Lowe and Lowe, "Reciprocal Ecology," 1–14. The "reciprocal ecology" developed here deals with interhuman relationships only, using the metaperspective and tools of the study of natural biotic ecologies applied to the study of human ecologies.

long-sensitive to the material world and to questions of connection and movement, some elements of Franciscan spirituality will be employed to explore ideas of ecological "home" and "homelessness" in vocational development. The discussion presented here rests on an assumption of three tensive powers: the power of *place*, the power of *nowhere*, and the power of *movement*. To suggest a way of integrating the operation of these powers, I will conclude by briefly describing the role of storytelling at my own institution.

RIVERS AND POPLARS: THE POWER OF PLACE

> By the rivers of Babylon
>   there we sat weeping
>   when we remembered Zion.
> On the poplars in its midst
>   we hung up our harps.
> For there our captors asked us
>   for the words of a song;
> Our tormentors, for joy:
>   "Sing for us a song of Zion!"
> But how could we sing a song of the Lord
>   in a foreign land? (Ps 137:1–4)[6]

As current or future employees of religious and non-profit institutions, stability and security are unlikely to be defining features of Christian ministers' professional lives. As denizens of a globalized culture and economy, they will communicate with people they cannot touch, eat food from they know not where, and relocate themselves, perhaps often. They will almost certainly spend considerable time in what anthropologist Marc Augé calls "empirical non-places," meaning "spaces of circulation, consumption and communication": highways, airports, transit systems, and cyberspace.[7] They may very well be called to serve people who are migrants and refugees.[8] The very effects of climate disruption are placing new groups of refugees

6. All biblical references are taken from the New American Bible Revised Edition.

7. Augé, *Non-Places*, viii. Augé contrasts "non-place" with the more traditional "anthropological place." He identifies the current epoch with "supermodernity" and maintains it is marked by excess in three philosophical areas: those of time, space, and individuals.

8. To speak only of the Americas, the international aid organization Médecins San Frontières (Doctors Without Borders) reported in 2017 on the then "largely undeclared refugee crisis, with 500,000 people fleeing annually from El Salvador, Guatemala, and Honduras" (Médecins San Frontières, "Running from Violence," 4).

on the horizon of ministry.[9] The minister's degree of self-understanding, the effectiveness of her ministry, the maturity of her emotional and spiritual life, must all be understood in terms of an ecological *place*. When we speak of ecology as we would any other element of cultural context, we are in agreement with scholars such as geographer Nicholas Entriken, who holds that the "recognition of the full dimensionality of experience and the cognitive understanding of place is necessary to appreciate its significance in modern life."[10] Or, in the language of E. V. Walter's *Placeways: A Theory of Human Environment*, "We call locations of experience 'places.'"[11] To say that one's spiritual relationship to the environment (both natural and built) is significant, is to say along with Walter that "meaningless objects do not exist."[12] It is to suggest that the minister-in-formation is accompanied, not just by family of origin, current human community and cultural patterns, but by sidewalks, walls, rivers, trees, and animals. Here we are not speaking of universal, abstract "space" but of something closer to "home." In a sense, we might regard each person at new student orientation as derivative of a place—like Julien of Norwich or Anthony of Padua. At the same time, it should be noted that some people cannot identify as coming from one place, but as moving through several places. (Anthony is either "of Padua" or "of Lisbon," depending on who speaks of him.)

A history of actual movement from place to place might actually be a defining feature of many people who study and work in theology school. Indeed, even if an individual administrator does not seek to relocate, it is distinctly possible nowadays that the institution itself might move. Attention to the tangible characteristics—the ecology—of place could prove fruitful, as no one develops a vocation apart from environment, however multiplied or sequenced that environment may be. Moreover, it would be difficult to take particular places seriously without also taking seriously all the creatures that reside there. If movement from one linguistic world to another impacts professional development, is it possible that hearing a different birdsong (or none at all) outside the office window also changes us? In posing such a question, I am suggesting a function of creation beyond that of "book" to be read or as an aspect of self-care. Though both of these commonly-assigned roles are significant, they limit creation to a relatively

9. The United Nations Refugee Agency observes, "Families and communities have already started to suffer from disasters and the consequences of climate change, forced to leave their homes in search of a new beginning" (UNHCR, "Climate Change").

10. Entriken, *Betweenness of Place*, 132.

11. Walter, *Placeways*, 117.

12. Walter, *Placeways*, 137.

passive role. I am positing here a more mutual, active relationship, something more like family dynamics.

With the preceding in mind, the work of Douglas Christie is especially
relevant to our educational circumstances, particularly his discussion of
topos (place) as it relates to a practice of "contemplative ecology."[13] With
Christie we can arrive at an understanding of place as almost actively spiritually formative. This leads us to suspect that treating ecology as a category
for vocational maturation may prove fruitful. Drawing on the work of Keith
Basso among the Western Apache and on the insights of American pho-
tographer Robert Adams, Christie describes the contemplative practice of
seeing "more" in a place or thing, noting the revelatory power of things that
are not us:

> It is a way of seeing the world, a way of being in the world that
> allows us to cherish it with all the feeling we are capable of. It is
> a way of seeing that enables us to gauge the true significance of
> what we gaze upon. This kind of seeing is akin to what the early
> Christians meant when they spoke of theoria, that way of seeing
> into the heart of reality that sometimes revealed the very face of
> the Divine.[14]

It is also a way of seeing the world that might inform the development of
pastoral skills and professional ethics in ministry students. In referring to
human encounters with places or non-human beings as "seeing into the
heart of reality," Christie identifies a type of horizontal ecstasy available to
saints and other people whose gaze is turned not heavenward, but earthward.

I would suggest that it is this "way of seeing the world" which reveals
the cramped quarters of an ICU to be an intimate chapel for prayer. It is also
this "way of being in the world" which permits a fleeting moment of sorrow
at the sight of roadkill on the way to campus. The patient in the hospital
bed, alone and in pain, is seen for the sacred being he is. The dead animal,
whose praise of the Creator has been cut short, is mourned. Not even the
hospital equipment and the highway themselves are excluded from this way
of seeing and being, and their own "true significance" would be revealed
under an attentive-enough gaze. I wonder further if, rather than saying this
contemplative gaze "sometimes" reveals the Divine, we might say it *always*
reveals the Divine to those who have eyes to see. To refer to another of the
senses, is it possible to live as if our physical surroundings were *always* talking to us, telling us something about the Eternal? Do we have ears to hear?

---

13. Christie, *Blue Sapphire*, 102–140.

14. Christie, *Blue Sapphire*, 118.

With such an understanding of ecological contemplative practice and location, the student or the administrator is asked (as we so often do) to privilege the concrete and the particular over the ideal and the universal in theological reflection and in the performance of duties. Now, for the hard-pressed person charged with implementing programmatic changes while assisting a student in crisis before flying off to a conference, the suggestion that he stop what he is doing, walk outside, and contemplate a tree might be received as facile—even by the most sanguine and spiritually savvy of assistant deans. Likewise, expecting a student to attend to "place" or "home" with such seriousness is to take the demands of contextual theology perhaps to its very limits. Does it take it too far? This chapter began with an assertion that experiences in and with the rest of creation must be considered somewhat like familial realities in vocational development. In order to see what this might mean, we must do what our students are often asked to do in class: we must think about love.

When Nichols Entriken questions whether a "decentered universalism" can capture the full dimensionality of place,[15] Douglas Christie would appear to answer "no." The thoughts he pursues suggest that relationships with other particularities help make us who we are in a contemplative ecology. To reflect a bit more on the significance of place in vocational development, it will be helpful to turn to Christie's treatment of desire, sympathy, and love—*eros*—in our relationship with the natural world. Citing its use in Christian tradition and in contemporary ecological discourse, Christie writes that *eros* "refers to a longing to share in the life of another, whether that 'other' be understood as a person, a place, a non-human species, or God."[16] The term's increasing prominence in contemporary thought and practice points to "a growing recognition of the centrality of desire . . . for helping us understand who we are in the world."[17] One element of vocational development is to understand "who we are in the world." A practice of contemplating that very world may be helpful. Perhaps the overworked assistant dean mentioned above really should step outside for a bit and contemplate a tree.

In his discussion of place, desire, and other beings, Christie acknowledges the hypothesis and study of *biophilia*. It is Edward O. Wilson who has offered this increasingly well-known hypothesis on the connection between self-knowledge and ecological appreciation (as opposed to ecological perception). Wilson defines biophilia as "the innate tendency to focus on life

---

15. Entriken, *Betweeness of Places*, 130.

16. Christie, *Blue Sapphire*, 117.

17. Christie, *Blue Sapphire*, 117.

and lifelike processes," noting "to the degree we come to understand other organisms, we will place greater value on them, and on ourselves."[18] Within biophilia-inspired disciplines, it is the field of environmental psychology which presents itself as a way forward to administrators and the students they serve. In an examination of human-environmental interactions in 1993, the environmental psychologist Robert Ulrich described his field as "a small and peripheral subfield within psychology."[19] At that time he could remark on the "embryonic state of much biophilia-related research," observing "Only limited beginnings have been made in investigating certain issues that might have considerable scientific and social significance, such as identifying the human benefits or values that could be lost when natural areas are eliminated."[20] The field appears to have grown however, and by 2015, a work on biophilic architectural design could cite Urlich, E. O. Wilson, Stephen Kellert, and others with some confidence, agreeing that humans are part of nature and taking an approach that "focuses on our subconscious human responses to places."[21]

I would venture to say that many of my colleagues already work creatively with some awareness of these concepts: the registrar whose office space is warm and welcoming, the recruitment director whose open house event flows smoothly and comfortably. An appreciative inquiry into the practices of our respective institutions would no doubt reveal many such instances of life-focused design. The thrust here offers some encouragement to take ecology seriously in vocational development, in that it moves a discussion of environment beyond how we decorate the chapel to considerations of the human person in full. A biophilic approach offers insights from evolutionary and behavioral sciences that can inform ministerial preparation and professional growth. Might sensitivity to the power of place assist those administrators who must communicate necessary institutional changes to students and staff? Are there any implications here for our expectations of distance learning? As the formational context for students becomes, not the school campus, but their local environments, this last question takes on added weight.

---

18. Kellert and Wilson, *Biophilia Hypothesis*, 4–5. The therapeutic use of animals on campuses taps into insights from this hypothesis, though the practice may not reach the level of regard Christie, Kellert, and Wilson describe. I am reminded of a picture my niece texted me during finals week at her school. In it she is clearly delighted with the therapy llama provided by student services. The llama's feelings are impossible to ascertain in the photo.

19. Ulrich, "Biophilia, Biophobia," in Kellert and Wilson, *Biophilia Hypothesis*, 87.

20. Ulrich, "Biophilia, Biophobia," in Kellert and Wilson, *Biophilia Hypothesis*, 87

21. Sussman and Hollander, *Cognitive Architecture*, 156–57.

The disciplines so far touched on, however, cannot be expected to provide all the substance needed for the necessary theological reflection in a program for ministry or a career in student services. For a fuller understanding of what it means to take our physical location—our home—seriously, we can turn to scripture and to developments within Christian traditions. In recent decades and across denominations, much theological and pastoral work has been done to bring light, language, and life to Christian teaching on ecology. One of these efforts is Pope Francis's 2015 encyclical, *Laudato si'*. The document sounds a cautionary note about the "usefulness" of the natural world, even as it regards our own development. While it is good for us to gain self-understanding through relationship to the environment, that is not, Francis insists, why other things exist. Among many related matters, the pope writes, "The ultimate purpose of other creatures is not to be found in us. Rather, all creatures are moving forward with us toward a common point of arrival, which is God, in that transcendent fullness where the risen Christ embraces and illumines all things."[22] In this view, everything else has a vocation and a destiny. Neither my self-understanding nor my desire for meaning serve as reason for the existence of a mountain, a neutron star, or a bacterium. They are here at Someone else's pleasure. This introduction of the transcendent into our consideration of ecology and vocation leads to new questions. In *Laudato si'* we hear:

> The history of our friendship with God is always linked to particular places which take on an intensely personal meaning; we all remember places, and revisiting those memories does us much good. Anyone who has grown up in the hills or used to sit by the spring to drink, or played outdoors in the neighborhood square; going back to these places is a chance to recover something of their true selves.[23]

That recovery of "something of their true selves" is no small matter in the training and formation of Christian ministers. As a matter of professional integrity, the person granted a Master of Divinity degree is assumed to have a fairly high level of self-knowledge and what the Association of Theological Schools standards identify as "emotional and spiritual maturity." Ministry programs utilize case studies and theological reflection to get at these matters in seminars. Clinical Pastoral Education programs ask applicants to give full accounts of life and spiritual history. Perhaps we should imagine an MDiv program or a CPE application asking: Did you live with any animals in your home when you were growing up? If so, describe its/

22. Francis, *Laudato si'*, para. 83.
23. Francis, *Laudato si'*, para. 84.

their effect on your spiritual development. What birds lived on the same street as you? Have you been able to return to a childhood home? If so, what did it feel like? What trees surrounded you at different ministerial locations? What used to live on the land where you received your undergraduate degree? What is your favorite building on this campus? Why? What is the body of water closest to you now? What do you know about its health? Have you ever been forced to leave a place you love? Do you know anyone who has? Are these not questions of some developmental import? If professional ministers move from place to place, yet report little of their ecological relationships along the way, are they leaving something significant unexamined? I would argue that they are leaving out something very significant indeed.

Yet some spiritual traditions—including, at times, Christianity—are suspicious of relationships that seem to depend on materiality. Should we not voice some caution when we speak about the formative power of place? Can too great an attachment to a particular home be harmful to human ecology? In my own theology school, ongoing dialogue among community members help us navigate the when, where, and how of different devotional practices. Each particular devotion comes redolent with scents, tastes, sounds, gestures, and images of home for those who remember. Each offers the possibility of meaningful encounter for those who have no such memories. Each also carries a potential risk inherent within the matrix of theology and cultural expression: that the ritual and symbol might serve to legitimize as universal what may only be local. In my insistence on the role of ecology in vocation, I would not wish to lose sight of that risk.

This section on the power of place began with the opening verses of Psalm 137 on the remembrance of, and longing for, Zion. It is a text sometimes evoked in discussions of place and home. As we consider whether strong attachment to particular environments might be problematic for personal development, let us recall that the last line of the song goes like this: "Blessed is the one who seizes your children and smashes them against the rock" (Ps 137:9). Maybe things and places can have too much meaning. Maybe we see too much in them. Maybe they speak too loudly or, more likely, we misinterpret what they are saying. Paradoxically, ministry students who would be emotionally and spiritually mature need also to consider the reality of "nowhere" in a Christian understanding of ecology. Theology school professionals experiencing their own version of institutional climate change might do the same.

FOXES AND BIRDS: THE REALITY OF NOWHERE

> When Jesus saw a crowd around him, he gave orders to cross to
> the other side. A scribe approached and said to him, "Teacher,
> I will follow you wherever you go." Jesus answered him, "Foxes
> have dens and birds of the sky have nests, but the Son of Man
> has nowhere to rest his head." (Matt 8:18–20)

This poignant self-disclosure from an itinerant messiah should give
any Christian pause when discussing vocational context. It is another scripture passage that shows up in writings about the place of place in human
lives. It gives witness to much of the Incarnation's meaning and also to the
reality faced by all too many of God's children today. If, as expressed in
Psalm 137, too strong a care for home can lead to vilification and violence,
are there other ways we might approach spiritualities of place? When so
many humans and countless other species must flee or vanish from their
familiar environs, what right have others to wax nostalgic over a particular
creek, street corner, or office space? One scholar who sensitively interrogates
the meaning of home in religion is the humanist geographer Yi-Fu Tuan. In
his evocative work, *Religion: From Place to Placelessness,* Tuan argues for a
universal, rather than particular, sense of home as signifying a more highly-
developed spirituality. He maintains that for the "true followers" of "Buddha,
Jesus Christ and the great prophets of Israel . . . the shift from place to placelessness is not cause for regret, for to them the true home for human beings
is never a geographical place—a holy city or a mountain—somewhere on
Earth. It is always elsewhere."[24] As I have pondered for the last several years
how to deliver spiritual formation and student services in a world of com-
muters and online learning, these words give me pause. Our students are
"always elsewhere." Why interpret this negatively, as I have sometimes done
from the confines of my small department? Are they not also in their "true
home"? What makes Tuan's assertion compelling are first, the author's clear
appreciation of actual holy places across multiple traditions and second, his
reflection on supporting texts from within the traditions themselves. When
Tuan asks rhetorically, "What is the ultimate test of a religion?" he does not
locate an answer in "the sacred book, the magnificent house of worship, the
faithful community and communion."[25] He responds rather, "My answer
is the truly good person—a saint, if you will—someone embedded in this
world yet not 'of this world.'"[26] Here is an interesting contrast of views on

24. Tuan, *Religion*, x.

25. Tuan, *Religion*, 66.

26. Tuan, *Religion*, 66.

human ecology: the Roman pontiff offers that humans "recover something of their true selves" in earthly places, while the geographer insists that "out of this world" spirituality is the mark of religious progress across traditions. With this complicated non-conclusion regarding whether home or homelessness signify vocational maturity, we can still maintain that place and ecology matter, but we are left wondering how they matter.

The tension between these two spiritual perspectives on home—the universal and the particular—runs throughout Christian scripture and traditions, of course. Followers of the incarnate Christ make an implicit agreement to learn to live with that tension. He was himself born in a place, laid in a manger. And yet he had no place to lay his head. How does one dwell, much less serve, authentically on this planet while self and others are always in motion? I would suggest that we in theological education must apprehend with new urgency the ancient Christian exhortation to live truly in the world, though not utterly of it.

To reclaim and attempt this is to work with what personalist philosopher Erazim Kohák calls "the ontological root of the *movement of dwelling* . . . the strategy of the incarnation."[27] Returning to the institutional standard quoted at the opening of this chapter, I note once more that ecology matters in any understanding of a student's situation. If a ministry program "should foster the capacity to understand and assess one's tradition and identity," then that program should utilize its tradition along with current research in such a way that new ministers learn to speak in new ways of the natural world, of home and of homelessness. Before briefly indicating one Christian tradition's "take" on relating to the environment, I will reassert that, in ministerial formation, this relationship ought to be addressed as explicitly as any other aspect of students' circumstances.

PILGRIMS AND STRANGERS: ONE INSTITUTION'S RESPONSE TO THE REALITY OF MOVEMENT

> Let the brothers not make anything their own, neither house, nor place, nor anything at all. As pilgrims and strangers in this world, serving the Lord in poverty and humility, let them go seeking alms with confidence, and they should not be ashamed because, for our sakes, our Lord made Himself poor in this world.[28]

27. Kohák, "Of Dwelling and Wayfaring," 34 (emphasis added).

28. Armstrong et al., *Francis of Assisi*, 103.

To open a way for student services professionals to integrate and possibly resolve the tensions around "home" and "homelessness," I will examine the strategies of one particular stream within Christian spirituality: the Franciscan one. Like all movements within the broader tradition, it is both derivative and generative. While its expressions are decidedly Christocentric, much of what is found here can also be found in other spiritualities. Within its intuitive foundation and in the intellectual tradition that developed, we may find certain emphases to assist Christian practitioners who, as I have argued, must take ecology seriously. In this argument that ecology, generously interpreted, must be considered formative, I have cited the recent encyclical, *Laudato si'*. Before considering very briefly how a few Franciscan texts might support the integration of ecology and vocation, I will note one obvious feature of the substantive papal document: It takes its title from a Franciscan song about people, nature, and God.

The encyclical, "On Care for Our Common Home," is the Catholic Church's current commentary on interactions between humans and the environment. It repeatedly uses, but does not really define, the concept of "integral ecology," an evocative term "for a vision capable of taking into account every aspect of the global crisis . . . one which clearly respects its human and social dimensions."[29] These aspects of *Laudato si'* should encourage us to search the document for vocational development material. In that search we will observe that the encyclical draws explicitly on the person and writing of Francis of Assisi, taking its title from this repeated line in the saint's work, composed around 1225: "*Laudato si', mi' Signore*" or "Praised be you, my Lord."[30] The song itself, known as *The Canticle of the Creatures*, has been posited by some as "the supreme and most characteristic work by Francis."[31] It is not a song about animals, but of the elements as understood in medieval cosmology, and the circumstances of its composition are profoundly, excruciatingly human. To dispel any notion that the love for creation and Creator expressed therein depends on dreamy romanticism, we need only remember that the *Canticle* was composed by a man approaching death, nearly blind, in pain, and believing that his movement was falling apart around him. There are real pastoral implications in that. Moving forward with the recent encyclical and a long-lived spirituality before us as a tools for professional growth, it is possible to imagine one approach to the

29. *Laudato si'*, para. 137.

30. Carbajo Nuñez, *Sister Mother Earth*, 75n44.

31. For those interested in a thorough study of these terms as used by Francis of Assisi, see Warner, "Pilgrims and Strangers," 63–170.

question of ecology in vocation—one that unabashedly loves creation yet is quite at home with being "pilgrim and stranger."

In the theoretical framework being constructed here, the imminent and the transcendent are attended to, and a contemplative stance can be maintained through a variety of interpretations and practices. To illustrate for students and professionals the experience of being both at home and homeless in the world, I cite just two stories from Franciscan hagiography and two instructions from the saint's writings. Interpreting these sources today can help develop a Christian ecological sense within a certain capacity which theology schools seek to develop. As given in the opening of this chapter, it is "the capacity to understand and assess one's tradition and identity and to integrate materials from various theological disciplines . . . in ways that enhance ministry and cultivate emotional and spiritual maturity." I imagine every theology has its origin narrative and some stories of movement. The two proffered below are contemplative stories of ecology that remind me where I am, who I'm with, and where we are all going.

As Pope Francis has identified this planet as "our common home" and identified Francis of Assisi as "the example par excellence of care for the vulnerable and of an integral ecology lived out joyfully and authentically,"[32] it may behoove us to examine this fairly popular figure anew. St. Francis's intensely familial language in his encounters with creatures both "sensible" and "insensible" is a well-known manifestation of the charism. There is a kind of shameless biophilia in these encounters, indiscriminately shared. They seem to ask, with an almost presumptuous familiarity, "What is it like to be *you*?"[33] Offered here as narratives about being at home in the world are meetings with a rabbit and a fish:

> Once while he was staying near the town of Greccio, a certain brother brought him a live rabbit caught in a trap. Seeing it, the most blessed man was moved with tenderness. "Brother rabbit," he said, "come to me. Why did you let yourself get caught?" As soon as the brother holding it let go, the rabbit, without any prompting, took shelter with the holy man, as in a most secure place, resting in his bosom. After it had rested there a for a little while, the holy father, caressing it with motherly affection, let it go, so that now free it would return to the woods.[34]

32. *Laudato si'*, para. 10.

33. Something of this quality also appears in accounts of his conversion experience with the leper and in the accounts of his visiting Sultan Malik al-Kamil in Damietta in 1219 during the Fifth Crusade.

34. Armstrong, *Francis of Assisi*, 235.

One time while he was sitting in a little boat at the port on the Lake of Rieti, a fisherman caught a large fish, commonly called a tinca, and reverently offered it to him. He accepted it gladly and gratefully, calling it "brother." He put it back in the water next to the little boat, and with devotion blessed the name of the Lord. For some time the fish did not leave the spot but stayed next to the boat, playing in the water where he put it until, at the end of his prayer, the holy man of God gave it permission to leave.[35]

Aside from their charm, what might these vignettes bring to a sense of vocation? Readers might reflect on the early Christian understanding that holy people carry an aura of Eden about them. They might also study the stories as glimpses of the eschaton. Christian stories of saints and animals look backwards and forwards at the same time. This might inform an administrator's own interactions with her environment, however constrained those interactions might be. Yet there is more. The image of Francis reaching out to these creatures and greeting them is loaded with personal delight and recognition of a significant other. With this in mind, the assistant dean who steps out into a courtyard after a difficult meeting can do more than catch her breath. She can look to the bee in the flower pot as a marvelous, needed colleague.

The accounts of the rabbit and fish offer more than what first appears in them. In the received hagiography, we might notice the interesting appreciation that other humans have of the saint's interactions with animals. We can surmise that something edifying, or at least intriguing, happened for the *viewers* of these encounters. Both the rabbit and the fish had been caught as sources of food. Yet each creature, for some reason, is handed to Francis with the almost certain knowledge that he will eventually let the meal go free. Why? To see something remarkable on an otherwise dull day, perhaps. (I have sometimes wondered: Would anyone find *my* interactions so delightful, surprising, and memorable?) The gestures appear imprudent, if not downright wasteful of resources. Yet if we read these little stories generously, we might draw out something else: When each creature is brought to Francis, it prompts a lesson or a prayer from him. It seems the actual touching of others provokes the wisdom to be shared. He asks the rabbit "Why did you let yourself get caught?"—a question he often asked his human brothers regarding other matters. He prays with the fish "playing in the water" beside him. Those who heard these lessons and prayers heard them from a person who seemed to be utterly at home wherever he was, whether "near the town of Greccio" or "on the Lake of Rieti." Francis's itinerary, like

35. Armstrong, *Francis of Assisi,* 235–36.

that of Jesus, is dotted with actual places and embodied interactions. There is a groundedness in his journey, an emotional and spiritual maturity here that a modern mobile professional, passing through sequential vocations, might want to make his own.

Alongside the understanding of home that a student or administrator should attend to in an ecological context, there is the ever-present experience of homelessness which must be considered. My own small school may be considered a case in point. It began as a seminary for vowed men in Mission Santa Barbara, California. In the summer of 1968, it relocated to the Graduate Theological Union in Berkeley and began accepting laywomen and men. In 2013, after some study and prayer, it moved again. Today the school is affiliated with the University of San Diego, not far north of Tijuana, Mexico. I leave it for the reader to imagine the variety of anecdotes that accompany each of these moves. Going forward (and in what other direction may we truly go?) there is every expectation here that faculty, staff, and students will continue to remain open to call of God and the needs of God's people. What this openness entails remains to be seen, yet what also remains is—through story—the ability to give reason for the hope that is in us. For our school, in order to support the integration of theological concepts that we seek in ministerial formation and vocational development, we keep working with the stories we have received. In addition to love of creation, they also contain the language of pilgrims and strangers. They sustain us in times of change, as I imagine others' spiritual sources sustain them.[36]

Let us turn to another example of received story. It is the passage quoted at the opening of this section, from the 1223 "Later Rule" of St. Francis. This text, enshrined and codified in the early years of the Franciscan family's life, provides us with a glimpse of the pilgrim identity behind the "integral ecology" that Pope Francis sees exemplified in the saint.[37] It is good to remember that this rule was written in times of intense social and institutional change. In the cited passage, the brothers are being exhorted to a spirit of non-appropriation and to one of trust. He tells them as "pilgrims and strangers in this world" to serve the Lord "in poverty and humility" and advises them to "go seeking alms with confidence." The life of service

36. Needless to say, we are always interpreting the stories we receive and attending to the embedded idiosyncrasies. St. Francis, for example, did not learn to love *all* animals. He was suspicious of ants, who seemed to put no trust in Providence. This, along with the fact that his sincere love of poverty did not preclude his accepting Mount Alverno as a gift, rescues us from any temptation to mindless impersonation.

37. For the interpretation that follows I am indebted to William J. Short, OFM, "God of the Migrant, or God the Migrant?" a talk on Justice, Peace, and the Integrity of Creation given to the friars of St. Barbara Province, shared with the author on January 22, 2013.

suggested here is at once Earth-connected and utterly mobile. It allows for confident movement yet preserves the practitioner from what I would call an unhealthy detachment from the world and its inhabitants.

A second and last reading offered from the writings of St. Francis zooms in on the source of that pilgrim identity, the person of Jesus. In an earlier version of his Rule of Life, the saint had already explained why the brothers should never be ashamed to make their needs known to each other and to receive help from others. Rather good counsel, even for today's ministers. Francis asserts, as he does time and again, that they are to accept this pilgrim condition because Christ himself did:

> They must rejoice when they live among people considered of little value and looked down upon, among the poor and the powerless, the sick and the lepers, and the beggars by the wayside. When it is necessary, they may go for alms. Let them not be ashamed and remember moreover, that our Lord Jesus Christ . . . was poor and a stranger.[38]

With this, the human person is invited to pass through many places, not as someone with her eyes fixed on heaven, but with her eyes fixed on earth. As she seeks to follow the footprints of God Incarnate, she is reminded that Christ himself was connected to, and dependent on others. Jesus had no place in his own creation to lay his head, yet his wayfaring was not solitary.

CONCLUSION

Ecology matters in vocational development, and the interactions of students and administrators with their environment are shaping them as much as language, sexuality, and socioeconomic status might. The disciplines of anthropology, evolutionary science, geography, philosophy and environmental psychology present tools for our study of human interactions with the environment. These can be incorporated into co-curricular programming. Using just one tradition out of many—Franciscanism—an exploration of ecology as home has been possible. This tradition, while affectively engaged with creation, points to the significance of "pilgrim and stranger" as a type of solution for interacting with the world. Other spiritualities and academic disciplines may highlight different, fruitful approaches to the topic. It may be that some theology school professionals, like the students they serve, are both in place and placeless. In this study, I have named some of the sources for my own sense of "place," a modest grasp of "nowhere," and some

---

38. Armstrong, "Earlier Rule," 70.

acceptance of "movement" while reaching for an integrated ecology of professional life. Such considerations indicate that rivers and poplars, foxes and birds, pilgrims and strangers all matter deeply for vocations of care in a common home.

BIBLIOGRAPHY

Armstrong, Regis J., et al., eds. *Francis of Assisi: The Saint: Early Documents*. Vol. 1. New York: New City, 1999.
Association of Theological Schools (ATS). "Degree Program Standards." April 30, 2015. Online. https://www.ats.edu/uploads/accrediting/documents/standards-of-accreditation.pdf.
———. "Standards of Accreditation." April 30, 2015. Online. https://www.ats.edu/uploads/accrediting/documents/standards-of-accreditation.pdf.
Augé, Marc. *Non-Places: Introduction to the Anthropology of Supermodernity*. Translated by John Howe. London: Verso, 1995.
Basso, Keith. *Wisdom Sits in Places: Language and Landscape among the Western Apache*. Albuquerque: University of New Mexico Press, 1996.
Carbajo Nuñez, Martín. *Sister Mother Earth: Franciscan Roots of the "Laudato Si'."* Phoenix: Tau, 2017.
Christie, Douglas E. *The Blue Sapphire of the Mind: Notes for a Contemplative Ecology*. Oxford: Oxford University Press, 2013.
Entriken, J. Nichols. *The Betweenness of Place: Towards a Geography of Modernity*. Baltimore: Johns Hopkins University Press, 1991.
Francis. *Encyclical Letter Laudato Si': On Care for Our Common Home*. Washington, DC: United States Conference of Catholic Bishops, 2015.
Kellert, Stephen R., and Edward O. Wilson. *The Biophilia Hypothesis*. Washington, DC: Island, 1993.
Kohak, Erazim. "Of Dwelling and Wayfaring: A Quest for Metaphors." In *The Longing for Home*, edited by Leroy S. Rouner. Notre Dame: University of Notre Dame Press, 1996.
Lowe, Mary E., and Stephen D. Lowe. "Reciprocal Ecology: A Comprehensive Model of Spiritual Formation in Theological Formation." *Theological Education* 48.1 (2013) 1–14.
Médecins San Frontières. "Running from Violence in Central America: A Humanitarian Crisis." *Alert* 18.3 (2017) 2–7.
Short, William J. "God of the Migrant or God the Migrant? Reflections on Place and Movement from the Franciscan Tradition." Unpublished article. 2012.
Sussman, Ann, and Justin Hollander. *Cognitive Architecture: Designing for How We Respond to the Built Environment*. New York: Routledge, 2015.
Swanbrow Becker, Martin A., and David J. Drum. "Essential Counseling Knowledge and Skills to Prepare Student Affairs Staff to Promote Emotional Welling and to Intervene With Students in Distress." *Journal of College & Character* 16.4 (2015) 201–8.
Trice, Michael R. "A Future in the Hyphen: The Dawning of the Faculty-Administrator." *Theological Education* 49.2 (2015) 45–57.

Tuan, Yi-Fu. *Religion: From Place to Placelessness*. Chicago: University of Chicago Press, 2010.

Ulrich, Roger S. "Biophilia, Biophobia, and Natural Landscapes." In *The Biophilia Hypothesis*, edited by Stephen R. Kellert and Edward O. Wilson, 73–136. Washington, DC: Island, 1993.

United Nations High Commission on Refugees (UNHCR). "Climate Change and Disaster Displacement." *UNHCR—USA*. Online. https://www.unhcr.org/climate-change-and-disasters.html.

Walter, E. V. *Placeways: A Theory of Human Environment*. Chapel Hill: University of North Carolina Press, 1988.

Warner, Keith Douglass. "Pilgrims and Strangers: The Evangelical Spirituality of Itinerancy of the Early Franciscan Friars." *Spirit and Life* 10 (2000) 63–170.

PART TWO

Called or Captive?

CHAPTER 6

The Lord Requires *What* of Me?

Answering a Call to Student Services in Theological Education

C. MARK BATTEN
and SHELLY E. HART

INTRODUCTION

GIVEN THE UNSTABLE REALITY we too often live and experience in the modern North American context, the community engagement, public theology, critical scholarship, and moral leadership of the students with whom we work in theological education is crucial, even essential, to fostering the continuing transformation of faith communities and the world. Our roles as student services personnel in helping these students navigate their theological education, fully embracing their own calls and preparing for whatever the future holds, allow us to be companions and sometimes even midwives on their journeys. In our daily work, we are attending not only the needs of our students but also our individual and collective call as people of faith to seek justice and build God's kingdom. It is exhilarating and exhausting sacred work, a vocation that requires us to exercise a variety of gifts and skills and often to pray for the fruits of the spirit (patience, kindness, and self-control to name but a few) to be abundant within us and within the students with whom we work as their discernment processes and formation unfold.

Having spent ten and twenty-one years respectively doing the work of theological education administration, we have found ourselves at first unexpectedly, but over time, increasingly and undeniably called to this particular vocation. Rather than experiencing this as a call away from ministry, our calls into theological education administration and to student services work have revealed to us a particular way in which our own gifts are suited to serve our neighbors and to work toward making the kingdom of God a reality in the here and now. Remaining passionate about the work of ministry, we engage daily in respectful, meaning-seeking conversations with prospective and current students as they discern how they are uniquely gifted to create positive change in the world. As we support students in utilizing the resources of theological education to form and equip them to do the work they are called to do, we fulfill our own vocations.

In this essay we will share our collective wisdom—which has been gained through thirty-plus years of combined experience in recruitment, admissions, communications, financial aid, and student records work—about the meaning we have found in asking better questions focused on how God wants to use us and the student services communities to which we belong to aid in the formation of religious leaders for this place and time. We will reflect on the prophet Micah's call in Micah 6:8 to "seek justice, love kindness, and [journey][1] humbly with God" as a framework and context for our work as well as why this field is a place in which our particular gifts align with the needs of students and our institutions as we cope with the ever-evolving landscapes of theological education and religious leadership.

CONTEXT

Like many student personnel administrators, we each stumbled across our gifts and call to this particular ministry by doing the work. Serving as a seminary administrator was not an option we explored in our denominational ministry discernment processes nor was it something suggested to us by our college nor seminary professors. Teacher, author, and activist Parker Palmer argues that, "Discovering vocation does not mean scrambling toward some prize just beyond my reach but accepting the reassurance of true

---

1. While the ending phrase of Micah 6:8 is appropriately and most commonly translated: "And humbly to walk with your God." See Brown et al., *Brown-Driver-Briggs*, 229–37, regarding the translation of the Hebrew word הלך (hâlak), meaning go, come, walk. We have chosen to replace "walk" with "journey" out of our commitment to be inclusive of people with disabilities and in affirmation that those who do not or cannot walk are not excluded from humbly traveling their spiritual paths with God as their companion.

self I already possess."[2] In student services work, we found our gifts being used and our own "deep gladness"[3] coming alive. In our particular cases, we followed similar paths, starting as students in seminary ourselves, becoming admissions work-study students to help make ends meet and to contribute back to our schools, and then seizing opportunities to transition to full-time student services work as we discerned our true callings. We were fortunate to find mentors who recognized our gifts and helped us to grow our capacities to serve students well. And while our work has been and is valuable to our institutions, the value of our work to the students whom we serve is the critical center of our own vocations.

As we continue to embrace our calls to student-centered student services in theological education, we find increasingly that every best practice in our work involves collaboration. As we have journeyed through various positions and functions in student services, we have naturally brought our previous experiences with us, allowing us to understand the necessary connections between the various parts of the work in our schools. While just doing the overwhelming amount of work on our own plates often seems the most critical thing we can do to help our students, making time to collaborate with colleagues across our institutions will ultimately help us to give our best to the students we serve. Similarly, taking time to learn from colleagues, whether they are in other schools of the Association of Theological Schools (ATS) or in other types of institutions altogether, can help us innovate in our own work. Though we must do our own part to "seek justice, love kindness, and [journey] humbly with God," none of us can complete the work of building God's kingdom on our own. Like members of the body that the apostle Paul describes in 1 Corinthians 12, members of seminary communities need each other in order to do the work to which we are called, and, as student personnel administrators, our primary work is to serve the students who are called to study in our institutions. Our schools would not exist without students, and students are becoming increasingly hard to attract for many of our institutions because of the myriad changes happening in the North American religious landscape and in society in general. This is yet another reason why working together is so vital. Every member of the body is part of the recruitment and student service efforts of our schools in some way. Rather than embracing only our own piece of the puzzle, we can contribute the most when we each connect our own gifts with those of our colleagues and all work together toward living into the vision and mission

2. Palmer, *Let Your Life Speak*, 10.

3. Buechner, *Wishful Thinking*, 118–19.

of our schools in order to contribute to the larger ongoing transformation of religious leadership and the world.

WHAT DOES THE LORD REQUIRE OF US?

For those who embrace theological education administration and student services work as a vocation, a ministry, and a calling, what is required of us goes beyond the words of our job descriptions. Certainly, we must fulfill the duties to which we are assigned by our supervisors and uphold the policies of our institutions. Yet there is more to our work than any job description could state. While there are a variety of ways to frame a conversation about embracing our work as a vocation, we find the words in Micah 6:8 an empowering context and framework. If we seek justice in our work, we will serve all of our students well and empower them to seek justice in their own work. If we love kindness (also often translated as mercy[4]), we will move beyond tolerance to embracing students and colleagues so that we can find a new level of working together. And if we journey humbly with God we will nurture our own souls and relationship with the divine so that we may be sustained in our work.

SEEKING JUSTICE

What might it look like to seek justice in the context of our student services work? First and foremost, we believe it means advocating for students, especially those who may be on the margins of our communities. International students, non-native English speakers, students of color, students with disabilities, students who struggle academically or financially, students who are in the minority for any reason may need us to advocate for them and to empower them to advocate for themselves. Depending upon our particular roles, student services personnel often have a chance to know students more fully than others in our institutions, especially if we approach our work with a posture of care and openness. We often know the structures of our institutions in ways that students cannot know them, therefore, we have power to help students navigate those structures. But a word of caution: we must listen carefully to our students so that we can learn what their needs are rather than assuming we know. Advocacy must not turn into paternalism.

---

4. The Hebrew word חֶסֶד (*che·sed*) is commonly translated into English as kindness (NRSV, ESV, and others) or mercy (NKJV, NIV, and others). See semantic translation references in Brown et al., *Brown-Driver-Briggs*, 338–39, for the nuances of meaning for חֶסֶד (*che·sed*).

Also, when students express concerns or issues to us, our first job is to believe them and to listen for understanding rather than immediately trying to explain the issue away or even to fix it. Once students have shared their need with us and we have reflected back what we think we know back to them, then we can ask if they need our help. Sometimes they may just need someone to listen. Sometimes they need advice about how to proceed. Sometimes they need to know what we are willing and able to do on their behalf or to whom we can refer them for help. When we have cultivated collaborations with other personnel across (and sometimes outside) our institutions we can readily work together to provide webs of support for students as specific needs arise.

Seeking justice does not mean that our students always get what they want. In fact, one of the hardest lessons to learn in our work is that sometimes the divine "yes" is in the "no" we provide through gracious boundaries. For example, students who are struggling academically often need to be placed on probation and a reduced course load, not as a punishment, but as a way to give them a chance to succeed by giving appropriate boundaries that they are unlikely to choose for themselves. Similarly, it can be heartbreaking to discontinue a student who has many gifts for ministry and scholarship but who continually withdraws from or fails classes despite the kind of gracious boundaries described above. However, it is not just or ethical for us to continue taking tuition dollars from a student who is not in a position to succeed in making satisfactory academic progress at this time in his or her journey. Such a "no" need not always be understood as permanent, but it may be the best and the most just thing for this student in these circumstances at this time.

Seeking justice in our work also means taking responsibility to do our part to confront systemic injustice within our institutions and in our larger communities. Over the past several years, Candler School of Theology students have increasingly expressed a heightened need to address institutional and societal racism and the resulting injustices, from microaggressions in the classroom to police killings of unarmed black men in our city, the disproportionate incarceration of black and brown bodies in our state and across our country, and so many other manifestations. The resulting institutional responses and student actions have been multifaceted, including unconscious bias training for faculty and staff, racial healing retreats for faculty, staff, students, and administrators, University-wide protests led by theology students, prophetic convocation addresses, and more. We are not only preparing students to be leaders for justice in the future, we are following their lead in seeking justice here and now within our institutions and in the communities beyond them. Recently, the Candler Staff Advisory

Council offered an opportunity for staff members to participate in an ongoing discussion group centered around the theme of racial realities. While taking the time to participate involves a sacrifice of time and energy as well as experiencing painful, vulnerable, and difficult conversations, those participating believe that the work of fighting racial injustice and promoting racial healing is critically important both within our school community and for furthering our individual and collective abilities to seek justice beyond our walls as well.

MODELING MERCY AND KINDNESS

In her book *Braving the Wilderness*, Brené Brown challenges leaders to be fully accountable for their treatment of one's neighbors and their authentic story. She references the current cultural rhetoric of *dehumanization*, the stripping of dignity.

> Dehumanizing and holding people accountable are mutually exclusive. Humiliation and dehumanizing are not accountability or social justice tools, they're emotional offloading at best, emotional self-indulgence at worst. Our faith asks us to find the face of God in everyone we meet. When we desecrate their divinity, we desecrate our own, and we betray our faith.[5]

In our work with students, we are seeking justice, in part, by extending mercy and kindness through validation of students and colleagues, even if it means putting ourselves in a vulnerable position to do so. Our work requires a particular blend of vulnerability—on the part of both the student and the administrator. At any point in a student's relationship with our institution, they may feel led to share a story that expresses their own vulnerability and openness. It is likely these moments of sharing, whether about anxiety and need or celebration, may have previously been met with misunderstanding and distasteful responses that undermine the validation of their particular experience. In our work, in which we are training leaders who we hope will faithfully reflect the gospel,[6] we ourselves must model integrity, compassion and solidarity as we seek the face of God by listening to, caring for, and responding to students.

5. Brown, *Braving the Wilderness*, 76.

6. While we are writing out of Christian contexts, we recognize that some institutions and programs within institutions are multifaith or educate students who claim no faith at all. We believe the values implied from Christian concepts such as the gospel, the body of Christ, etc. can be applied universally in the form of love, justice, respect, mercy, etc.

Listening and caring is a ministry of presence. Our decisions and responses have significant impact on students as they seek clarity and viable options for resolutions to problems. Validation takes many forms and our investment can either solve a problem just for today or extend support that benefits the student long term. Brown continues, "Challenging ourselves to live by higher standards requires constant diligence and awareness."[7] Higher standards is not used here as a cliché. Responding to an evolving student dynamic—how they navigate their identity, interact interculturally, and embody their beliefs—involves challenges that require us to be diligent in cultivating our awareness of a student's experiences outside our institutions and the other dynamics that might influence their communication. Consider the following example.

There was a student who came to seminary with a background in graphic design. This student's vocational interest centered around the use of art as a practice for healing and holistic well-being. Participating in the work-study program this student assisted the seminary's communications staff with the creation of a vast array of graphic assets used for digital and print publications. The seminary experience was, at times, difficult for this student. During a particularly tough semester, the student's emotional health was becoming increasingly unstable. In a regular meeting with a supervisor to review recent design projects the student erupted in exasperation that the supervisor could offer such critical assessment about a particular design. In that moment the supervisor realized that the feedback spoken was being actualized by the student at an individual, personal level instead of being understood as constructive criticism about particular elements of the project.

After a necessary pause in the conversation to restore centeredness, the supervisor exercised vulnerability—in this case a sensitive pastoral response—and offered space for the student to discuss the trigger that led to such an outburst. Feeling the power shift and kindness in the supervisor's response, the student shared that the current process of assessing the work was a constant reminder of a previous working relationship in which the only feedback typically offered was fault-finding. For over a year the student had been traversing through discomfort, hiding within a darkness of disapproval and judgment based on prior encounters, but had not been provided space to share the difficulty.

As the conversation continued, the student and the supervisor began to establish a process that first valued affirmation and gratitude. Once the positive aspects were fully expressed, then the constructive assessment or

7. Brown, *Braving the Wilderness*, 76.

criticism would be offered. This seems like a simplistic process to adopt. However, in an environment where seminary personnel increasingly find themselves pulled between multiple responsibilities and day-to-day strains mute our abilities to fully attend to building rewarding relationships with students and with colleagues, the routine manner of reply is to quickly re-lay what needs to get done to complete a project instead of offering mercy and kindness, acknowledging appreciation for another's effort and energy. Additionally, in this particular scenario the student had been functioning out of previous dehumanization, as described by Brown, that provided a destructive framework out of which the student reacted.

"Darkness is not the whole of the story—every pilgrimage has pas-sages of loveliness and joy—but it is the part of the story most often left untold," Parker Palmer reflects on the process of becoming one's self. "The experience of darkness has been essential to my coming into selfhood, and telling the truth about that fact helps me stay in the light."[8]

Efforts to instill healthy relationships with appropriate boundaries are necessary in our work with students. At the same time, so is healthy dialogue. We must develop and continually fine tune our ability to be truth tellers and to share our own vulnerability in appropriate ways. "Many young people today journey in the dark, as the young always have, and we elders do them a disservice when we withhold the shadowy parts of our lives,"[9] Palmer reminds us. Considering our own past vulnerabilities and the pro-cess we underwent to be successful, to change the narrative of our lives, is an important chapter of our own vocational journey and equally important in our support of others as they traverse in and out of darkness and light in the context of their theological education.

We read of a discouraged Elijah in 1 Kings and a cast out Hagar in Genesis, yet we also read of a courageous Elijah and a brave Hagar. These stories begin with defeat and insecurity, but they move toward faithful-ness and clarification of purpose due to God's compassion and mercy. In the context of our work in student services, being truth tellers means con-tinuing to navigate the ever-evolving student dynamic and experience. In an opening worship service at Wake Forest University School of Divinity during a recent new student orientation, a second-year Master of Divin-ity student proclaimed to the entering class, "None of us fit in, but we all belong here." Despite a mainstream culture in which the powerful oppress the weak, the unloved find no hospitality, and the voiceless have difficulty finding space to proclaim their truth, seminaries have the opportunity to

8. Palmer, *Let Your Life Speak*, 18.

9. Palmer, *Let Your Life Speak*, 18.

build a coalition of support for students and model what belonging to a loving, kind, and merciful community truly means. Wake Forest University School of Divinity has been intentional within our learning community to model the demographic diversity of communal life in the United States. One of the benefits is that faculty, staff, and students find themselves engaging in conversations of many vibrant and brilliant hues. Together, in a safe and courageous community, they practice justice, mercy, and kindness as they discuss deeply personal matters of faith, reflect on classroom learnings, and enjoy lively banter. These conversations permeate through community life—at the twice-weekly community lunches, weekly coffee hours, internship cohort meetings, and impromptu hallway exchanges. Although the end result is not always agreement, students are actively building community and intercultural engagement practices that will impact their future work as religious leaders, where their acts of discovering, knowing, and transforming will flourish by way of listening, understanding, and risk-taking.

Our task as student services personnel is to be courageous and brave, willing to venture into the wilderness with students who are searching and taking risks, to hold their discouragement and worry and at the same time extend mercy and kindness—or loveliness and joy as Palmer describes—helping to break them out of their dark places so that flourishing can be restored. When we faithfully take these actions to genuinely connect with students, we invite them to reclaim and affirm their value. We also empower them to share their own vulnerability with others in their community, opening the possibility of exponential impact. This intentional modeling of kindness and mercy is likely to beget kindness and mercy over and over again—a "pay it forward" ideal which can expand our whole communities into brave spaces where everyone can find belonging.

EMBRACING OUR CALLS THROUGH [JOURNEYING] HUMBLY WITH GOD

In her wonderful book, *Redeeming Administration*, Ann Garrido dedicates a chapter to the ways the work of administration can help us grow in the virtue of humility. Like Brené Brown, Garrido describes this virtue first in terms of vulnerability:

> Administration has the capacity to make us appropriately vulnerable, which is a wonderfully holy thing. First, administration helps us gather a more accurate, truthful picture of ourselves. It puts us in situations that we would not otherwise confront, allowing us to see how we handle certain kinds of demands and

pressures. It is stressful enough that we can't manage to put on a good face week after week, month after month without our true selves coming to the surface.[10]

Garrido claims that once our true self is out in the open for others to observe, we have the chance to embrace holy humility, that is to say, we can embrace a true and balanced picture of ourselves.[11] In our work, we will have chances to recognize and admit our faults and foibles as well as to better understand our strengths and accomplishments. Garrido argues that without humility the picture of ourselves as we truly are is distorted and when that is the case, "there is no way that we can be in honest and truthful relationships with others, and consequently there is no way that we can participate in God's Trinitarian life."[12] If we understand God as Trinitarian, then we contend that God's very nature is relational, mutually vulnerable, and authentic. As those made in God's image we are called to live likewise in order to be our fullest selves.

The gift of humility offers us each the chance to be who we are in our work spaces. When we can admit our mistakes, celebrate our gifts, and be genuine in our relationships, we are much more likely to thrive than when we spend our energy projecting a false image of our own perfection. Even the most seasoned among us has room to continue to learn and grow in our roles and how we relate to ourselves and others as we nurture the next generation of leaders who seek to shape communities that will thrive.

Garrido also describes the story of Mary and Martha (Luke 10) in her chapter on humility, saying, "the voice of Jesus in the situation is not a critique of service . . . but rather a concern about the anxiety and worry the exercise of leadership is causing in Martha. Perhaps Jesus is saying that the one thing needed in leaders is the capacity to first sit down and listen for a while, rather than engage in endless activity."[13] For those of us in student personnel administration, journeying humbly with God may in part mean taking time away from the overwhelming busy nature of our jobs to listen to the voice of God speaking to us both through cultivating our own inner spiritual lives and through the community around us. Our days are so filled with our overflowing inboxes, meetings to attend, and data to crunch that we hardly have time to go down the hall to refill our water bottles. Nevertheless, we invite you (and ourselves) to imagine how to carve out time each day to pause to pray or attend chapel worship (if it isn't your direct responsibility

10. Garrido, *Redeeming Administration*, 83.

11. Garrido, *Redeeming Administration*, 84.

12. Garrido, *Redeeming Administration*, 85–86.

13. Garrido, *Redeeming Administration*, 88.

to be there already) or go to an event that will feed your spirit. If we do not occasionally, at the least, make time for such things, we are in danger of becoming exhausted, snappish, and even burned out. As Parker Palmer asserts, "Self-care is never a selfish act—it is simply good stewardship of the only gift I have, the gift I was put on earth to offer others. Anytime we can listen to true self and give the care it requires, we do it not only for ourselves, but for the many others whose lives we touch."[14]

FINAL REFLECTIONS

Douglas J. Schuurman in *Vocation: Discerning Our Callings in Life* summarizes the connectivity of our vocations as uniting "not only with the Life of God in whom we live and move and have our being . . . but also our past, present, and future as a liturgy of sin, forgiveness, and renewal."[15] Vocation as liturgy creates a beautiful metaphor for our work in student services. Liturgy is a creative expression of beliefs and ideals that seeks action-oriented service to God and community. Liturgy seeks a new creation grounded in justice, hope, equitable provisions, equal rights, safety, and security for all of God's beloved creatures. Our vocation in serving students engaged in theological education supports the work of seeing this new creation realized. If we seek justice in our work, students will be empowered to seek justice in their own work. If we practice mercy and kindness, we begin to model understanding and wholeness, embracing the image of God in each person we encounter and in ourselves. If we journey humbly with God, the intentional nurturing of our connection with the divine source of our own vocation and calling will embolden our students to faithfully participate in self-reflective spiritual practices such as prayer, meditation, and study.

Near the end of his work, Schuurman asks how vocation shapes our identity—how we make decisions, our behaviors and attitudes—in a particular place or sphere. His response? "Vocation encourages Christians[16] to see themselves as created and redeemed by God's grace, so that they will express their love for God and God's world through these spheres. In all of them Christians should exhibit the fruit of the Spirit."[17] Our response? The work of student services in theological education empowers us to express

14. Palmer, *Let Your Life Speak*, 30–31.

15. Schuurman, *Vocation*, 66.

16. While Schuurman writes out of a Christian context, we believe that the more general term "people of faith" would equally apply. Faithful people from many traditions can embrace vocation as a way to see themselves as created in the divine image.

17. Schuurman, *Vocation*, 151.

our love of God and God's creation by using our gifts to minister to, for, and with students who are being formed as transformational leaders for communities of faith and the world. The decisions we make on a daily basis to practice our values (justice, mercy, kindness, openness, respect, vulnerability, humility) within the context of our work, allow us to serve students well and to model for them a kind of leadership and service that we pray will empower them to "seek justice, love kindness, and [journey] humbly with God" during their sojourns in our seminary communities and throughout all of their lives and work.

As you seek to embrace your own vocation in theological education student services, we leave you with this benediction, a blessing titled "For a New Position" by Irish poet and teacher John O'Donohue:

> May your . . . work excite your heart,
> Kindle in your mind a creativity
> To journey beyond the old limits
> Of all that has become wearisome.
> May this work challenge you toward
> New frontiers that will emerge
> As you begin to approach them,
> Calling forth from you the full force
> And depth of your undiscovered gifts.
> May the work fit the rhythms of your soul,
> Enabling you to draw from the invisible
> New ideas and a vision that will inspire.
> Remember to be kind
> To those who [you encounter in your] work . . .
> Endeavor to remain aware
> Of the quiet world
> That lives behind each face.
> Be fair in your expectations,
> Compassionate in your criticism.
> May you have the grace of encouragement
> To awaken the gift in the other's heart,
> Building in them the confidence
> To follow the call of the gift.
> May you come to know that work
> Which emerges from the mind of love
> Will have beauty and form.
> May this . . . work be worthy
> Of the Energy of your heart
> And the light of your thought.
> May your work assume

A proper space in your life;
Instead of owning or using you,
May it challenge and refine you,
Bringing you further
Into the wonder of your heart.[18]

May it be so for you. Amen.

BIBLIOGRAPHY

Brown, Brené. *Braving the Wilderness*. New York: Vermilion, 2017.
Brown, Francis, et al. *The Brown-Driver-Briggs Hebrew and English Lexicon*. Peabody, MA: Hendrickson, 2007.
Buechner, Frederick. *Wishful Thinking: A Seeker's ABC*. New York: HarperCollins, 1993.
Garrido, Ann M. *Redeeming Administration: 12 Spiritual Habits for Catholic Leaders in Parishes, Schools, Religious Communities, and Other Institutions*. Notre Dame: Ave Maria, 2013.
O'Donohue, John. "For a New Position." In *To Bless the Space Between Us: A Book of Blessings*, by John O'Donohue, 20–22. New York: Doubleday, 2008.
Palmer, Parker J. *Let Your Life Speak: Listening for the Voice of Vocation*. San Francisco: Jossey-Bass, 2000.
Schuurman, Douglas J. *Vocation: Discerning Our Callings in Life*. Grand Rapids: Eerdmans, 2004.

18. O'Donohue, "For a New Position," 20–22.

CHAPTER 7

Meaning, Messaging, and Money

Navigating the Challenges and Opportunities for Seminary Enrollment

GRAHAM MCKEAGUE
and ASHLEY NICHOLS VANBEMMELEN

INTRODUCTION

Seminaries operate at the nexus of ministry and higher education, shaped by both worlds in an era marked by change. Increasingly, seminaries must make a case for the value of religious education in a world increasingly shaped by the language and policies of efficiency, return on investment, and measurable outcomes. This time of change provides both challenges and opportunities for enrollment offices. We employ a case study approach to examine some of the current practices within seminary enrollment, presenting our work within the "reflective practitioner"[1] approach generally, and specifically as a task of "sensemaking." Bolman and Gallos note the importance of sensemaking for academic leadership stating that it is "a personal, interpretative, action-oriented process involving three basic steps: noticing things, interpreting them, and deciding what to do about

---

1. Schön, *Reflective Practitioner*, 49–69.

them."[2] Weick, Sutcliffe and Obstfeld add that sensemaking is a way to make "salient categories"[3] within organizations as a step towards action. As such, sensemaking can be used a means to organize in the midst of confusion, to label and categorize through reflecting and interpreting, and is useful for informed action. This chapter applies a process of sensemaking to seminary enrollment at a mid-sized, evangelical, Association of Theological Schools (ATS) accredited institution embedded within a larger university, and presents the categories of meaning, messaging, and money as a framework for discussion.

MEANING

Clydesdale's study of eighty-eight Christian undergraduate institutions provides a helpful entry-point into a discussion of seminary enrollment and *meaning*. His work highlights the importance of talking with students about vocation as it relates to their formal education. Clydesdale writes, "a major disadvantage [of a postmodern world] is the fact that it assigns individuals the task of navigating life's purpose amid ever-churning seas of meaning. . . . The majority of college students seek a meaningful life, and most are willing to hear any narrative of purpose that is genuinely conveyed."[4] To this we might add that the majority of seminary students also seek this same meaningful life and narrative of purpose. In our experience, though prospective seminary students have already identified a larger vocational trajectory oriented towards ministry, they are often following a path of vocational discernment that is highly individualized and largely based on a sense of personal calling. Prospective students often arrive at seminary with a generalized sense of calling, an understanding of themselves as people and ministry leaders that is still being formed, and with a limited concept of what ministry options may be available to them as a career.

Our argument is that seminary enrollment professionals are uniquely placed to provide what Clydesdale calls a "narrative of purpose,"[5] one that builds from whatever stage of development and knowledge a student presents. We see this process occurring across three levels: first, at the individual-level where the enrollment professional seeks to further understand the personal narrative of the prospective student. How does seminary further prepare someone for ministry in response to a sense of vocational calling?

2. Bolman and Gallos, *Reframing Academic Leadership*, 29–30.

3. Weick et al., "Sensemaking," 409.

4. Clydesdale, *Purposeful Graduate*, 21.

5. Clydesdale, *Purposeful Graduate*, 21.

Over time enrollment professionals learn and categorize the narratives of many individuals, both those who chose to attend seminary, and those that do not. Drawing from this archive of narratives can be very beneficial in guiding prospective students. We have observed how a seminary education profoundly shapes individuals in their understanding of what ministry is, the ways in which it is practiced, and in their personal growth. Often students do not have a clear sense of who they are and where they might be headed, and that reality, rather than presenting a challenge, provides great opportunity for enrollment teams in working with students.

Second, telling the institutional narrative, including the historical and theological tradition, along with a vision for the future. How does the seminary understand its role within a larger university context, as part of a denomination, or within society? In our experience, potential students are very interested in hearing clear responses to these types of questions. A common question from prospective students in our particular case was, "What type of school are you?," a question that invites the telling of our institutional narrative, in our case, a seminary founded in the 1940s, rooted in the Baptist tradition, but now a multidenominational evangelical school. Prospective students often ask about how we envision the seminary today and how it might develop over time. What does the curriculum emphasize? What are faculty teaching about and researching? What's the seminary's connection with larger social questions? In this way, prospective students are seeking to align their own individual sense of meaning and purpose with an institution. We also encourage potential students to consider how they might contribute to the ongoing life of the seminary, shaping it in important ways as students and later as alumni. This has been an especially important conversation for students of color and female students in seeking to anticipate their sense of belonging within the seminary community.

Third, the larger narrative of God's redeeming work in the world. Over the years, this has perhaps stood out as one of the most important aspects of seminary enrollment in defining meaning. In our experience, students frequently come to seminary with minimal understanding of the larger narrative of God's work in the world as presented in Scripture. We consider two frameworks in particular to be helpful examples in describing what this larger narrative entails: First, the Creation-Fall-Redemption framework as presented by Wolters,[6] or second, the "grand narrative" idea presented by Christopher Wright.[7] One of the greatest points of meaning is found in showing students how their own decisions regarding seminary are part of

6. Wolters, *Creation Regained*, 12.

7. Wright, *Mission of God*, 47.

the larger narrative of participating in the mission of God, reorienting their decisions around God's plans and purposes, rather than simply the fulfillment of the individual.

In considering all three levels of meaning, how might we, as enrollment professionals, meet this challenge to work with students in a way that speaks to meaning and purpose? Veith and Ristuccia state that we should exercise "our imagination so that it accords with God's imagination—that is, his creation, his purposes, and his works of grace, all of which he reveals in his word."[8] Our experience is that there are tremendous opportunities to work with students who come to seminary hungry for that type of educational experience, to understand God's word more fully, to exercise their imaginations more freely, and cultivate a worldview that is deepened and meaningful in service to God.

MESSAGING

We turn now to consider how meaning is communicated. We posit that meaning must be accurately and efficiently turned into messaging for prospective students and stakeholders. Each school stakes their claim to a unique identity, distinguished faculty members, and academically robust programs. Thinking about messaging across the three levels already presented, how might the enrollment office help students in the process of their individual discernment. Perhaps the following questions can guide these discussions:

- What is the value of theological education? How do we meet the need for students to discern their calling and direction?

- Ask prospective students to reflect on their own story and what has led them to this point.

- Have prospective students consider who else in their life has helped to affirm their decision to consider seminary.

Second, how do we (as institutions) accurately share the message about who we are and who we want to become? How do we attract students who fit the narrative of our school? How do we keep up with the changes in marketing and advertising when Facebook, Google, and Instagram seem to be releasing new features on a constant basis? The following questions may be helpful for consideration:

8. Veith and Ristuccia, *Imagination Redeemed*, 93.

- Who are we as an institution? How do our mission, vision, and values impact the work we do?

- Who are our stakeholders and what messaging do they need or expect from us? How do we meet this need now and in the future?

- What do we need prospective students to know about who we are? Are these factors compelling?

- What type of student are we hoping to recruit? Think critically about diversity: gender, race, ethnicity, ability, socioeconomic status, theological position, denomination, etc. Do we represent our student population effectively across marketing platforms?

- What does our school provide that will be unique or exceptional for students? What are some compelling ways to share this narrative?

A significant challenge with messaging is the ever-changing nature of marketing platforms. Fifteen years ago, most schools relied heavily on print materials and travel to undergraduate institutions to communicate their message. Today, schools need a comprehensive marketing plan including print, radio, social media, search engine marketing, retargeting, email list campaigns, banner ads, blogs, and podcasts. When building a comprehensive marketing plan, enrollment professionals need to consider the core messages of the institution. It is key to build messages that complement and expand on one another across platforms. For example, a professor has written a new book that the school would like to feature; the professor records a short lecture or podcast about the book which is then edited and turned into a blog post. Key phrases or quotes can be used to promote the book across Twitter, Facebook, and Instagram. An email campaign with a free chapter download can be sent to church or alumni lists. These are just a few ways in which one message or product can be promoted across multiple platforms for multiple stakeholders.

Enrollment professionals have the opportunity to carefully craft the message of the institution in order to effectively communicate the meaning of theological education and the unique aspects of our schools. The messages need to sound compelling to an ever-changing digital generation of millennials and generation Z students, while still reaching the fifty-plus demographic growing across ATS schools. Millennials and Generation Z typically value honesty in a narrative, and they can see through the spin of traditional marketing and stock photos. They care about creation, social change, and advocacy, while being less religiously affiliated than previous generations.[9] Our narratives need to honestly speak to the concerns of these potential students while faithfully representing our institutions and programs.

A significant task in honest representation is a narrative that speaks to student experience, formational development, cost of completion, and ramifications on job and family life. We do no favors to our students when we garner interest with one narrative, then students discover another reality upon enrollment. The "narrative of purpose" (noting Clydesdale's language) we communicate must be true to who we are and the work we do as an institution, not an inflated story of who we wish we were. When we engage students with honest rhetoric regarding a typical student's experience, expected formational growth, and the implications for family life and finances, we are more likely to increase retention percentages and see students realize degree completion. In our case, we have worked to specifically outline cost per credit, total cost per program, expected grant/scholarship funding, anticipated federal loan eligibility, average time commitment per class, and formational enhancement opportunities. In addition, we consider how we can address the third aspect of meaning, where students have a clearer understanding of what it takes to enroll in seminary, but also participate in the larger work of God in the work. Our messaging must be able to point students to this larger purpose.

From our experience, we also suggest that messaging needs to occur from departments outside of recruitment as a significant opportunity for most schools. At our institution, we have developed an Intercultural Lecture Series and Talking Points program that has a regular blog and multiple mini-conferences throughout the year. These programs have provided the faculty and administration with an outlet to develop the school's narrative in partnership with the enrollment staff. The blog highlights faculty research, publications, and speaking engagements as well as provides encouragement and advice for ministry and counseling professionals. Through the mini-conferences, popular topics in evangelicalism are addressed; including Christian social ethics, creation, sexuality, addiction, women's issues, and race relations. These external facing events provide the institution a space to engage churches, non-profit leaders, educators, lay leaders, alumni, and other stakeholders with an example of how faith communities can engage deeply in important conversations, thereby highlighting the value of the scholarship in supporting the work of ministry.

9. Pew Research Center, "Age Gap in Religion," 30–49.

MONEY

Conversations about money are unavoidable. We are continually considering ways to enhance the student experience, improve student services, endow additional scholarships, and fund marketing campaigns. Many seminaries are dependent on tuition dollars and scholarship funding in order to support the financial viability of the school. If students do not attend, tuition cannot be collected and scholarship funds sit unused. This presents an increasing need for recruitment and retention models that support the flow of funding into the institution, adding additional pressure to the work of enrollment.

This broader challenge is seen across ATS schools where we see a decline in overall FTE headcounts. In 2007, 41.5 percent of member schools had a FTE equivalent of more than 150 students.[10] By 2017, the number of schools with more than 150 FTE has decreased to 31.1 percent.[11] In the same ten-year period, overall headcount has decreased by almost seven thousand students while ATS has added eighteen new member schools.[12] The number of schools enrolling students had increased while the number of students enrolling has decreased. Schools are pursuing a shrinking population of seminary students, causing enrollment offices to adjust budgets to account for less income, increase tuition, or find new streams of revenue.

At our institution, we have pursued a combination of all three methods listed above. In recent years we have had to adjust the expenditure budget, yet the budget for marketing and advertising has not kept up with the demand of messaging platforms. The funding needed for social media, pay-per-click (PPC) advertising, and brand campaigns has grown significantly without allocations to match the need. It is impossible for most seminaries to fund these campaigns without crippling the budget. The work of enrollment management includes allocating and evaluating spending each year to match actual enrollment revenue.

Increasing tuition has become commonplace for many institutions to maintain revenue. However, this creates a tension when the cost of tuition feels unmanageable to prospective students expecting modest salaries upon graduation. Therefore, the identification of new revenue streams to address student cost-of-attendance has become a major focus for many institutions, including ours. Under the leadership of our Academic Dean, departments across campus (Administration, Alumni Relations, Advancement,

---

10. See table 1.5-A in ATS, "2007–2008 Data Tables."

11. See table 1.5-A in ATS, "2017–2018 Data Tables."

12. See table 1.5-A in ATS, "2007–2008 Data Tables"; "2017–2018 Data Tables."

Admissions, Marketing) have worked together to identify new scholarship funding, communicate with the local community, and recruit additional students. This has enabled the enrollment office to increase and diversify the student body (enrolling over two hundred urban leaders in ten years; increasing the MDiv by twenty-five students) by providing scholarships that lower the total cost of attendance (50–75 percent tuition scholarship).

With the support of a grant from the Lilly Endowment, we developed an advanced standing program that awards student graduate credit for advanced-level undergraduate coursework. This decreases the length and cost of graduate programs enabling us to provide students with more educational resources on fundraising, financial advising, budgeting, and debt repayment, leading to more fiscally educated ministry leaders. One practical method of delivering this information has been a "Steps for Success" session within our New Student Orientation program, where fiscal literacy is addressed in depth.

Several new initiatives remain as future endeavors or opportunities for our small staff. With the increase of more than forty-five students to our Master of Arts (MA). in Counseling program due to the addition of an online modality, we have recognized the need for flexibility in scheduling and robust online programs. Through listening to the needs of current students, our constituents, and market research, two new MA level degrees are under consideration for the next year. We also recognize the need for a strong alumni relations department. Alumni are often the best brand awareness champions. Yet, we do not have personnel resources to adequately cultivate and develop seminary alumni. We have discussed the need for a brand champion program within our current student body. Current students have access to markets through churches, ministries, and community engagement. Selecting fifteen-to-twenty students within the seminary population and investing resources to train them as brand champions and send out into their communities can provide additional leads for an admissions team to cultivate.

In sum, we have found it increasingly important for enrollment professionals to have direct conversations with students about money. The decrease in enrollment across ATS schools has made it apparent that changes are needed to remain viable. New initiatives and programs can only come to fruition with the support of faculty, advancement, marketing, and administrative professionals on campus. These endeavors cannot be managed alone. Enrollment professionals are uniquely positioned to positively impact change within their theological school context in light of the changing financial models.

CONCLUSION

Enrollment professionals have a critical role in any graduate theological school. With the responsibility of recruiting and retaining students, enrollment professionals must think strategically about the challenges and opportunities in meaning, messaging, and money. By knowing their institution and having a deep belief in theological education, enrollment professionals can communicate a narrative of meaning to potential students and additional stakeholders. They can work with faculty and alumni to affirm the importance of developing students within a multidisciplinary approach that encourages vocational discernment. Enrollment professionals use this lens of meaning to craft compelling messages that can be used across traditional and digital platforms. At its best, messaging allows us to reach students and stakeholders in a targeted way that draws them into the larger narrative of the school and their place in the redemptive story of God's purposes in the world. While enrollment goals need to be reached and revenue projections met, the role of enrollment staff provides the unique opportunity to step into a prospective student's journey, hear their narrative, and help them begin to see themselves in the larger redemption story.

BIBLIOGRAPHY

Association of Theological Schools (ATS). "2007–2008 Annual Data Tables." Online. https://www.ats.edu/uploads/resources/institutional-data/annual-data-tables/2007-2008-annual-data-tables.pdf.
———. "2017–2018 Annual Data Tables." https://www.ats.edu/uploads/resources/institutional-data/annual-data-tables/2017-2018-annual-data-tables.pdf.
Bolman, Lee G., and Joan V. Gallos. *Reframing Academic Leadership*. San Francisco: Jossey-Bass, 2011.
Clydesdale, Timothy T. *The Purposeful Graduate: Why Colleges Must Talk to Students about Vocation*. Chicago: University of Chicago Press, 2015.
Pew Research Center. "The Age Gap in Religion Around the World." *Pew Research Center*, June 13, 2018. Online. https://www.pewforum.org/2018/06/13/the-age-gap-in-religion-around-the-world.
Schön, Donald A. *The Reflective Practitioner: How Professionals Think in Action*. New York: Basic, 1983.
Veith, Gene E., Jr., and Matthew P. Ristuccia. *Imagination Redeemed: Glorifying God with a Neglected Part of Your Mind*. Wheaton, IL: Crossway, 2015.
Weick, Karl E., et al. "Organizing and the Process of Sensemaking." *Organization Science* 16.4 (2005) 409–421.
Wolters, Albert M. *Creation Regained: Biblical Basics for a Reformational Worldview*. 2nd ed. Grand Rapids: Eerdmans, 2005.
Wright, Christopher J. H. *The Mission of God: Unlocking the Bible's Grand Narrative*. Downers Grove, IL: InterVarsity, 2006.

CHAPTER 8

Bureaucratic Grace

The Role of the Registrar in Theological Education

Vince McGlothin-Eller

THE LEARNING THAT TAKES place in the classroom, whether physical or virtual, is obviously key to the educational institution. Teachers and students come together in classes to share ideas, to impart knowledge, and, hopefully, to gain a bit of wisdom. But outside of the classroom, administrators throughout the educational institution make sure that all other matters that make learning possible are taken care of. Students must be reviewed for admission and for financial aid; tuition must be charged and collected; calendars and course schedules must be published; and records related to classes and student registrations must be kept. This is but a simplistic overview of all the work that goes on behind the scenes, all designed to support student success.

In many ways, this is not unlike the appointment of the first Hellenistic ministers in the book of Acts (6:1–7). Recognizing a need that could best be met by other members of the community, the apostles worked with the rest of the community to identify those with the gifts and graces to do the additional work needed in the community. The seven that were identified then took on these additional roles, allowing the apostles to continue their own parts of the ministry. The apostles and the seven worked together towards a common goal though they each had a different role to play. In the same way, the faculty and administrative professionals in the school each have their own roles to focus on. Each is supporting the education of the students, but where the faculty focus most explicitly on direct education, student services professionals support the other work that is also necessary to keep the community functioning.

The registrar sits at the center of the web of intersecting roles and responsibilities that make it possible for students to learn. At the most basic level, the registrar is "the steward of the academic record and the keeper of institutional data."[1] The registrar sits at the intersection between student services and academic programs, in many ways not falling fully into either category, though often reporting to the academic dean or to the head of enrollment management. Registrars manage the registration process and often assist with student advising. Registrars must be able to communicate effectively to multiple constituencies through regular communication and the publication of policies, procedures, and course information. The registrar is often involved in data collection and reporting as well as performing research on program performance and assessments.

Each of these areas is directly connected to and helps to support the learning and experience of students. Because these areas of responsibility that fall to the registrar are somewhat varied, there are certain key qualities that are beneficial for anyone working in that office. While these qualities are related to the tasks for which the registrar is responsible, these are general descriptors related to the person of the registrar and not necessarily about specific responsibilities. These qualities are extremely useful traits for a registrar to have and should be considered when hiring a registrar or anyone working in that office.

As should be apparent given the data-related tasks that fall to the registrar, the first quality that the registrar should possess is a *keen attention to detail*. So much of the work of the registrar relates to entering and maintaining data that this is a necessity. If the data is not cared for, all the other jobs that flow from that data are potentially compromised. Data that is entered incorrectly can skew statistics, block enrollment, or (like a misfiled folder) create difficulties in locating a student record. So the registrar needs to pay attention to how data is being entered and always be on the lookout for ways to increase accuracy.

In addition, the registrar must have *impeccable integrity*. There will be times in each registrar's career when this integrity will be challenged—by a student who wants a grade change or to jump ahead on a waitlist; a faculty member or other administrator who wants access to privileged information;

---

1. AACRAO, *Registrar's Basic Guide*, i.

or possibly a president that suggests your job might be at risk if you don't bend the rules a little. But "as the steward of the academic record and the keeper of institutional data,"[2] integrity is key, especially in the face of colleagues or superiors. This does not mean there is no room for grace, but it does mean being clear about why grace is being offered when it does occur.

In some ways flowing from the previous two qualities, registrars must also *be good with puzzles.*[3] The registrar must be able to take the data that is available and work out all of the potential outcomes that are possible with that information. While a negative decision may need to be made for the sake of integrity, grace is shown by also sharing possible solutions to the problem. What options are available to a student that, due to circumstances beyond their control, has moved to another state but still wants to finish the degree? How can they complete the program while maintaining institutional standards and offering high quality education? What are the exceptions that can be made, and what are the processes for seeking those exceptions? This is all part of the information that the registrar must possess, and a small window on how the registrar supports student success even through difficult times and situations.

One additional quality that is key to the theological school registrar is to *understand themselves as a servant leader within the community.* Their leadership and decisions should always be tempered by an attitude of grace—grace not only in the sense of that forgiveness which Christ exemplifies but also in the sense of having a disposition of kindness and courtesy. The registrar must lead with compassion, recognizing the constantly changing struggles that students face and the fact that all fall short from time to time. This graceful attitude should be apparent not only in interactions with students but also in the registrar's presence in administrative meetings and daily tasks. Ultimately, as outlined further below, the theological school registrar is serving the students by supporting their success as well as the church by supporting the process of preparation for ministry.

While these personal qualities should be at the core of the registrar, it is at least as important for a registrar to have the competence to do the day-to-day work of the office. Thankfully, several good resources are available to

2. AACRAO, *Registrar's Basic Guide*, i.

3. While this is certainly related to problem solving, which will be discussed further below, I am distinguishing this as a way of being that relates more to how someone views the world and less about being able to apply logic to a given situation. For me, this quality is about the ability to intuitively see how things are connected and, therefore, the ability to see all the possible outcomes from a given decision or action. This quality can perhaps be honed by different types of puzzles or games, such as jigsaw puzzles. Games like Qwirkle and Q-bitz, available from MindWare, are ideal for exercising the type of thinking and visualization I am suggesting here.

assist the registrar with becoming more competent in their areas of responsibility—from professional organizations to books to monthly newsletters.[4] These resources help the registrar with the day-to-day work of the job and keep registrars up to date on changes in federal policies, available solutions, and best practices for addressing the needs of students and institutions. Though they sometimes have different responsibilities due to school size and denominational responsibilities (which will be expanded on later in this chapter), theological school registrars are encouraged to take advantage of these resources.

In general, the tasks of the registrar can be summarized into three broad areas of responsibility: (1) accountability, (2) privacy, and (3) problem-solving. All of the traditional functions of the registrar fall into one of these areas. It should be remembered that the end goal of all of this is to help students be successful in their programs, while also recognizing that success can take many forms. Sometimes student success does not look like what is expected; hence the need for grace.

ACCOUNTABILITY

The idea of accountability in higher education is multi-layered. Students are accountable to institutional rules, policies, and program requirements. Schools are accountable to their own policies as well as other stakeholders such as trustees, accreditors, the state (or states) in which they function, and, possibly, to the federal Department of Education. In the case of theological schools, they are often related to one or more denominations that must be considered as well. Often the registrar is the primary person in the school tasked with maintaining these many levels of accountability. Because the registrar sits at the intersection of so much of the educational data flowing through the school, the registrar often holds the first level of responsibility for academic policies and procedures both internally and externally.

At the student level, the registrar's primary accountability is to the students' educational records. This means facilitating registration, performing program reviews and degree audits, and developing processes and procedures to make all of that possible. Due to the close proximity to student

4. The American Association of Collegiate Registrars and Admissions Officers (AACRAO) is the premiere professional association for registrars in higher education. They offer several publications touching on the various general roles that the registrar plays in the institution, from data maintenance, to the academic record, to the Family Educational Rights and Privacy Act (FERPA). See AACRAO, "Online Bookstore." See also the higher education newsletters and journals, including Hope, *Successful Registrar*, available from Jossey-Bass.

educational records, registrars are also responsible for interpreting and holding students accountable to academic policies, whether they be the rules of the institution or other rules by which the school is bound.

Because of this responsibility, it is important for registrars to be a part of all institutional committees related to academics, with at least voice if not vote. This includes program and degree committees and faculty meetings. The registrar must know the "ins and outs" of every program and any related policies or other requirements that might impact a student's ability to complete the program. This way they can interpret institutional policies to students and others within the institution. This is best accomplished when registrars are a part of the conversations and, therefore, have the context for the meaning behind various policies. Being included in conversations related to student educational requirements and policies also allows the registrar to inject grace into the conversation as an advocate for the needs of students. Because of their knowledge of student educational needs, registrars can highlight or raise questions about the impact of certain decisions on student success. In places where the registrar is not currently present in these sorts of meetings, the registrar should speak with their supervisor to ask about the possibility.

At the institutional level, the registrar must also be aware of the policies of accreditors, governing boards, and trustees, as well as any federal laws that apply. For seminary registrars that are embedded in a larger university, there are additional school policies that may need to be accounted for, such as a university registrar's office that cares for transcripts and sets policies related to educational records. The registrar's knowledge of policies and requirements not only keeps the students accountable but also the school itself. When new programs are being developed, the knowledgeable registrar keeps the school on task and aware of any relevant policies or laws that may impact the proposed program, be it a new online or hybrid program, a partnership with another school, or a denominational requirement that has been overlooked.

During a recent curriculum revision, an initial revision draft for one program did not account for certain denominational requirements for ordination. While most of the requirements were accounted for, two courses were missing in the initial proposal. I was able to bring my knowledge of the educational requirements as well as data I had researched showing the number of students on the ordination track who had completed that program in recent years into the conversation and assure that the two courses were again included. This saved future students potential headaches down the road and assured the seminary would be able to offer the programs that students need in order to complete educational requirements.

An additional aspect of keeping the school accountable to accrediting bodies, registrars are often directly involved in annual reporting to outside bodies. These reports help to show how the school is performing educationally and how it is following the policies that are in place. These reports may be to federal or state agencies, accreditors, denominations, and/or trustees. In order to prepare these reports, the registrar needs to know the educational and student data better than anyone else in the institution. As far as possible, the registrar should be the chief report writer for educational data in the institution. This will require special training as well as a close relationship with the database administrator or other IT professionals on campus.

PRIVACY

In some ways, privacy is a subset of accountability. However, based on federal guidelines and concerns about identity theft, it stands alone as a unique area of responsibility. For those schools that accept any form of federal aid (student loans are the primary means of participating in federal aid programs for theological schools), they must abide by the Family Educational Rights and Privacy Act (FERPA).[5] This federal law protects student data and outlines how that data may or may not be shared with others.[6]

In short, there are certain data that may be freely shared publicly about students, though students have the right of keeping even that information private. This is often called "directory information" as it is the type of information most often to be found in a student directory, such as name, picture, and contact information. Schools may choose to limit this further and are under no obligation to release data about students even if it is considered public information.[7]

Any other personally identifiable information related to student records must be kept private and cannot be shared internally or externally

5. For a basic overview with links to resources for specific target groups, see US Department of Education, "FERPA." For the current full text of the law, see US Department of Education, "FERPA Regulations."

6. While FERPA is the primary federal law related to student privacy, registrars should also be familiar with HIPAA and/or consumer protection policies as these may also relate to student information.

7. As an example, I have been asked on occasion by outside companies and organizations for student lists so that they could contact students for promotional or commercial purposes. Though this information is technically considered public, I always declined to provide information in these cases. This may not be the case for theological schools that are a part of larger schools or public universities that are subject to Freedom of Information requests. Be sure to verify your responsibility as an employee of the school.

to anyone who does not have a need to know. While one would obviously not share the student files locked in office cabinets with the general public, there are other practices about which they must be just as careful. Any information that the school does not consider directory information must be protected. Grades or other personal information about students cannot be shared with parents or spouses without permission from the student. Academic information cannot be shared with another administrator if it doesn't relate to their job function. While an academic advisor may have right of access to a student's file, the right extends only to students for whom they are responsible and is not blanket permission to access all student files. Being an employee of the institution does not automatically give someone right of access.

Perhaps most crucial for theological schools, under federal policy religious affiliation can never be considered directory information. This means student information cannot be released to denominations on request based solely on the criteria of denominational membership since this would by default personally identify religious affiliation. Denominational bodies can ask for verification of student enrollment if they have a name already, but they cannot simply be given a list of all students belonging to that denomination who are already attending the school. One option to address this matter would be to request for students to sign a waiver that specifically gives the school permission to release information in this context. If your school does this, you should also be clear about the wording of the waiver. Information can only be released for students that have signed a waiver and only for the specific purpose(s) outlined in the waiver. The waiver does not (or at least should not) constitute blanket permission to release religious information.

The Ministerial Educational Fund reporting that United Methodist schools do every two years is a perfect example of this point. To receive denominational funding, United Methodist theological schools must submit comprehensive reports of all United Methodist students attending the school as well as recent graduates. These reports require not only names, but additional information about educational programs and annual conferences where students are members. Obviously, this would run afoul of FERPA requirements. To get around this, several schools have developed waivers that must be signed by students annually. The purpose of these waivers is for the student to grant the school permission to list denominational affiliation in internal reports and directories and to release that information to denominational representatives on request. Even so (and well within their rights), several students do not grant the waiver and must be asked each time in order for their data to be shared. Failure to grant the waiver results in anonymous data being submitted. This can have quite an impact on the funds available to the school. Even still, care must be taken to complete the process accurately and with integrity.

While not all theological schools technically fall under FERPA (those that do not participate in federal aid programs are not necessarily subject to this federal law), the guidelines set forth in FERPA are a good baseline for all schools. Even if not compelled by federal law to do so, it is still good policy to protect student privacy as far as possible. The practice of confidentiality with student records sets a good example for those that will be religious leaders and who may therefore have access to private or privileged information about members of their congregations.

PROBLEM-SOLVING

As stated before, the registrar needs to know the institution's academic data better than anyone else in the school. They need to know all of the requirements and policies of each of the academic programs at a moment's notice so that they can speak to faculty, other administrators, current students, or even prospective students. Registrars should also familiarize themselves with the basic policies and requirements that may be managed by other offices that have an impact on students, such as financial aid, international students, and Veterans Affairs. Their knowledge of all of the requirements related to the programs and their familiarity with the work of other offices will make it possible for them to answer specific questions, to advise students on potential courses or outcomes, to suggest recommended study plans, and to refer students to a more appropriate office for assistance when needed.

Registrars need to also be aware of general statistical trends for the institution so that they may recognize changes in enrollment or other school demographics. If the registrar notes a significant change in total enrollment or enrollment in a particular program from one year to the next or even one term to the next, they can alert other offices so that steps can be taken to identify any problems that may come about. This helps the institution to plan for the future and to make program and policy changes before issues become problematic. A general awareness of what other schools are doing or have done in similar situations also helps.

For example, an unexpected increase in the number of new students could mean additional seats will be needed in first-year courses. In this instance, good communication between the registrar and the admissions team is required. Once it is apparent that more new students are expected than the number of seats currently planned, steps may be taken through the dean and department chairs to address the increased need, hopefully before it becomes a problem for the new students.

By drawing on their knowledge, available data, and awareness of the ways various campus responsibilities intersect, registrars are in a position to look at multiple possible solutions or outcomes for any particular action. This allows them to make recommendations not only to address problems that may arise but also to recommend programs or policies that may enhance programs already in place. As demographics change, what changes might the institution need to make to better serve currently underserved populations? An awareness of the data and possible solutions is key to answering these questions.

Recently, there was a student that had initially started the Master of Divinity program some eight years ago. While they started well in their first term, they then entered a pattern of registering enough courses to qualify for aid and then withdrawing from courses towards the end of the term. After a few terms of this, they became ineligible for federal aid since they were no longer making satisfactory academic progress. Without aid eligibility, they soon became inactive. Fast forward to last year when this student reapplied to start the Master of Divinity program all over again. The question quickly arose of the student's eligibility for loan aid. Because of my awareness of the student's situation, both the reasons that had led to the previous problems and the change in circumstances that had led them to reapply, I was able to work with the financial aid director to advocate on the side of grace and allow the student another opportunity to fulfill their call with us.

While the general areas of responsibility above apply to all registrars regardless of type of school, there are some distinct differences for registrars in theological schools. Some of these differences make the job slightly easier, while some add an additional layer of responsibility. As most theological schools are graduate institutions, they typically do not have to deal with issues specific to undergraduate students. Most theological schools do not have to relate to high schools, student parents, or the most common standardized tests. While it may be helpful to be aware of how policies like common core or No Child Left Behind affect the way students approach schools and learning in general, theological schools are not directly responsible to those acts. Most theological school registrars do not need to be concerned about NCAA eligibility rules unless they happen to be a part of a larger school that is concerned about the impact on a favorite team in the coming season.

Particularly for those that are standalone schools, though there are some related implications for schools that are part of larger universities, theological schools tend to be on the smaller side. While this in itself is not a bad thing, it does change the way they have to think about enrollment and the solutions to student problems. As wonderful a resource as organizations like AACRAO are, their annual meetings and training opportunities tend to be geared more towards large universities with significant resources. This does not mean that these groups have nothing to offer, but any solutions learned about through AACRAO must be taken with a healthy dose of skepticism or adaptation.[8]

A good supplement and/or alternative to the various AACRAO events is the ATS Student Personnel Administrators Network (SPAN) meeting that takes place each spring. As this is an ATS event, it is specific to theological schools. While obviously not on the same scale as an AACRAO event, it is a good meeting for discussing problems common to theological schools and for networking with colleagues that face the same types of issues with similar access to resources. There is also a SPAN listserv that members can participate in to ask questions of colleagues about best practices or possible solutions to problems.[9]

Due to the size of many theological schools, many registrars carry multiple titles with related and occasionally unrelated responsibilities. In addition to responsibilities for the registrar's office, many registrars carry additional responsibilities related to academic advising, institutional assessment, and technology support. Some are responsible for external relationships or continuing education. The registrar may even carry faculty rank and responsibilities. In many schools, the registrar essentially functions with the responsibility and authority of an associate dean, but rarely with the recognition or title. Even so, it is important to consider how these additional responsibilities, related as they may be, impact the primary work of registrar. How will a registrar who also supports IT approach the job differently? Will this affect their ability to accomplish the day-to-day work of the registrar's office? There is no single answer to these questions, but the size of theological schools and the nature of the education being provided makes it a necessary question to consider.

---

8. AACRAO offers a variety of meetings and workshops annually that can be of benefit to registrars. Each meeting usually includes a FERPA update that helps to keep registrars aware of any changes to federal policy that may impact their work. These meetings are also a good way to learn about best practices for common problems and to hear about novel approaches to addressing these problems. Annual meetings and workshops include "Registrar 101," "Registrar 201," "SEM Conference," "AACRAO Annual Meeting," and "Technology and Transfer Conference" (see AACRAO, "Meetings").

9. For additional information about SPAN, the annual meeting, and a sign-up for the listserv, see ATS, "Student Personnel Administrators."

DENOMINATIONAL CONSIDERATIONS

But perhaps the biggest difference between theological schools and most other schools in higher education is the relationship to the church. Most theological schools relate to a primary denomination, and some may have significant numbers of students from other denominations as well. Just as there is a layer of accountability to accrediting bodies and state governments, theological school registrars also must be aware of the rules related to particular denominational affiliation(s). This relationship to the church has particular implications for how theological schools approach the work of education in general and, therefore, on how registrars approach their work in particular.

The first need is an awareness of the requirements and expectations that the primary denomination being served has for those pursuing ordained ministry. In order to best guide students in their educational process and in order to provide them the information they need not only to graduate but to go forward towards professional ministry, the registrar should know all of the curricular and co-curricular requirements the student may need. While the Master of Divinity is the primary degree for this purpose, many denominations have specific requirements that may be optional in some programs, particularly at schools that serve more than one denomination. For example, United Methodist students must complete a course in United Methodist History even though it may not be required of all Master of Divinity students. An awareness of these rules as well as a good working relationship with denominational leadership to whom the registrar can go for questions is vital.

As registrar, I was in frequent conversation with directors at the General Board of Higher Education and Ministry of The United Methodist Church as well as annual conference Boards of Ordained Ministry. I had met many of them personally and they had learned to trust my knowledge and insights as well, so it became something of a two-way collaboration. There was a recent student that had completed a Master of Arts degree at a previous school that was not approved by The United Methodist Church even though it was fully accredited by ATS. After reviewing their educational records, a decision came that they were expected to either complete a full Master of Divinity (minus any transfer credits we approved) or to go through an alternative but not easily understood educational route that would end with no degree but would lead to ordination. The student was in tears when they came to my office to discuss the situation. After reviewing the relevant educational requirements and the work completed by the student previously, I was able to propose a plan for them that would end in a Master of Arts, meet all of the denominational expectations, and save the student at least three courses that they ultimately did not need. After reviewing the letter, I wrote on the student's behalf and the proposed educational plan, the denomination approved the plan and the student was able to graduate a semester ahead of schedule and continue towards ordination. Without a thorough knowledge of United Methodist educational requirements, this would not have been possible.

Beyond helping students meet the educational requirements for ordination, theological schools and their registrars must also remember that they serve the church. And not simply a particular denomination or even the big 'C' church, but all of the people who make up the church. The students that come through the halls of theological schools will go on to serve those people. This in some ways shifts the registrar's responsibilities from that of simply a job to a ministry. The registrar is serving the very people of the church by supporting student learning, which leads to certain questions. How will the people respond to what the students are learning? Are the students learning what they need to know to lead the people already in the church today? What about in five or ten years? While other schools may also concern themselves with the job skills their students are learning, the very nature of the church necessarily changes the language theological schools use for the conversation about student learning and preparedness. The registrar must consider the outcome for not just the students but also the people of the church as courses are planned, policies created, and academic records reviewed.

Related but slightly different is the fact that theological schools are preparing religious leaders. While most registrars will not spend much time in the classroom with students, students will interact with the registrar throughout their education. Maybe it will be through public communications or through additional advising or even through academic probation. Whatever the case, registrars have something to teach about the nature of leadership and the nature of grace. How can the registrar make sure that the administrative work of the school is also an example of the work of grace?

FINAL THOUGHTS

Years after my own formal theological education had been completed, I was bemoaning one of my least favorite tasks to a faculty colleague—academic probation and dismissal. I know it is necessary work, but I still hated being the bearer of news that was often unwelcome. Once I was done expressing this thought, this professor proceeded to give me a new lesson on grace.

Grace, he said, can only be offered after a judgement has been made. Grace without judgement is meaningless. Only by completing the task that I found so distasteful could grace become possible in the given situation.

In this particular example, the grace is ultimately offered by someone else. And yet, grace is also embodied in the approach to the task. On the one hand, a computer can be programmed to automatically review student academic standing on a particular date using particular criteria and then automatically generate letters and notifications to all requisite parties to notify them of the decision. The program could then automatically register the details in the database and place whatever blocks might be necessary, all without a person needing to be involved at all. But this misses our calling as theological schools and as the people who serve them. Instead, a good registrar will review the data and make a decision while also determining any alternatives or next steps that might be possible. Is there something that can be done to reverse the decision? Is there some mitigating circumstance that could be taken into account for an appeal? Or, perhaps, is time away with the possibility of return later just what that student needs at that time? Sometimes the decision simply has to be made. Even then, the decision can be made and communicated in as graceful a manner as possible.

In the end, the registrar is one of, if not, the most essential administrator in most schools. Registrars often have the widest range of access to institutional data and bear the bulk of responsibility for protecting student records and communicating institutional policies and procedures. Due to the nature and size of theological schools, these responsibilities are compressed to an even greater weight, and registrars in theological schools may find their responsibilities far exceed the traditional roles of the registrar. In many ways, this is true of the students with whom the registrar will interact—students who are preparing to be religious leaders and who will find themselves responsible for everything from preaching on Sunday mornings to congregational care to making sure the heat is turned on before services. For those of us who accept the call to serve as a registrar in a theological school, the care with which we approach this ministry and the grace that we show in our interactions with others will hopefully model for the students the same grace they need to take into their own ministry settings.

BIBLIOGRAPHY

American Association of Collegiate Registrars and Admissions Officers (AACRAO). *2016 Academic Record and Transcript Guide.* Washington, DC: AACRAO, 2015.
———. *Curriculum Management and the Role of the Registrar.* Washington, DC: AACRAO, 2016.

———. "Meetings." Online. https://www.aacrao.org/events-training/meetings.

———. "Online Bookstore." Online. http://www.aacrao.org/publications.

———. *Professional Development Guide for Registrars: A Self-Assessment.* Washington, DC: AACRAO, 2018.

———. *Registrar's Basic Guide.* Washington, DC: AACRAO, 2018.

———. *Student Records Management: Retention, Disposal, and Archive of Student Records.* Washington, DC: AACRAO, 2014.

Association of Theological Schools (ATS). "Student Personnel Administrators." Online. http://ats.edu/resources/administrators/student-personnel-administrators.

Falkner, Tina, and LeRoy Rooker, eds. *2012 FERPA Guide.* Washington, DC: AACRAO, 2012.

———. *2013 FERPA Quick Guide.* Washington, DC: AACRAO, 2013.

"The Family Educational Rights and Privacy Act of 1974, 20 USC § 1232g; 34 CFR Part 99." In *The FERPA Answer Book for Higher Education Professionals,* edited by Aileen Gelpi and Clifford A Ramirez. San Francisco, CA: Jossey-Bass, 2009.

Hope, Joan, ed. *The Successful Registrar.* 18 volumes. Jossey-Bass: 2000–2018.

Klein-Collins, Rebecca. *Assessment's New Role in Degree Completion: A Registrar's Primer on Prior Learning Assessment and Competency-Based Education.* Washington, DC: AACRAO, 2014.

Lauren, Barbara, ed. *The Registrar's Guide: Evolving Best Practices in Records and Registration.* Washington, DC: AACRAO, 2006.

Montgomery, Jessica, ed. *The Transfer Handbook: Promoting Student Success.* Washington, DC: AACRAO, 2015.

US Department of Education. "Family Educational Rights and Privacy Act (FERPA)." March 1, 2018. Online. https://www2.ed.gov/policy/gen/guid/fpco/ferpa/index.html.

———. "FERPA Regulations: 34 CFR Part 99—Family Educational Rights And Privacy." Online. https://studentprivacy.ed.gov/node/548.

CHAPTER 9

Communicating Culture through Admissions

ADAM J. POLUZZI

INTRODUCTION

THIS CHAPTER IDENTIFIES STRATEGIES admissions officers might consider using to communicate culture with prospective applicants. The chapter is based on a research study, conducted as part of my doctoral work,[1] which focused on the role of the admissions officer related to communicating culture. Two hundred thirty-six theological school admissions officers were contacted via a web-based survey about institutional culture, how institutional culture is communicated to prospective students, and how admissions officers learn their institution's culture. In-depth interviews with eight admissions officers were conducted, exploring questions of effective mechanisms of communication and challenges specific to the field of theological school admissions. This research identifies and describes how admissions professionals communicate culture to applicants, what channels of communication they perceive as most effective, and how they describe and understand their particular schools' cultures. The findings also suggest that many admissions officers view their work in admissions as a ministry,

1. See Poluzzi, "Communicating Culture in Graduate Admissions." For further reading, my full dissertation, which contains complete details on the research study and more findings, is available via ProQuest.

while simultaneously remaining aware of the challenges of rapidly chang-ing technologies and demographics, as well as the realities of the current landscape of theological education.

Communicating the distinct culture of a particular school or program is one of the most important and powerful ways an institution can differenti-ate itself in a competitive enrollment market. An understanding of a school's particular culture can help shape the choice applicants face when deciding where to enroll. This idea is not exclusive to education, as seen in organi-zational culture's relationship to corporate brand identities and customer loyalty.[2] In the education world, however, culture's role in the enrollment process is different from many of the other factors often cited by students when making their decisions. Variables like cost, geographic location, and size are inflexible factors that are mostly closed to interpretation.[3] Culture, on the other hand, can be experienced, observed, and interpreted,[4] allow-ing it to serve as a key factor in differentiating schools.

Theological graduate education presents a perfect test case for how culture might affect enrollment, given its particular set of challenges.[5] The Association of Theological Schools (ATS) has recently reported multiple school closings and only limited institutional enrollment growth—with a slight 0.5 percent decline in enrollment from 2018 to 2019 across all ATS schools.[6] This volatility has required institutions to seriously focus on en-rollment, considering such issues as marketing, recruitment, financial aid management, and course offerings to attract the best students possible given the changing and challenging enrollment environment.

In order for theological schools to compete for the limited number of students that exist, it is essential for schools to identify what is special or unique about their school: their particular culture. Culture is variously

2. Guckian et al., "Few Bad Apples," 29–41; Sellers, "IBM Exec."

3. Stiber, "Characterizing the Decision Process [Doctoral Programs]," 13–26; "Characterizing the Decision Process [Master's Programs]," 91–107.

4. Magolda, "What Our Rituals Tell Us," 2–8.

5. See Pew Research Center, "What Surveys Say About Worship Attendance"; Schindler, *Catholicism and Secularization*; Weddell, *Forming Intentional Disciples*. Faith and religion have recently faced particular challenges related to culture. For example, secularization in America has negatively affected the place and role of religion within society. Additionally, many Americans have stopped attending mainline churches, no longer feeling connected to their traditional faith communities. Abuse scandals and financial issues within the Catholic and Protestant churches have accelerated this de-cline. Finally, the job market for theology school graduates is limited and the existing positions often pay very little. As a result of these challenges, many schools connected to these faiths have recently faced enrollment difficulties.

6. ATS, "2019–2020 Annual Data Tables."

defined as a term and often elusive to describe.[7] I define culture as the behaviors, rituals, values, customs, traits, and way of life of a specific community. In thinking about how a place feels or what makes it distinctive or particular—that is its culture. Culture can be an important and influential factor on enrollment. Although culture may not be the only unique factor, the communication of culture can help potential students gain an impression of what it might be like to become part of that institution's community. Because religious identity, community, and culture are so intimately connected,[8] prospective theology students may have higher expectations of culture than applicants in other disciplines. These expectations include questions of how a school's particular culture supports and connects with their educational experiences and future ministries. As a result, admissions officers must develop strategies to effectively relate a school's culture to applicants. The decision on how to portray culture—which aspects of the culture to highlight and which tools and methods to use—can vary. An institutional advantage in the competition among different schools for students comes from the ability to best communicate the nature of an institution's culture.

This chapter is organized into five sections. The first section provides an overview of culture and its role in the admissions process, with ATS admission officers providing their perspectives on culture's role in their admissions processes. During interviews,[9] I asked each participant to describe his or her school's particular culture. A representative sampling of those answers is included in this section. The second section identifies and discusses the methods of communication used by admissions officers. Section three discusses how survey and interview participants rated the effectiveness of individual methods of communication at portraying a school's culture. A major goal of this research was to learn about admissions officers' perceptions of what methods of communication were viewed as most effective. The "effectiveness" of a method refers to its success in influencing students' decisions to apply and enroll. The fourth section provides recommendations for future practice based on the results of the study. These recommendations will hopefully be useful to those directly involved in admission and recruitment activities, as well as to those charged with supervising or hiring

---

7. Kezar and Eckel, "Effect of Institutional Culture," 436–60; Kuh, "Assessing Campus Environments," 30–48; Kuh and Whitt, *Invisible Tapestry*; Simplico, "University Culture," 336–39; Smart et al., "Roles of Institutional Cultures," 256–81.

8. Tisdell, *Exploring Spirituality and Culture*, 45–66.

9. Throughout the chapter, I have included direct quotations from participants, which give the best and most authentic indication of how admissions officers reflect on their work. I have used pseudonyms and redacted any identifying terms when presenting these quotes.

admissions officers. The chapter concludes with a discussion and summary of the overall results of the study.

CULTURE AND THE ADMISSIONS PROCESS

Culture matters in the admissions process and research shows that admissions officers incorporate culture into their recruitment strategies at a high level. All survey participants indicated that they incorporated culture to some degree, with 59 percent of the sample reporting that they incorporated culture very much. Similarly, survey participants indicated a high perception of culture's importance in students' decision-making, with 93 percent of survey respondents indicating that culture was of highest or high importance.

Throughout the interviews for this study, participants shared their perceptions of culture's importance. Most participants ranked culture among the top three factors they believed were important to prospective students. Other factors mentioned as top reasons students enrolled included financial aid, location, and academic offerings. However, culture's importance was seen as the factor that might help students decide between two schools if other factors, like cost, were equal. Matthew, who attended the school where he now works, shared his impression of the power of culture in decision-making: "If someone really falls in love with the place, it's not going to matter how much [it costs], I knew I was going to come here no matter what. If I got in I knew they could have charged me extra and I would have shown up."

Many participants reported that "fit" was a very important concept and directly related to school culture. One survey respondent shared that at his school "students achieve better and are more holistically healthy when they feel like they are in the right place for their personality and interests." Additionally, culture can serve as an important factor in guiding the types of students that admissions officers seek during the recruitment process. As Andrew noted: "Culture affects the type of students we look for, you know, students with more ministry and different experiences. Bringing together students with diverse experiences is very important for us."

Interestingly, admissions officers often talk about culture in similar ways, regardless of their schools' religious traditions or theological approaches. Although some participants indicated they preferred the terms "narrative," "environment," or "community" to describe how a school feels, the aspects of the description are alike. For example, when asked to provide buzzwords that described their schools' communities, the most frequently occurring terms included: community, academic excellence/academic rigor, accessible faculty, spiritual formation, and diverse/diversity/inclusive.

The following interview excerpts address the question of how participants would describe their schools' cultures to prospective students. As Sarah explained, culture was an important tool for differentiating her school from its competitors:

> I need to immediately define how we are different than our competitors and I would say that our culture has been our brand. Our students are very independent, they're very inclusive. We're very pro LGBTQ. We embrace people who are not necessarily [redacted, denomination/ethnic group[10]] by birth but invite people who are making decisions to be [redacted, religion] by choice and wish to study it in a graduate program. So, the more that I can talk about the types of individuals who come to our school, I think I'm much more successful.

For Matthew, the discussion of culture begins with the availability of strong scholarship guided by incredible people:

> I would say that we're an ecumenically Christian environment. Our dean likes to say that we are proudly Christian but not narrowly so. We do not have a specific theological lens through which we filter our teachings, we simply give you the best available scholarship and practice as possible, and we manifest that in a variety of ways. But what makes it more than just an average seminary experience are the people here. The people here are really incredible, and we're a world-class research university, but we have amazing students who come to us from all over the country and the world.

For Ellen, the presentation of her school's culture is contextual, depending on the student. In a similar way, however, her description includes what the community is like and highlights some distinct features of campus life, including faculty involvement:

> I only ever talk about culture in context of the student's interests and needs. We talk more about what it feels like to be on campus, what it feels like to participate in the community as a commuter student (whether that means physically or online), and that includes aspects of our curriculum, the way our faculty teach, what it's like to be in the classroom here, which we think

10. I have redacted words that would indicate a specific religion, denomination, or ethnic group.

is probably different from what it's like to be in the classroom at other schools in the area. The fact that we are a residential campus and that half of our faculty lives on campus makes our community life very distinctive.

She went on to point out that there is often great similarity in how ATS admissions officers verbally describe culture:

In my experience of observing what schools say about themselves, and then actually participating in a virtual recruiting fair, it's odd, but schools use a lot of the same language to talk about themselves. What we think is distinctive, ain't so distinctive. It's being talked about all over the place, so I try to highlight the factors that are contributing to community life. Lots of schools talk about their faith community, but what makes the community distinct is that you can't just use buzzwords. You have to be able to illustrate what that means in that specific context. "Yes! We have a wonderful faith community!" Everybody is saying this, but they need to demonstrate it.

Appropriately, the remainder of this chapter describes how admissions officers attempt to demonstrate these differences and communicate their unique cultures.

METHODS OF COMMUNICATING CULTURE

Admissions officers use several methods for communicating culture during the admissions process. There are two different approaches through which the communication of culture occurs: *explicit* methods and *implicit* methods of communication. Explicit methods employ outward actions, events, and tools to intentionally convey messages about a school's culture. In contrast, implicit methods are subtler and include ideas, attitudes, and approaches that subliminally deliver culture messages. This section further details and provides examples of each of these methods.

Explicit Methods

Explicit methods of communication directly deliver messages about culture to prospective students. I have organized explicit methods into three categories: in-person channels, virtual channels, and quasi-virtual channels of communication.

In-Person Channels

On-campus visits and events, off-campus recruitment at conferences and graduate school fairs, and interviews are examples of in-person channels for communicating culture. In-person channels involve person-to-person interactions, with admissions officers indicating a strong preference for face-to-face and on-campus interactions whenever possible. The on-campus visit—the most commonly identified example of an in-person channel—may include a campus tour; conversations with different constituencies within the school, including admissions staff members, current students, and faculty members; opportunities to participate in a class session; and other activities central to the culture of the school (e.g., liturgies, daily coffee breaks, shared meals).

Additional in-person mechanisms exist, including interviews with applicants and on-the-road recruitment events. Off-campus events lack the advantage of having the school's environment to provide cultural context. Instead, admissions officers must use their communication skills to describe and create an image of the school. Although off-campus events prevent admissions officers from actually showing the school community to a prospective student, the face-to-face conversation still allows questions to be answered and clarified and for the prospective student to have a personal interaction with at least one representative from the school.

Virtual Channels

Opportunities to interact with students in person do not always exist. Additionally, the first point of contact for the majority of potential students is through a school's website, printed viewbook, or other virtual channel of communication. Virtual channels of communication are tools created by admissions officers (often in conjunction with other institutional representatives) to convey culture and other information on behalf of the school. Prospective students experience these channels independently, without the presence of an institutional representative to guide them. Unlike in-person channels, virtual channels are not interactive and rely on human initiative to update them.

Quasi-Virtual Channels

Advances in technology are blurring the lines between in-person and virtual channels by creating ways for people to interact without being face-to-face.

These quasi-virtual channels provide the opportunity for virtual in-person interactions to take place. Quasi-virtual channels can stand alone as individual forms of communication or can help enhance static websites with interactive tools.

For example, phone and email communication allows admissions officers the ability to interact back and forth with prospective students without having to be in the same place. Video conferencing can allow the admissions officer and prospective student to see each other during conversations. Social media platforms have made digital interactions even more sophisticated. Interactions and types of content seem unlimited, with the option to post photographs, videos, and news items, and to comment back and forth on others' posts, as well. Social media also provides an opportunity to engage admitted students with the larger student community, creating interactions for applicants with school culture before they arrive to campus. Used in this manner, social media can also be used to keep students engaged after attending an on-campus, in-person event. Relationships formed among admitted students can be maintained by keeping in touch through Facebook, Twitter, Instagram, and other social media channels.

Implicit Methods

Another category of communication that emerged from the interviews was less obvious and less tangible. These implicit methods of communicating culture are subtler than the overt channels of communication described above. Instead, implicit methods include attitudes and approaches that indirectly convey images of a school's culture to prospective students. Implicit methods can include hospitality and customer service, inclusion and diversity, enthusiasm, and honesty. This section briefly explores how admissions officers use these implicit methods.

Hospitality and Service

Admissions officers reported that customer service[11] could communicate a school's culture through the hospitality delivered during the admissions process. The welcome that prospective students receive during the admissions process can signal a larger school culture that includes the ethos of support and care. Admissions officers indicated their awareness of the treatment of

11. Although some audiences may prefer not to label students as customers, many admissions officers used the term "customer service" in describing their work. Findings indicate that the term "customer service" is part of many admissions office cultures.

applicants and that treatment's impact on enrollment decisions. Having a positive experience during the application process, one survey participant noted, was going to matter after students were admitted, which in turn would matter when they make their choices to enroll.

Honesty and Authenticity

Many admissions officers indicated the importance of authentically communicating the characteristics of their schools. This focus on authenticity and honesty connects to the practice of discernment, figuring out what God wants us to do, that many working in theological school admissions described. While it is often applied in the Catholic context, discernment is a spiritual practice used by many Christians, and also found in other traditions.[12] In the *Spiritual Exercises*, St. Ignatius of Loyola, the founder of the Jesuits, offered guidance for discerning what God wants for each of us in this life. This approach is a distinctive characteristic of Ignatian spirituality, involving information gathering, mindfulness, prayer, and reflection to make judgments, to distinguish among, and to understand the implications of different courses of action.[13] Many admissions officers already value student discernment and are willing to have conversations with applicants that include questions, such as "where is God calling me?" "what is my vocation?" and "is the timing right for me to pursue studies?" The findings indicated that admissions officers approached these conversations in a ministerial way, by providing open, honest answers about the field of graduate theology and about their schools in general. Many admissions officers also noted that their applicants viewed the application process as a time for discernment. Accurately and authentically representing one's whole school, as opposed to only highlighting certain positive aspects, appears to be central to the way many admissions officers working at theological schools approach their roles.

Diversity and Inclusion

In describing culture, some admissions officers commented on their schools' openness to diversity. They spoke comfortably about their schools' approaches to multiple dimensions of diversity, including race, ethnicity, and sexual orientation. There was an awareness that not every student's

12. Luévano, "Catholic Discernment," 39–52.

13. Fleming, *What is Ignatian Spirituality?*, 89–94.

experience would be the same and that a recruitment plan must acknowledge that an applicant's background might influence the details he or she searched for during the application process.

Enthusiasm and Support

Admissions officers recognized that choosing a school was a complicated process for applicants that involved weighing both factual and emotional aspects. During interviews, when I asked admissions officers to pretend I was an applicant and describe their school's cultures to me, it became clear that they showed enthusiasm for their specific schools and for the study of theology. Enthusiasm, on the part of an admissions officer, could potentially help an applicant emotionally connect with a school, by helping them get excited about potentially enrolling that school. Additionally, in periods of challenge, change, or adjustment at a particular school, admissions officers must remain aware that their communication of cultural changes, if not presented positively, could imply an unenthusiastic reception of that change and affect applicants' impressions of the school.

Both explicit and implicit methods of communicating culture play important roles in the recruitment and enrollment processes. Having identified the ways culture can be communicated during the admissions process, the next section explores admissions officers' perceptions of the effectiveness of these different methods at communicating culture.

PERCEPTIONS OF EFFECTIVENESS

As defined earlier, the effectiveness of a method of communication refers to its success in influencing students' decisions to apply and enroll. This section explores how admissions officers view the effectiveness of in-person, virtual, and quasi-virtual channels. The section concludes with a discussion of how admissions officers indicate they assess which communication strategies are successful.

Overwhelmingly, survey participants cited face-to-face, on-campus visits and events as the channel of communication they perceived as most effective. Following on-campus visits and events, the next highest rated channels were quasi-virtual forms of outreach: telephone calls and e-mails to prospective students. On average, in-person channels scored highest, followed by quasi-virtual channels, and finally virtual channels. These averages suggest that the more interactive and personal a channel is, the more effective it is perceived.

In discussing the perceived effectiveness of on-campus visits and events with interview participants, it became clear why this mechanism, in particular, was viewed so highly. It is not that the idea of an in-person visit is unique; rather, it is the opportunity for prospective students to engage with individual, unique members of the school's community. The majority of admissions officers indicated they facilitate some form of campus visit so that applicants gain a full sense of the school's culture. Constance believed that her school's visit days were most effective because they were authentic, noting: "it's not a polished production for the sake of this day—whatever happens here is real." The on-campus visit has the opportunity to not only show off the school's setting, but also to help prospective students connect with the community. As one admissions officer indicated:

> You can read about culture in a viewbook, but it's something different to experience it. And it's something you can read on a website—what a great community, or this is our community or we're a community or whatever—but then you come here and have a tour . . . or you see faculty having lunch with students. Any number of things communicates community in a way that words alone cannot.

The ability to (1) show not just tell and (2) foster authentic, personal experiences keeps on-campus visits and events at the top of the list for effective mechanisms of communicating culture.

Although the majority of admissions officers rated on-campus, face-to-face interactions high in perceived effectiveness, realism about on-campus limitations also existed. Many prospective students never get to visit campus. Admissions officers explained that there were several reasons preventing students from visiting, including time constraints, financial reasons, and distance. Other students, they explained, prefer online communications and would rather engage with the school virtually, without committing to anything. Even at theological schools, where ideas of community, formation, and experiential and faith-based learning emerge more prominently than in other graduate disciplines, admissions officers believed that most students first encounter a school virtually through the website before setting foot on campus (if they ever do). Ellen explained these challenges:

> Face-to-face is always going to be the most effective at really conveying reality, but, increasingly, we are seeing a population that is inclined towards online education. As much as I think for ministry and theological education, face-to-face is the ideal, that's not going to be the first encounter for most people. Students are willing to forego face-to-face contact for convenience.

> Therefore, schools have to be effective at communicating what
> their environment is like in a medium that is unnatural for us.
> That's likely going to be online, on the web. Maybe e-mail. It
> could be a text. But it's web-based. It's the art of compromise.

Given this technological reality, admissions officers must attempt to be effective at communicating culture both in-person and virtually. They must
also be aware that most students' first impressions of a school's culture will
be made online, through virtual mechanisms, like school websites, and proceed from there. Admissions officers must strategize how to make virtual
mechanisms as effective as possible.

Websites

Virtual mechanisms, in order to be as effective as possible, require technical expertise and constant updating. Many admissions officers recognized
these challenges, admitting they would like the text and other content on
their websites updated more often than is currently occurring. As Joseph
explained, his school's website consisted mostly of text that had been im-
ported from his school's printed viewbook and academic catalog:

> But I think if you look on our website and if you look at our
> materials they're pretty anemic. I mean we have not done a good
> job—we don't have good materials. Like if you go to our website,
> there'll be three paragraphs on a degree. It's not interactive, it's
> not robust in any way saying this is why you should come here,
> this degree is fantastic, you know?

In interviews, most participants indicated that their websites needed significant improvement. Others talked about enhancements that were recently
made or would be made soon, but shared the frustration that their websites
needed improvement.

In some cases, the available technology did not support the changes
that were wanted or needed. Matthew could identify what he would like
added to the website but did not have the technical knowledge to create the
content himself. Multimedia, including video, was cited as an improvement
that would be welcomed and very helpful in showcasing the culture of a
school. Video content has the ability to actually show, not just talk about, a
school's culture. However, as Matthew confided, creating multimedia content often requires a specialized skill set:

> I would love to see more videos on there, short two to four
> minute videos. I think that would be a really good way to talk

about each of the degree programs and the different aspects of
the school that are unique. I'd love to see the website be a little
bit more updated but I am not a web designer, I do not know
what goes into web design.

For others, website changes were scheduled to be made, but were not happening fast enough. As Ellen pointed out, the admissions season is cyclical and, therefore, there is a specific window of time when changes would impact the communication of culture the most: "There is a new website coming. It's just not coming yet. And in admissions, we already know . . . we needed it last spring."

As a result of technical limitations, interview participants also expressed a concern that their websites did not accurately represent the school's culture and all that it could offer its students. As one participant pointed out: "It's frustrating to know that that is the web representation from us and that we have all these other things that are so incredible and the website looks like it was designed in 1997." For those admissions officers who perceived the website as an effective tool at communicating culture, this constant push to assess and improve the website's content was a recurring theme.

Despite identifying the website as his most important recruitment tool, Matthew recognized, as many other admissions officers did, that his website and the skills needed to maintain it required improvement. These skills include writing for the web, time management in order to make updates, and the ability to add media and other quasi-virtual channels (e.g., blogs, social media) directly to the website.

Social Media

Most admissions officers indicated they use some form of social media as part of their communications plan. Instagram, Twitter, and Facebook were the most commonly cited social media platforms. Interview participants explained that the time investment in using social media was very high, but that the advantage to using social media was in the opportunity to diversify content through different posts. For example, they could create a post highlighting a faculty publication and then later in the day post a reminder about student social events. The ability to showcase different aspects of a school through social media helps admissions officers represent the full culture of a school.

Social media tools also help engage prospective students with each other and the larger school community. Matthew indicated that social media was useful for pushing information about different aspects of school culture (upcoming research conferences, housing opportunities, faculty updates) as well as logistical updates (e.g., application requirements, commitment deadline reminders). Social media also provides an opportunity to engage admitted students with the larger student community, helping them to interact with school culture before arriving to campus. He shared his approach to social media:

> We use social to get them excited about meeting their cohort, to get them talking to one another. To get them, you know, because then they can direct message each other about their anxieties and their fears and what they're excited about and to post things like that. And then also we use it to disseminate information and so we'll say things like you gotta have your decisions to us by April 15th. You've got to, here are some housing units that are coming up, here's a job opportunity in a local thing that people want you to know about, things like that. Here's a conference—I just posted about a conference yesterday.

Used in this manner, social media can also be used to keep students engaged after attending an on-campus, in-person event. Follow-up information from the admissions office can be pushed to attendees. Relationships formed among admitted students can be maintained by keeping in touch through a school's social media channels.

Figuring Out What Works

Questions regarding the assessment of communication methods were asked on the survey and during interview conversations. Survey respondents noted that questionnaires administered by ATS were useful in figuring out what methods were effective during the recruitment process. The ATS Entering and Graduating Student Questionnaires ask a number of overarching demographic and student life questions, as well as a limited number of questions about the student's recruitment and application experience. Individual schools distribute the pre-made surveys to their students, but schools have the option to add additional school-specific questions. This function allows admissions officers the opportunity to ask more probing questions regarding specific aspects of the recruitment process, including the communication of culture. This information can then be used to "fine tune" and update recruiting strategies.

Joseph expressed a concern about how to track the many different points of contact that take place between school and applicant. While it may be easy for admissions officers to collect contact information from applicants, it can be harder to determine which point of contact was most effective. As Joseph pointed out, without a sophisticated customer relationship management (CRM) system, it can be difficult to determine whether a printed viewbook or a monthly email correspondence was the more effective method of communication. This lack of clarity could potentially affect knowing how to follow up with applicants effectively. Survey and other interview participants shared this concern. Many respondents indicated a desire for the ability to better track students who participated in an on-campus event, met with an admissions officer on-the-road, or who requested information virtually, for the purpose of determining whether prospective students gained a better understanding of school culture. These findings suggest a strong need for greater technology in order to better measure and assess success in communicating culture.

RECOMMENDATIONS FOR FUTURE PRACTICE

This section presents practical recommendations for those working in admissions, and for those who might supervise or hire admissions officers. The importance of discernment is highlighted, as well as the significance of customer service, relationship building, and technical expertise.

Supporting Discernment within the Admissions Process

Research findings indicate that admissions officers are aware that prospective students engage in discernment throughout the enrollment process. Many described a culture of discernment when working with potential students, viewing their work in admissions as a ministry in and of itself. The recognition by admissions officers that prospective students engage in discernment distinguishes the theology admissions process as one of constant reflection and consultation. As many of the participants in this study indicated, it is advantageous for admissions officers to recognize and support the discernment taking place throughout the enrollment process. The key for admissions officers is maintaining the ability to provide students with the honesty and authenticity they need to discern, while still maintaining enrollment numbers to promote the good financial stability of their schools.

Hiring and Training Issues

In order to grasp the culture of a school and be successful in an admissions role, it is not essential that a candidate be an alumnus of the school. Research shows there is little difference in how admissions officers, whether or not they attended the school at which they now work, value culture's role in the recruitment process. In fact, the findings indicate there may be an advantage to candidates coming from outside of the school, since they can bring in different perspectives and often have previous experience in admissions. Beyond a candidate's educational history, there are other factors to consider during the hiring process that could potentially indicate a candidate's successful transition into an admissions role.

Forming Relationships and Adapting to Change

First, the ability for an individual to form relationships with a number of different constituencies appears to be key. These relationships include the individual's direct supervisor, from whom the admissions officer may seek guidance regarding key aspects of the school's culture, and faculty members, who are often involved in the admissions process. Many admissions officers feature faculty involvement in their description of school culture. Fostering strong faculty alliances allows the admissions office the ability to access faculty members during the recruitment process. In a similar way, successful candidates must also be able to form strong relationships with current students. Students also play an important part in recruitment, serving as ambassadors, tour guides, and conversation partners for applicants. During her interview, Sarah indicated her ability to seek out allies as she learned her school's culture:

> In order to really imbibe and understand the culture, I made a concerted effort to meet with people and I knew who the strong people were, I knew who the sleepers were, I knew who had charisma, I knew who had a pulse and was innovative. I would say that there was a fairly consistent understanding and expression of the culture of this school.

To assess the ability to build relationships during the hiring process, a search committee should consider a job applicant's previous experience. An invitation to share prior examples of relationship or consensus building may be helpful. Asking the candidate to research the school's website or other communications and then share a few aspects of culture he or she felt were important would also be a potential way to evaluate these qualities. Given the volatility in theological school enrollment in recent years, it may also be important to assess a candidate's ability to adapt to change, handle pressure, and balance competing interests. Admissions officers must be ready to react to strategic changes, so that adjustments in recruitment practices can be made without negatively impacting enrollments.

Customer Service Excellence

The importance of a strong customer service background should not be overlooked in searching for any admissions position. Many described the idea of customer service as providing care, support, and the welcoming of applicants, rather than high-pressured sales tactics. Some participants indicated there was a negative stigma associated with viewing admissions work as sales and reinforced that they did not view their work in this way. Sarah took a different approach to the idea of selling. By treating it as a positive concept, selling has become something essential to her school's livelihood and reflective of her school's culture, which is focused on care for individual students. Sarah shared:

> At our senior staff meeting, we're talking about how to sell. So we're taking the dirtiness out of selling and saying it's an integral part of everything we're doing. We have to sell and it's okay to promote, to explain, to engage, this is all about customer satisfaction and knowing what your commodity is really and how to get people excited about it. It isn't dirty anymore.

Sarah and her team have focused on connecting the idea of selling to proactively advancing the school's mission and communicating that mission to a larger audience. At her school, selling is a necessary mechanism for engaging and exciting potential applicants. The remainder of this section offers three additional considerations regarding customer service related to the hiring process.

FIRST IMPRESSIONS MATTER

The hospitality, support, and welcome that admissions officers provide applicants can potentially create an impression of the entire school and student experience. Admissions officers are often cognizant of how impressions send implicit messages of culture to applicants. A positive, hospitable experience, for example, can help deliver an implicit message of warmth about the school culture and community. Job applicants for admissions positions must be able to exude this warmth and hospitality.

Understanding Applicant Concerns

Successful admissions officers understand the concerns and challenges of the application process and help their applicants navigate that process. Research findings identify the importance of helping counsel and guide applicants through the admissions process. This may involve the ability to explain specific required elements of the application or it may involve recognizing that an applicant just needs a short email to confirm and reassure him or her that materials have been received. Often, patience, clarity, and attention to detail are required for excellent applicant service.

Experiences Are Everything

There was overwhelming agreement by admissions officers that on-campus events were most effective in driving enrollment. Therefore, job applicants for admissions positions must be able to illustrate that they can help craft these impactful experiences for prospective students. To be considered during the hiring process: someone who cannot create positive, impactful experiences risks creating a negative perception for the school.

To gauge excellence in customer service, hiring committees must be aware of all of the job applicant's interactions with the committee (e.g., first contact, cover letter quality, first moments of the interview as the candidate is meeting the committee). Situational questions, which ask the candidate to respond to "real-life" applicant concerns, may be both helpful and revealing in terms of an individual's approach to hospitality and service.

Technical Skills and Design Ability

Recognizing that increasingly more admissions experiences occur virtually, it is essential that an admissions candidate possess some understanding of digital marketing and communications. As more admissions tools (e.g., online application systems, database query tools, filing systems) are digitized, strong technical skills should also be required of potential admissions employees. At a minimum, job applicants should be conversational in areas of marketing and design, including web, print, and video design. Many admissions officers indicated a need for specific technical and design skills—especially skills that would allow them to make "on-the-fly" updates to websites and online admissions tools, as well as interact with design and information technology employees.

Hiring committees should look for previous experience with systems that track interactions with prospective students (i.e., CRM systems), as well as familiarity with other online communications and data mining tools. Ideally, the candidate would possess both the customer service skills described above and the analytical mindset to access and utilize admissions data in an effective way.

Professional Development Issues

Supporting a newly hired admissions officer once she or he begins is as important as hiring the right candidate for the admissions role. This study suggests that not all admissions officers receive the support they require. Supervisors should encourage new employees to take advantage of professional development opportunities that already exist. Enrollment management organizations like NAGAP (the Association for Graduate Enrollment Management) and AACRAO (the American Association of Collegiate Registrars and Admissions Officers) offer multiple conferences, workshops, and consulting options, which serve the needs of admissions novices to experts. An opportunity within the theological discipline to connect and learn is offered by the ATS Student Personnel Administrators' Network (SPAN), which offers an annual conference and ongoing resources.

FINAL THOUGHTS

Culture's role in the admissions process has been shown to be a crucial and influential one. As admissions officers create recruiting strategies to reach out to potential students, culture is highly integrated into these plans. Likewise, admissions officers believe culture is a highly important factor in converting admitted applicants to enrolled students. Although culture is not the sole element in these decisions—factors like financial aid and location are also perceived to play a large part in decisions—culture is unique because its communication can be malleable. Admissions officers can create and refine channels of communication to showcase and emphasize specific aspects of school culture. Additionally, through implicit actions, they can transmit different qualities of the culture in order to appeal and attract certain students. For this reason, culture remains a powerful factor in influencing enrollment decisions.

Despite the context of an advancing technological world, face-to-face interactions were shown to be the method of communication most valued by admissions officers for passing culture on to applicants. A challenge for admissions officers in the years to come will be to maintain this commitment to face-to-face methods of communicating in a world that may—or may have already—become more reliant on digital communications than in-person ones. For theological school admissions officers, this means figuring out how to facilitate and support the student discernment process in a digital, virtual way. This work becomes more important each year, as admissions officers must seek new strategies to effectively communicate culture and positively affect student enrollments amid constant challenges in graduate theological education.

BIBLIOGRAPHY

Association of Theological Schools (ATS). "2019–2020 Annual Data Tables." Online. https://www.ats.edu/uploads/resources/institutional-data/annual-data-tables/2019-2020%20Annual%20Data%20Tables.pdf.

Fleming, David L. *What is Ignatian Spirituality?* Chicago: Loyola, 2008.

Guckian, Meaghan L., et al. "'A Few Bad Apples' or 'Rotten to the Core': Perceptions of Corporate Culture Drive Brand Engagement After Corporate Scandal." *Journal of Consumer Behavior* 17 (2018) 29–41.

Kezar, Adrianna, and Peter D. Eckel. "The Effect of Institutional Culture on Change Strategies in Higher Education: Universal Principles or Culturally Responsive Concepts?" *The Journal of Higher Education* 73.4 (2002) 436–60.

Kuh, George D. "Assessing Campus Environments." In *Handbook on Student Affairs Administration,* edited by Margaret J. Barr, 30–48. San Francisco: National Association of Student Personnel Administrators/Jossey-Bass, 1993.

Kuh, George D., and E. J. Whitt. *The Invisible Tapestry: Culture in American Colleges and Universities.* Las Vegas: Association for the Study of Higher Education, 1988.

Luévano, Rafael. "Catholic Discernment with a View of Buddhist Internal Clarity." *Buddhist Christian Studies* 29 (2009) 39–52.

Magolda, P. M. "What Our Rituals Tell Us About Community on Campus: A Look at the Campus Tour" *About Campus* 5.6 (2001) 2–8.

Pew Research Center. "What Surveys Say About Worship Attendance—and Why Some Stay Home." *Pew Research Center,* September 13, 2013. Online. http://www.pewresearch.org/fact-tank/2013/09/13/what-surveys-say-about-worship-attendance-and-why-some-stay-home.

Poluzzi, Adam J. "Communicating Culture in Graduate Admissions." PhD diss., Boston College, 2015.

Schindler, David L., ed. *Catholicism and Secularization in America: Essays on Nature, Grace, and Culture.* Huntington, IN: Our Sunday Visitor, 1990.

Sellers, Patricia. "IBM Exec: Culture Is Your Company's No. 1 Asset." *Fortune,* March 10, 2011. Online. http://fortune.com/2011/03/10/ibm-exec-culture-is-your-companys-no-1-asset.

Simplico, Joseph. "The University Culture." *Education* 133.2 (2012) 336–39.

Smart, John C., et al. "The Roles of Institutional Cultures and Decision Approaches in Promoting Organizational Effectiveness in Two-Year Colleges." *Journal of Higher Education* 68.3 (1997) 256–81.

Stiber, Gregory. "Characterizing the Decision Process Leading to Enrollment in Doctoral Programs: Theory, Application, and Practice." *Journal of Marketing for Higher Education* 10.1 (2000) 13–26.

———. "Characterizing the Decision Process Leading to Enrollment in Master's Programs: Further Application of the Enrollment Process Model." *Journal of Marketing and Higher Education* 11.2 (2001) 91–107.

Tisdell, Elizabeth J. *Exploring Spirituality and Culture in Adult and Higher Education.* San Francisco, CA: Jossey-Bass, 2013.

Weddell, Sherry A. *Forming Intentional Disciples: The Path to Knowing and Following Jesus.* Huntington, IN: Our Sunday Visitor, 2012.

CHAPTER 10

Before the Buck Stops
Managing Crisis to Avoid Chaos

PAMELA R. LIGHTSEY

PROLOGUE

ACADEMIC YEAR 2014–2015 WAS one of the most formative times of my career as an administrator. That was the year I began to learn, really learn, about responding to crisis in schools of theology and more broadly speaking in local communities. My conversations and presence in a number of contexts helped me adjust my perspective so as to see the benefits of a number of approaches and the danger of operating from a solely conciliatory management approach which has the *veneer of repair* as its ultimate orientation.

As a mechanism of normative and hierarchical models of higher education administration, repairing conflict through *conciliatory* crisis management is often the means by which schools attempt to declare they are being respectful and "willing to work with" students who raise concerns. This is a fairly common management approach that can easily mask deceitful practices under disguised traits—the veneer—of "inclusive" and "agreeable." I am of the opinion that solely using conciliatory management merely passes the buck, passes problem solving responsibilities from one department or administrator to another or from one era of time to another.

It is will-o-the-wisp in nature; an exasperating vacuous effort because the orientation towards repair is not equivalent to actually fixing the root problem. We spend a great of time repairing issues by conciliatory patchwork. At a time of rising campus protests, administrators must be prepared to resolve, not to *handle* conflict; to fix—even if it means tearing away and casting off internal defective or unnecessary parts—rather than to cover up our deficiencies.

I'm not advocating that administrators can resolve all problems, especially all acts of bigotry on campuses. I do feel that our work absolutely must include trying to create a culture of respect and equal opportunities for learning for all our students, faculty, and staff. The only way we can make that a reality is by listening to students and our diverse constituency to determine how we are doing and to implement changes to bring that vision of equal, fair, and just education to fruition.

Therefore, this chapter is not meant as a panacea for responding to campus crisis. Rather, it is what I hope will be a useful analysis, albeit more reflective, than some who are looking for concrete answers desire. Why should such a reflection matter to you, the reader? What value is a reflection over and against the limitless manuscripts on conflict resolution or models of administrative leadership—using qualitative and quantitative research—within the academy? Better yet, of what use is this chapter if it does not make as primary these expert resources? Certainly, these are all valid concerns. However, my goal in this chapter is to pull from history's vast repository of data to detail those multiple events where the buck of responsibility was simply passed on to the next generation of leadership, or for the purposes of this chapter, passed on to the next generation of academic leadership who—especially when it came to protests against discrimination—too often handled the crisis only to satiate the students or donors of that moment or era. In light of the historical review, this chapter will also consider crisis as a learning opportunity that comes so that our schools may respond and fix challenges.

RUMINATION

Admittedly, I write this article from the perspective of having been *handled* at times as a student and as an administrator. From the handling of being forced to integrate southern white schools to witnessing the handling of black students—and black faculty—across universities and schools of theology during the height of the #BlackLivesMatter movement, the response of mostly predominately white schools is filled with predictable actions (which

I will cover, though not fully, in this chapter) that never quite get to the crux of the matter. Instead, actions are put in place to satiate or mitigate rather than making the deep sacrifice to address what has been an ongoing national dilemma: racism.

Though ongoing, the ways racism is deployed has changed. In fact, at the beginning of this new century a new term is used to describe the often subtly hostile, discriminatory, and racist comments and actions directed towards students of color, *microaggressions*. For instance, first generation Asian Americans frequently report hearing, "Your English is really good!" from white students and faculty.

To be sure, racism is the common denominator across many of the campus protests from the twentieth century to now. The insistence on the part of students that schools join the effort to eradicate racism either by ending institutionalized racism and/or combatting structural racism in our world will return, refusing to be set aside, by each new generation of students desirous of living in a world where human rights is a reality for all persons. As a female, African American, queer lesbian administrator I walk a very tenuous path during these times. I feel quite strongly a longing to be helpful in the work to end oppression even as a representative of the institution that is the subject of protest. It is a multiple bind the likes of which has been acknowledged in a recent report led by the Association of Theological Schools:

> Literature is abundant in its claim that institutional realities present double, triple, multiple binds for constituents of color and women constituents: there are almost always too few individuals committed to institutional change around diversity, and the limited decision-making positions that constituents of color and women constituents hold further accentuate power asymmetries.[1]

The limited number of senior administrators who are persons of color within theological schools places a heavy burden on those of us who fill these positions. Often, there is the perceived notion that we are involved in all the actual decision-making taking place when in fact, decisions and the authority and power to make the most crucial decisions at times involves an unfolding, unforeseen power dynamic. Deans of Students and Directors of Diversity and Inclusion can find that what they were told during the hiring process about their authority to make decisions about co-curricular matters is not at all consistent with reality. Uncomfortable decisions for the institution's hierarchy can be—and often is—relegated to these administrators

1. Aleshire and Jennings, "ATS Work."

during times of student dissatisfaction. Moreover, these administrators may find the buck resting at their doors initially; they may easily find themselves being asked to be the face of poor institutional governance—with little to no true authority to make final decisions—during the initial moments/hours of student protests. It is important to note that in healthy academic institutional governance, boundaries are established and adhered to that prevent oppressive power dynamics. Yet, during times of crisis, struggles can and do at times emerge between the day-to-day decision-making administrators, faculty, boards of trustees and donors.

Perhaps, the strongest pull for me during these difficult seasons of unrest exists as a result of my educational upbringing. I was reared, like many African American children of the 60s, by teachers and parents who believed that education was the means by which true liberation and economic well-being would be realized. Not many generations removed from the painful era when African slaves were prohibited from learning to read or write, we, the progeny of slaves, entered schools—segregated though they were—with the encouragement that "you can make it if you get that education." Black feminist bell hooks's recollection of her early years in school is not unlike my own:

> Almost all our teachers at Booker T. Washington were black women. They were committed to nurturing intellect so that we could become scholars, thinkers, and cultural workers—black folks who used our "minds." We learned early that our devotion to learning, to the life of the mind, was a counter-hegemonic act, a fundamental way to resist every strategy of white racist colonization.[2]

As a counter-hegemonic act, education meant freedom: "The emphasis on education as necessary for liberation that black people made in slavery and then on into reconstruction informed our lives."[3] After years of viewing education, particularly learning to read and write, as a goal that had life-threatening consequences, here we were, finally able to have access to the primary academic instruments upon which we believed our predicament in life would be improved.

This way of thinking about and approaching an education remains a difficult disposition in a system that articulates its purpose as "equipping students to lead" which would be commendable but for the fact that it is embedded in an academic ideology that too often views students as recipients rather than participants in the teaching process. Education is arduous

2. hooks, *Teaching to Transgress*.
3. hooks, *Teaching to Transgress*.

at best when faculty serve only as distributors of a cache of facts rather than conveyors of ideas which they and students will spend time analyzing for the truths they may reveal. Coming from a model of education as an important mechanism in the quest for liberation and justice, it is difficult not to value student unrest as a clue that the education they are receiving is not being understood as liberative. It is a struggle not to hear their challenges as an opportunity to reevaluate how it is that we are indeed "equipping" students. Protests remind us that the worth of what is being taught and how we administer our degree programs need to be deconstructed and reviewed frequently.

The model of teaching that Dr. hooks remembers and many teachers of my day utilized taught us the value of digging, uncovering, and daring to ask questions of the material presented as established truths. What is more, we learned that this practice was important for every facet of our lives; to first free our minds from the incumbrances of honoring what white people told us was truth for the benefit of seeing another reality and therefore a better day. For me then, it is no small wonder that it was black students who dealt such a fatal blow to Jim Crow and desegregating schools through sit-ins and freedom rides. These university and seminary students utilized their analytical skills to address the cultural questions and issues of their lives. They brought to the halls of academia the frustrations and divisions happening within the nation, most often on the matters related to race and war. These were matters that could not be brisk classroom analysis as Conrad Cherry, Distinguished Professor Emeritus of Religious Studies at Indiana University notes in his work, *Hurrying Toward Zion*:

> Some of the clearest lessons about race and racism, however, were not taught in divinity school ethics courses, nor even in the fieldwork designed to give those courses practical significance. They were taught, instead, in the schools' pursuit of policies and practices of racial integration within their own university communities. Early in their histories, the nondenominational and Methodist divinity schools in the North led the way in the integration of institutions of higher education through their admission of black students, and many of those students went on to distinguished careers.[4]

Through what was understood as a *gradualist*[5] approach to integration, black students began to slowly fill the halls of schools of theology such as Perkins School of Theology at Southern Methodist University:

4. Cherry, *Hurrying toward Zion.*
5. See Cherry's review of Perkins' dean, Merrimon Cunninggim, who felt that this

The recruitment of full-time black students at Perkins was taken quietly and uneventfully. In the fall semester of 1952, five regularly enrolled black students, representing three different Protestant denominations, were admitted to the divinity school at SMU, and, despite some struggles owing to weakness of academic preparation, they were to receive their diplomas three years later as the first blacks to be awarded academic degrees by the University.[6]

These students attended classes without much fanfare and, at the behest of key administrators avoided calling attention to themselves. Their admission to these schools of theology were seen as a moral imperative. The nature of the schools themselves were seen as antithetical to the mission of the church. The secular world was increasingly taking up the matter of civil rights, particularly demonstrated—at the time—by the Supreme Court Decision known as Brown vs. Board of Education that ruled school segregation as unconstitutional.

This changed during the sixties student movement. Nonviolent direct action was used to agitate for justice. The tactics of this effort included freedom rides to the south and sit-ins to denounce segregation and injustices. This was largely student-led work—most notably the Student Nonviolent Coordinating Committee (SNCC) though their work was often supported by persons who felt a deep commitment to their goals. For instance, at Boston University School of Theology, faculty and students joined the work of its greatest student, Rev. Martin Luther King Jr., as he became the leading face of the Sixties' civil rights movement. Students not only demanded the end of segregation and racism at the university but many boarded buses as freedom fighters traveling to southern Jim Crow cities.

However, while schools of theology, particularly in southern regions of the country, might have been willing to gradually admit black students, their moral sensibilities had not matured enough to accept these students without stipulations that demanded the students not "rock the boat"—if you will—within the school's largely still segregated order. Considering this, there is perhaps no better example of when that order was best tested in a southern university than the case of James Lawson at Vanderbilt Divinity School.

Lawson, was a member of the racially segregated Methodist Church. During those years, its African American members were part of the

strategy for integration "called for patient education of the opponents of integration and alleviation of their fears of different races" (Cherry, *Hurrying toward Zion*, 201).

6. Cherry, *Hurrying toward Zion*, 199–200.

jurisdiction known as the Central Jurisdiction. Its African American members were well aware of the moral pretense of the denomination. This was the climate of the denomination and the school. Lawson, a chief organizer of the sit-ins of the time, was even at that time, one of the nation's leading progenitors of civil disobedience and student of Gandhian nonviolence. "In February 1960, Lawson helped to organize (but at that time did not participate in) a series of sit-ins at Nashville lunch counters that provoked violent reactions from a group of angry white citizens."[7]

Typical of the day, though it had been "tolerant" of Lawson's actions to live and move around the city and campus as any other student—rather than maintain a low-profile—the angry publicity the sit-ins brought to the university was more than the school's chief administrators had the will to handle. The University issued a swift demand of Lawson to "advise the protesters to desist from sit-ins" or be expelled from the school.[8] Refusing, Lawson was expelled.

The reaction to Lawson's expulsion was swift. To their credit, faculty of the Divinity School responded in support of Lawson, even lodging a formal complaint and threats of resignation from many of the faculty. All to no avail:

> Lawson's expulsion from Vanderbilt Divinity School and the resulting resignations of faculty members in protest embroiled the campus and the Nashville community in a nationally reported controversy for months in the spring of 1960. Eventually, a compromise was forged to stop most of the resignations and allow Lawson to complete his degree in Nashville. Lawson instead chose to transfer to Boston University.[9]

Clearly, in the case of integration of African American students into predominantly white schools of theology, the gradualist model could only be employed for a limited time. Moreover, as said earlier, the school taught what it thought about racism and the social gospel not in its classroom but through its administrative actions.

Often, there was not enough time to take a gradualist approach, especially in the late Sixties. For example, in the tense days after the assassination of Rev. Dr. Martin Luther King, Jr. as the nation was awash with protests and riots on the streets and demonstrations, Columbia University Students for Democratic Society and the Student Afro-American Society held three of the school's administrators in its Hamilton Hall, including Henry S.

7. Cherry, *Hurrying toward Zion*, 207.

8. Cherry, *Hurrying toward Zion*, 207.

9. "Rev. James Lawson."

Coleman, then acting dean,[10] for three days. SNCC representative H. Rap Brown and Stokley Carmichael, CORE, and other local community activists joined the students in acts of solidarity.

The cause of the student protest was "Columbia's plans to build a gymnasium in a nearby [Harlem] park, among other things"[11] as well as the school's known participation in war weapons research with the Institute for Defense Analysis (IDA):[12]

> The tension continued despite the release of Henry Coleman, acting dean of Columbia College, and two associates. They had been held in Coleman's office in Hamilton Hall since Tuesday afternoon. Students revealed them at 3:30 p.m. yesterday.[13]

Police eventually arrested over seven hundred demonstrators, the university cut ties with IDA, plans for the gymnasium were dropped and though initial suffering financial damage, the university would rise to become one of the most prominent liberal universities in the nation. In addition, what happened at Columbia shows that campus protest can be a mix of a number of pressing issues of the time. Most notably, not only were there protests against racism, the campus protests of the Sixties also included uproar against American participation in war:

> The civil-rights movement of the late 1950s and early 1960s mobilized college students, both black and white, to a degree never before witnessed. But the Sixties student movement occupies an uneasy position in American history. On its fundamental planks—antiwar, antiracism, antipatriarchy—the movement scored major victories.[14]

In fact, the season of civil rights protest would barely begin to lessen when students would take up the anti-war cry. For instance, in March of 1968, students at NY University, aware of Dow Chemical's complicity in the manufacturing of napalm chemicals, staged a massive protest against the company and the US military's use of chemical warfare against the Vietnamese people.

Lest we over-romanticize the danger of the times, I hope the reader will keep in mind that most twentieth-century campus protests have been

10. An interesting note on the life of Dean Coleman can be found in Martin, "Henry S. Coleman."

11. Martin, "Henry S. Coleman."

12. Columbia University 1968, "Strike Coordinating Committee."

13. Benes and Mulligan, "Columbia University Students."

14. Dickey, "Revolution on America's Campuses."

very dangerous undertakings by students in responses to rising tensions within the nation. For instance, the Kent State University Massacre is one of the most horrible in the history of campus protests: .

> On May 4, 1970, members of the Ohio National Guard fired into a crowd of Kent State University demonstrators, killing four and wounding nine Kent State students. The impact of the shootings was dramatic. The event triggered a nationwide student strike that forced hundreds of colleges and universities to close.[15]

Yet students and faculty were willing, courageously willing, to put their very lives—physically and vocationally—on the line believing the ultimate fruits of these protests would improve the conditions on college, university, and seminary campuses. Student protestors took to—rather took—the halls of academe with intentional methodology to bring about change. Their nonviolent practice included long sit-ins, marches, and a process to ensure campus presidents and boards of trustees would listen to their demands and negotiations that produced helpful initiatives to resolve the injustices of the time. Many of today's humanity programs'—such as gender studies and racial-ethnic centers (e.g., African American Studies Department, Feminist Studies)—more diverse faculty hiring practices, as well as the hiring of senior administrators with titles that include "diversity" "equity" and/or "inclusion" are directly related to campus protests. Student leaders of campus protests unintentionally learn important lesson and some go on to be leaders on a national level.[16]

These measures were well received but not considered alembic actions in the face of institutionalized bigotry. Despite the moral discordance within predominantly white schools of theology, students of color were able to cut through the antinomic pedagogy that articulated a God of justice and hope while the prevailing nature of the curriculum itself was a display of the superiority of white scholarship. That is, until we reached the most recent phase of the movement to end white supremacist culture on university campuses and schools of theology.

The twenty-first-century era of student protests—including embracing Occupy Wall Street and the Black Lives Matter movement—tend to continue a history of demands for curriculum changes, and, like the demands

15. Lewis and Hensley, "May 4 Shootings."

16. Such as Representative John Lewis and Senators Bernie Sanders and Hillary Clinton. "At the University of Chicago, Bernie Sanders led a student chapter of the Congress of Racial Equality and was arrested; at Wellesley, Hillary Clinton led a two-day student strike and was offered a job after graduation with community organizer Saul Alinsky" (Dickey, "Revolution on America's Campuses").

of decades before, students' demands include retirement or dismissal of key administrators (e.g., presidents and deans) and the hiring of faculty and/or staff from particular demographic contexts. 2018's LGBTQIA+ Duke Divinity students' protest included a State of the School Address that made use of technology (webpage, YouTube video) to make their case and list their demands for public view.[17] This came pretty much on the heels of the spring 2017 internal clashes between some of the school's faculty over the matter of racial-equity training culminating with the resignation of one of its faculty,[18] as well as concern expressed by African American students about the ethos of the school and very serious unchecked racist behavior:

> "One of my classmates was sitting in a class, and she texted me and asked me to come to her class because a student was in her class saying, 'N****** like you come here and think that you can just change everything. Why don't you just learn what Jesus is really about?'" said Amber Burgin, president of the Black Seminarians Union, who is in her third year at Duke Divinity. "We are in classes trying to pull each other out of class to hear people making inappropriate slurs, like a white student calling someone a jigaboo and then claiming they didn't know what that means. Or a white classmate calling a black classmate 'ghetto.' . . . I've had classmates who have had to take leave; I've had classmates who have left the program because they were tired of being treated in such a way." Burgin stressed that the intolerant atmosphere also targets Latino and LGBTQ students.[19]

While this narrative may seem shocking to the reader, exchanges similar to this occur on campuses across the country on a daily basis. Duke Divinity is not unique. Among schools of theology has been #SeminaryWhileBlack launched by African American students at Fuller Theological Seminary in Pasadena, California[20] and students who marched in protest to Candler School of Theology at Emory University bestowing a Distinguished Alumni Awards on alumni, the Reverend H. Eddie Fox, who is known for his advocacy against full inclusion of LGBTQ persons within the United Methodist Church.[21]

All this to show that the nettlesome task of responding to bigotry at our schools is a consistent crisis which though not always apparent is likely

17. "LGBTQIA+ State of the School Address."

18. Dreher, "Duke Divinity Crisis."

19. Kenny, "Black Ministry Students At Duke."

20. Beard, "Black Students at Fuller."

21. Blevins, "Protest Greets Rev. H. Eddie Fox."

just bubbling below the surface of many campus communities. As society has changed, so too have the ways schools have dealt with conflict and protest. Sexual harassment (Title IX), the Americans with Disabilities Act (ADA), the Family Educational Rights and Privacy Act (FERPA) require knowledge and skills of administrators in ensuring the rights of students, staff, and faculty. The complex approaches to managing a safe and respectful learning environment means the buck not only stops with the head of the school but it lands on the desk of a number of administrators who must work together to make sure schools comply with law while at the same time avoid and/or resolve conflict before the incidents reach full protest mode.

Historically, the ways senior administration responded to tensions and protests on campus have primarily been to (1) ignore; (2) shut down through use of expulsion, arrests, and firing faculty; (3) gradual change acceptable to the status quo; (4) negotiation and mediation (e.g., conflict resolution practices); (5) secure legal counsel for adjudication; (6) develop new co-curricular programs; and (7) create new positions and curriculum. But what have we learned from crisis, especially student protests that can be adopted as an ongoing, not reactive, approach to school administration?

PREPARING FOR THE PREDICTABLE

As I noted in the beginning of this chapter, using conciliatory crisis management as the go-to means of resolving campus conflict should never be seen as the gold standard. Moreover, if the crisis reaches the level of full-scale marches, sit-ins, etc, this type of crisis management—especially if it is merely a method to cool things rather than solve the actual problem at hand—has the potential of infuriating students and extending the time it takes to reach resolution. Though one always hopes for an academic year without crisis, in reality each new term, each new class of students, each new faculty or staff hire, ushers in the potential for deep conflicts, hard feelings and potential protests (seen and unseen). Rather than be in a reactive mode to these tensions, senior administrators must be prepared for the predictable time of conflict.

Proper preparation entails considering what our schools articulate about the ethos of its campus with prospective students and the surrounding community. A sure way to fester hostility on our campuses often starts by the difference in the way the school is described to prospective students over and against what those students find to be the true state of the school as they start their coursework.

Is it really a "diverse community"? Are the voices of conservative and liberal thinkers equally respected? Will students who have very differing theological views than the vast majority of persons teaching and learning at the school feel welcomed? How is "diversity" actively honored in the classroom, in curriculum, and during co-curricular activities? What institutional systems are in place to make sure that what the school says of itself in its branding, mission, and vision is in fact reality? Do the administrators or faculty who are tasked with leading these systems have not only voice but the decision-making authority and funding to enact change and resolve disputes? These are the type of hard questions schools need to ask, examine thoroughly with a neutral party, and take measures to address with the oversight of the Board of Trustees.

I suggest utilizing a neutral party because administrators in charge of managing institutions have a way of protecting the long-held image of the institution and may likely be blind to the actual day-to-day realities experienced by faculty and students. In fact, outside review teams of administrators among the Association of Theological Schools may or may not be helpful. Neutral must mean inviting persons who have no relationship (past or current) with the school and no potential gain by pulling back the layers of the school's work and revealing unhealthy cultural practices—some information which may be quite confidential in nature.

Does the institutional system(s) in place include a process for conflict resolution that is known by the entire community, not merely students? What specific education and certifications for conflict resolution and/or mediation does the person/team that addresses conflict have and what continuing education are they required to complete? To whom are they accountable and do they really have authority to function as tasked?

The history I have covered includes a history of schools creating offices of "Diversity and Inclusion" (or similarly named) that are not central to the overall functioning of the school. Tucked away from the heart of the school, how can these administrators have their pulse on the problems emerging and discussed among students? What guidelines must be put in place so as not to tokenize its student liaisons?

There are vast opportunities for these administrators, but they cannot efficiently function in seclusion and as sole administrators chatting it up with a few students here and there. Like any other administrator, those who work in the area of diversity and inclusion need to possess a sense of how the entire institutional parts connect and work together with the hope of providing a seamless system. In addition, they cannot function well by being mere figureheads with little to no decision-making authority. They must be trusted to do the work, held accountable as they work but never—and especially not in this position—micromanaged.

Accountability seems to be an idea tossed about by administrators—and yes, students—without much thought. Mostly, I hear this spoken as a way of saying the people who are doing the work must be trustworthy and they must honor those for who and with whom they work by being responsible to the hopes, dreams, and visions of this representative body. To operate in a truly accountable posture is to understand how the work of your particular office impacts other parts of the school, cultivates success or breeds hostility within the entire community.

Perhaps nothing is as divisive as an attitude of tolerance for breeding hostility and promoting conflict in academic settings. This is why the gradualist approach of the Sixties was doomed to fail. This is why that same approach which reappeared during the #BlackLivesMatter and LGBTQ protests is as ineffective. By tolerance, I mean the exercise of those with power and privilege to "allow" the presence and/or participation of minorities in limited fashion. At universities such as Vanderbilt—in the Fifties and Sixties—it showed up in the way schools allowed the admission of black students as long as they kept a low profile and did not demand anything more than was offered.

Ultimately, I have learned that tolerance of this type only postpones an inevitable disruption. Students will demand our schools make changes even as our society changes. Now, whether or not such change is for the public good, will—and should—be a matter of transparent, respectful conversations that interrogate the actual viability of the change that is being demanded. Simply put, when students demand change, it is within our responsibility as institutions of higher education not to immediately dismiss their ideas but rather to initiate dialogue, do the research, and invoke collaboration towards resolution. Failing this, schools are likely to see more campus disruption. It is a truth; disruption is a student methodology for communication.

That said, the disruption itself is an opportunity, as I said at the beginning of this chapter, for growth. Proper management of crisis must always consider the tension that has risen as one of the ways students are signaling their desire to be in helpful conversation with the administrators of the school. If we enter into these situations with the intention of silencing, pacifying, or with the posture that the institution and the students are adversaries, we have already passed a fine opportunity to improve our work on to another generation or—as is frequently the case—another teaching institution (school, agency, or organic intellectuals). In an era where "alternative facts"[22] are on the rise, our very success in this work has the potential to impact the wellbeing of the nation.

BIBLIOGRAPHY

Aleshire, Daniel O., and Willie James Jennings. "ATS Work through the Committee on Race and Ethnicity, 2000–2014." *Theological Education* 50.2 (2017) 21–46.

Beard, Charlotte. "Black Students at Fuller Launch #SeminaryWhileBlack Protest." *Faithfully Magazine* (blog), July 16, 2018. Online. https://faithfullymagazine.com/black-students-fuller-protest.

Benes, Edward, and Arthur Mulligan. "Columbia University Students Barricade the Dean's Office in 1968." *New York Daily News*, April 25, 1968. Online. https://www.nydailynews.com/new-york/manhattan/columbia-students-barricade-dean-office-1969-article-1.2188331.

Blevins, John. "Protest Greets the Honoring of Rev. H. Eddie Fox at Emory's Candler School of Theology." *Religion Dispatches* (blog), December 12, 2013. Online. http://religiondispatches.org/protest-greets-the-honoring-of-rev-h-eddie-fox-at-emorys-candler-school-of-theology.

Cherry, Conrad. *Hurrying toward Zion: Universities, Divinity Schools, and American Protestantism.* Bloomington: Indiana University Press, 1995.

Columbia University 1968 (@1968CU). 2018. "'The Strike Coordinating Committee reiterates that our six demands, including the demand for amnesty, must be met.' #CU1968." Twitter, April 26, 2018, 4:35 p.m. https://twitter.com/1968CU/status/989649072809304068.

Dickey, Jack. "The Revolution on America's Campuses." *Time*, May 31, 2016. Online. http://time.com/4347099/college-campus-protests.

Dreher, Rod. "Duke Divinity Crisis: The Documents Are Out." *The American Conservative* (blog), May 7, 2017. Online. https://www.theamericanconservative.com/dreher/duke-divinity-crisis-griffiths-documents.

hooks, bell. *Teaching to Transgress: Education as the Practice of Freedom.* New York: Routledge, 1994.

Kenny, Carl. "Black Ministry Students At Duke Say They Face Unequal Treatment And Racism." *National Public Radio*, May 24, 2017. Online. https://www.npr.org/sections/codeswitch/2017/05/24/467233031/black-ministry-students-at-duke-say-they-face-unequal-treatment-and-racism.

Lewis, Jerry M., and Thomas R. Hensley. "The May 4 Shootings at Kent State University: The Search for Historical Accuracy." *Ohio Council for the Social Studies Review* 34.1 (1998) 9–21. Online. https://www.kent.edu/may-4-historical-accuracy.

"LGBTQIA+ State of the School Address." *Making the House of Love* (blog), March 1, 2018. Online. https://houseoflovedds.wordpress.com/2018/03/01/lqbtqia-state-of-the-school-address.

Martin, Douglas. "Henry S. Coleman, 79, Dies; Hostage at Columbia in '68." *New York Times*, February 4, 2006. Online. https://www.nytimes.com/2006/02/04/nyregion/henry-s-coleman-79-dies-hostage-at-columbia-in-68.html.

---

22. A term unintentionally coined by US Counselor to the President, Kellyanne Conway.

"The Rev. James Lawson to Return to Vanderbilt as Visiting Professor." *Vanderbilt News*, January 1, 2006. Online. https://news.vanderbilt.edu/2006/01/19/the-rev-james-lawson-to-return-to-vanderbilt-as-visiting-professor-59113.

PART THREE

Building Institutional Capacity

CHAPTER 11

Staff Leadership

Forming Collaborative Teams
and Hospitable Academic Communities

Alexandria Hofmann Macias

ADMINISTRATION IN A CHANGING CONTEXT

The changes taking place in theological education demand strong leadership from theological schools. Schools that cultivate collaborative teams of faculty and staff will be best equipped to adapt. Changes in theological education are certainly not new. The meaning and purpose of accreditation has shifted over the last fifty years, from ensuring minimum standards of resources to an outcome-based, mission-oriented evaluation, made more complicated by of federal government regulations.[1] But now more than ever, students are pursuing theological education in less traditional ways, and schools are adapting their programs, policies, and course modalities to keep up with rapid change. My own institution has seen a decrease in traditional campus-based students alongside an increase in distance learners, on-campus students who also take online classes, and part-time students who work full-time. Distance learning and online education have been significant discussions in theological education for the last several years. As of July 2018, the Association of Theological Schools (ATS) Board of Commissioners had

1. Aleshire, "Fifty Years of Accrediting," 65–73.

approved 173 exceptions or experiments, reflecting the need for schools like mine to attempt new distance learning and other initiatives designed for more flexible delivery or to reach new markets.[2] Accreditation standards have shifted over the years in response to these kinds of changes in practice and will continue to evolve with the upcoming revisions.[3]

In the past, greater complexity led to the development and growing role of the academic dean, as well as the proliferation of more focused support staff positions.[4] Expansion of administrative authority has not always been welcome. Faculty skepticism of the academic dean role is a running theme in reflections from chief academic officers and in a comprehensive study of the role, but in general, faculty and deans respect each other and recognize one another's leadership as valid and beneficial.[5] In the recent years of economic downturn, more administrative shifts are taking place. Theological institutions have cut staff and faculty while other positions have gone unfilled after retirements and resignations. The remaining support staff positions have diversified to accommodate fewer resources and the growing complexity of program changes and additions to retain students.[6] Though the responsibilities of staff are increasing, their sphere of influence has not kept pace. Junior administrators and staff are too frequently excluded from decision-making conversations, and their positions are rarely considered leadership roles. The "support" in support staff has the unfortunate consequence of suggesting that they merely support the more legitimate leadership of faculty and deans rather than leading in the fullest sense. Yet, in the rapidly shifting context of theological education, recognizing staff leadership in its own right and incorporating staff leadership into the larger decision-making community are both necessities for survival and a calling to Christian hospitality. Schools that embrace staff leadership will not only make more informed decisions and implement program changes

2. ATS, "Approved Exceptions and Experiments."

3. Aleshire, "Fifty Years of Accrediting," 74–80.

4. McLean, *Leading from the Center*, 16–33. McLean describes the evolution of the academic dean role, since its beginnings in the late nineteenth century, as well as the current complexity of the role. She makes mention of the support staff positions that have grown alongside the dean.

5. Graham, "Vocation," 71–73. See also McLean, *Leading from the Center*, 113–18, 234–36. For an example of faculty skepticism of academic administration within the research university, see Ginsburg, *Fall of the Faculty*. McLean's research did not find this level of suspicion in theological schools, but my experience tells me that similar tensions may crop up when it comes to decision-making power.

6. For a recent example, the plenary panel for the 2019 SPAN Conference was entitled, "Our Changing Roles: Managing Multiple Functions for Student and Institutional Success."

more effectively, they will be more just institutions. This chapter will focus on how schools can empower staff and increase the effectiveness of their participation by reshaping cultural boundaries between faculty and staff, fostering meaningful dialogue, and protecting staff time for development and reflection.

ADAPTIVE LEADERSHIP AND CHANGING LEARNING COMMUNITIES

Theological higher education is certainly not alone in its attempts to grapple with change. The business sector has also responded to dramatic shifts in technology and global markets with new concepts of leadership, and we would do well to pay attention. Executive decision making, in which one leader largely determined the course of the organization, was once the norm. Business literature now recognizes the "incomplete leader" who understands their own limitations in an increasingly complex world and values the leadership capacity "throughout the organizational hierarchy—wherever expertise, vision, new ideas, and commitment are found."[7] In this model, leadership is not limited to a single individual or department but is distributed across the organization at all levels.

Proponents of adaptive leadership approaches also recognize leadership capacity outside of the executive office and go further to envision the organization as a learning community that eschews hierarchical boundaries in favor of collective wisdom. Adaptive challenges are those that press an organization to define and redefine core institutional values and set new directions under the threat of change or extinction. With an adaptive approach, leadership becomes less a top-down authoritative role and more the ability to facilitate a group learning process that leads to mobilization and change.[8] Leadership becomes the onus of each member of the group who "use one another as resources, often across boundaries, and learn their way to those solutions."[9]

Faculty and staff do not have the same perspective, and allowing room for both offers a fuller picture. A leadership model that incorporates different visions and interpretations means a process is messier, less clean-cut, and prone to conflict, and yet it recognizes that in changing times, all perspectives are necessary to feel out the next steps. Given the shifting context of theological education, schools will need to respond innovatively. To do

7. Ancona et al., "Incomplete Leader," 94.
8. Heifetz and Laurie, "Work of Leadership," 124.
9. Heifetz and Laurie, "Work of Leadership," 124.

that, they cannot afford to overlook the vantage point of staff. It is time for schools to recognize that in addition to being a learning community of faculty and students, there exists a learning community comprised of senior administration, faculty, junior administrators, and support staff.

ACADEMIC HOSPITALITY AND STAFF EMPOWERMENT

While business literature may provide helpful models, we must hold fast to our ultimate goals as theological institutions. We align ourselves with the life of Christ and the work of the church. As such an institution, we strive for more than teamwork, innovation, or financial success. We strive for the embodiment of the gospel through academic hospitality, a helpful bridge concept between the learning organizations of adaptive leadership and the world of theological education administration.[10] Hospitality, as a Christian virtue, is about crossing boundaries, the foreigner welcomed in. Staff may not be foreigners to the overall community, but unfortunately, they may be in decision-making and "leadership" spaces. A colleague, for example, once remarked that while she was often thanked, she did not feel truly appreciated because she was rarely asked for her opinion. Academic hospitality, in contrast, rejects the prestige economy prevalent in institutions of higher education.

To be an academically hospitable institution, staff must be considered worthy of more than appreciation for their service. They should be considered "worthy of intellectual attention," something that faculty already possess by virtue of their scholarship and their seat at the table of many institution-shaping conversations.[11] True, faculty have subject mastery and teaching expertise among other qualifications, but to fulfill their whole mission, schools need more than subject mastery. They need the practical experience of staff as well. As a learning community, grounded in the gospel, academic hospitality urges one to learn from the other. In this case, the "other" may not be a scholar of differing perspective but a colleague in a different role altogether offering practice-based expertise in addition to the theological training that many staff have as well.

---

10. See Bennett, *Academic Life*, 46–69, for an introduction to the term. See also Mutch, "Leading," 189, for the implications for administrative leadership in theological schools. For more on hospitality in higher education in general, see Palmer and Zajonc, *Heart of Higher Education*, esp. 125–49, in which they propose transformative conversations as the locus for integrative learning.

11. Bennett, *Academic Life*, 53.

In times of change, even in crisis, healthy schools will do more than survive; they will empower their staff, thereby developing the leadership potential of their whole team and creating a more just, more hospitable institution in the process. Of biblical examples of hospitality, Mutch writes, "Each stranger was a potential enemy, yet the welcome, provision, and protection regularly extended to the unfamiliar one witnesses to the sacredness of the responsibility."[12] It would indeed be sacred work to welcome, provide resources, and protect the voice and time of the staff. By letting go of meeting traditions that keep faculty and staff separate and giving staff opportunities to lead, by investing in the vocational development of staff, and by fostering an environment in which all are encouraged to contribute their judgment to decision-making, schools can empower staff and strengthen the learning community. With academic hospitality, staff and faculty find they are not strangers but co-learners discerning new ways of being a theological institution together.

Welcoming Across Boundaries

It is time that we let go of hierarchical traditions that separate faculty from staff when they no longer serve us. Though we have made significant progress in my institution, in the past it was not uncommon for the same information to be presented twice, once in the faculty meeting and once in the staff meeting, as if there were a policy against all parties being in the same room! Aside from the inefficiencies of such a structure, this sort of segregated meeting is a hindrance to building a successful team and a successful strategy for innovation. I am not suggesting we abandon all segregated meetings. There will always be spaces in which confidential information should only be shared with a select few, and there are certainly benefits to having spaces for employees in like fields. (A meeting can also be inefficient by having too many people involved!) However, when faced with a potential program innovation or shift in how we do business, if we fail to bring together key perspectives simply out of institutional convention, we lose the opportunity to understand the full scope of the venture and spot its weaknesses. Instead, we can empower staff by embracing more porous barriers and find strength in joining together in common discernment and purpose.

Staff are particularly adept at understanding the implications of a major decision. We know the details of course schedules, catalogs, handbooks, and websites. We attend to student questions, are keepers of policy, handle enrollment data, and facilitate co-curricular requirements. We also know

12. Mutch, "Leading," 188.

how these pieces contribute to the overall structure of student programs. A lived wisdom comes with working with students in this capacity. Like many other staff, my work includes both large scale and detailed responsibilities. I have been a part of a major curriculum overhaul, multiple new program implementations, partnerships with several entities, self-studies and accreditation visits, and assessment structure overhauls in addition to the daily tasks of the academic office. Such variation allows staff to maintain both a microscopic view and a macroscopic view, both of which are critical for setting new institutional direction.

In times of change, it is imperative that we incorporate these perspectives. While institutions may preserve faculty-only voting structures, they should certainly open dialogue within meetings of business. Institutions striving for academic hospitality may choose to forgo the "faculty" designation, labeling them simply "business meetings" to remind that staff members present will bring their perspective. Similarly, in lieu of regular staff meetings, mixed role committees may be appropriate for addressing issues of process or logistics. The goal is not to add more meetings to the already full plate of staff members (or faculty for that matter) but to be strategic about which meetings would benefit from their judgment and including those critical voices from the start. The criterion for attendance and voice does not rely then on the membership of the individual, faculty or staff, but rather on the perspective that one brings to the subject at hand. Institutions will need to adjust as appropriate to their own context, but the academic hospitality of extending invitations to staff in institutional or program decision-making meetings is a necessity for institutions to flourish.

Protecting Staff Voice

Allowing space at the table for staff is not enough. Senior administrators must empower them by promoting and protecting their voices within that space. Mutch argues that a primary responsibility of the academic dean is to cultivate academic hospitality through "conversation, community, and compassion."[13] Deans are key players in creating cultures of conversation, encouraging contribution from all, and establishing norms to discourage talking over and other habits that stifle dialogue. We do well to remember that "true conversation is marked by humility, identifying the other as a necessary participant in one's own learning."[14] If we are committed to being a learning community, we will allow ourselves to be shaped by others—even

13. Mutch, "Leading," 189.
14. Mutch, "Leading," 191.

if the others are not traditional scholars—and the more we are accustomed to hearing each other's voices, the more we can focus on the important tasks ahead of us.

Voicing that which is difficult to hear is a key aspect of leadership, one that staff enact each time they have a finger on the pulse of the institution and provide a challenge to the status quo. Receiving and considering such challenges, however, is a key characteristic of an academically hospitable institution. Schools must be comfortable with and encourage interjections that disrupt or are unpopular; these can be profoundly important. In fact, allowing dissenting voices to arise "is the foundation of an organization that is willing to experiment and learn."[15] While protections exist for tenured faculty (even tenure-track positions may be hesitant to voice dissent), there are few for staff. It becomes the responsibility of the dean to acknowledge that opinions may conflict but that the community considers and values each. For staff, speaking up can feel like putting oneself in a precarious position, but crucial to leadership is "turning up the heat" of the room so that participants are fully engaged and take ownership of the group outcome.[16] Having the support of their dean enables staff to step into that leadership with greater confidence. Not all staff contributions will be subversive. On the contrary, including staff perspective is sure to provide insight into student-centered innovation and unleash creative energy. They can be some of the students' greatest advocates and some of the most committed to the school's mission. Still we should not be afraid of conflict. It can be quite healthy. When dissenting views are in dialogue, issues are exposed and real progress can take place. It is possible to balance heated dialogue with compassion and humility.[17] These are not mutually exclusive. On the contrary, we may find this is sacred ground.

Providing Time for Development and Call

Staff are empowered when schools invest in their professional development and sense of call. Though there are reflections on the distinct vocational call of chief academic officers, there has been little comparable attention given to support staff.[18] Similarly, while ATS has demonstrated commitment to staff development through conference and workshop opportunities over

15. Heifetz and Laurie, "Work of Leadership," 129.

16. Heifetz et al., *Practice of Adaptive Leadership*, 159–61.

17. See Garrido, *Redeeming Conflict*, 89–111, for more on emotion and conflict. The entire text is pertinent to this conversation.

18. See, for example, Graham, "Vocation," 63–74.

the years, the standards addressing their development are thin.[19] Schools that want to empower their staff should encourage their participation in the Student Personnel Administrators Network conference and other ATS sponsored workshops, as well as joining other professional networks and learning opportunities. Reading, either for best practices or devotionally, as a staff community is another way of promoting development. Just as faculty have scholarship expectations, there must be a mutual commitment between staff and institution to staff training and scholarship. These not only benefit the individual but also keep the school within best practices and enhance institutional learning.

To reap the most benefit for staff and school, staff must have a sense of God's calling within their day-to-day work. They must find meaning and connection between God's calling, institutional mission, and their role within the institution.[20] To foster this, institutions must protect staff time by providing space for reflection and by keeping workloads manageable. With diversified responsibilities ever increasing, so does the noise that drowns out the voice of God within. Increased collaborative work (tasks that require connecting with more and more internal and external constituencies) is a by-product of rapid change and global technologies and can lead to staff burnout.[21] Much of collaborative work that occupies staff time involves email and answering questions from students, instructors, and other staff. It is the busy-work of the day, and out of proportion, it can pull one away from important projects and inhibit the reflection and bigger picture thinking that comes during quiet downtime.[22] Time to think is not just a necessity for deans and faculty but for leaders at all levels of authority. Individuals are refreshed and institutions benefit from focused work time. Furthermore, schools need authentic leaders who live integrated, balanced lives that allow time for self, families, and larger communities in addition to vocations.[23]

19. See Graham, "Evolution," 97–118. See also ATS, "General Institutional Standards," for standards regarding staff (23), library staff (11), and general personnel (25).

20. For an exploration of vocation and calling in administrative positions that is as applicable to support staff as top administrators, see Garrido, *Redeeming Administration*. Garrido makes the case that administration is a true ministry. The staff team at my institution used this text as the start of our monthly meetings and found it affirming for our work together.

21. Cross et al., "Collaboration without Burnout," 134–35; Cross et al., "Collaborative Overload," 76–77.

22. Note the distinction between the collaborative work in Mutch, "Leading," 190–91, which leads to meaningful collegial conversation, and the everyday, mundane collaborative work of emails and phone calls found in Cross et al., "Collaboration without Burnout," 134–35.

23. George et al, "Discovering Your Authentic Leadership," 136–37.

When we have time for rest and reflection, we are better able to lead with integrity. Theological schools encourage boundaries and self-care for our students; we should encourage the same for employees of all levels with our communal practices and institutional structures.

Protected time becomes especially important in times of institutional strain when schools may be inclined to say "yes" to more initiatives in the hopes of drawing in more students. We do not always know which initiatives will prove fruitful, but we can be discerning and choose carefully so that we limit undue burden for staff with little payoff for the institution. Not only is it acceptable to say "no" to a new idea or another exception, it can demonstrate a positive commitment to a greater value. Institutions may not be able to provide a staff equivalent to faculty sabbaticals, but they can better support them by simplifying programs, revamping inefficient administrative structures, and streamlining processes. These adjustments can trim down the excessive collaborative work to allow time for the more meaningful collegial conversation. This is a higher-level collaborative work that better supports students and fosters faculty and staff teamwork. Supporting staff to expend their energies where it counts and streamline practices that waste time will give them the bandwidth, the slowness of breath, to better discern God's call on their life and work and to put it into practice.

CONCLUSION: ASSESSMENT AS ACADEMIC HOSPITALITY

In my institution's last self-study, the evaluation committee rightly pointed out that we did not have the culture of assessment that we needed to grow. As a result, our dean of faculty created a three-person assessment taskforce. In addition to traveling to and learning from two institutions known for their understanding and execution of quality program assessment, two of us continued our assessment education with a master's-level course, a resource available to us as a seminary embedded in a university. As a team, we revamped our assessment plans, implementing a major new component: a faculty jury process in which small interdisciplinary teams collectively evaluate our programs by judging student artifacts against a rubric. We close faculty juries with a large debrief of findings and discern communally the changes that we will make to address problem areas we have uncovered.

At our last session, I found myself at the head of the table looking out at the room full of faculty—many of whom have been my own professors—drawing out the conversation, helping to make connections, allowing concerns to come to the surface so that they could be tested, and steering our group to the task at hand, the purpose behind it, and ultimately to our program outcomes. I left the meeting feeling refreshed despite our hard work, knowing that faculty had felt similarly invigorated by the process.

This group learning would not have been possible had we held to past barriers between faculty and staff. Instead, our dean recognized staff leadership capacity, encouraged our professional development, and provided the opportunity to exercise leadership and have a significant voice in the direction of the school. It has been a learning process for all, and we are finding new ways of working together to tackle issues before us. We are beginning this process, but my hope is that this shift in culture will continue to be fruitful. The challenges facing theological schools are significant, and schools that embrace staff leadership to form collaborative teams and hospitable academic communities with faculty and senior administrators will thrive.

BIBLIOGRAPHY

Aleshire, Daniel O. "Fifty Years of Accrediting Theological Schools." *Theological Education* 49.1 (2014) 63–80.

Ancona, Deborah, et al. "In Praise of the Incomplete Leader." *Harvard Business Review* 85.2 (2007) 92–100.

Association of Theological Schools (ATS). "Approved Exceptions and Experiments." Online. https://ats.edu/member-schools/approved-exceptions-and-experiments.

——. "General Institutional Standards." Online. https://www.ats.edu/uploads/accrediting/documents/general-institutional-standards.pdf.

Bennett, John B. *Academic Life: Hospitality, Ethics, and Spirituality.* Bolton, MA: Anker, 2003.

Billman, Kathleen D., and Bruce C. Birch. *C(H)AOS Theory: Reflections of Chief Academic Officers in Theological Education.* Grand Rapids: Eerdmans, 2011.

Cross, Rob, et al. "Collaborative Overload." *Harvard Business Review* 94.1 (2016) 74–79.

Cross, Rob, et al. "Collaboration without Burnout." *Harvard Business Review* 96.4 (2018) 134–37.

Garrido, Ann M. *Redeeming Administration: 12 Spiritual Habits for Catholic Leaders in Parishes, Schools, Religious Communities, and Other Institutions.* Notre Dame: Ave Maria, 2013.

——. *Redeeming Conflict: 12 Habits for Christian Leaders.* Notre Dame: Ave Maria, 2016.

George, Bill, et al. "Discovering Your Authentic Leadership." *Harvard Business Review* 85.2 (2007) 129–38.

Ginsberg, Benjamin. *The Fall of the Faculty: The Rise of the All-Administrative University and Why It Matters.* New York: Oxford University Press, 2011.

Graham, Stephen R. "The Evolution of Leadership Education at ATS." *Theological Education* 52.1 (2018) 97–118.

————. "The Vocation of the Academic Dean." In *C(H)AOS Theory: Reflections of Chief Academic Officers in Theological Education*, edited by Kathleen D. Billman and Bruce C. Birch, 63–74. Grand Rapids: Eerdmans, 2011.

Harvard Business Review. *On Leadership*. HBR's 10 Must Reads. Boston: Harvard Business Review Press, 2011.

Heifetz, Ronald A., and Donald L. Laurie. "The Work of Leadership." *Harvard Business Review* 75.1 (1997) 124–34.

Heifetz, Ronald A., et al. *The Practice of Adaptive Leadership: Tools and Tactics for Changing Your Organization and the World*. Boston: Harvard Business Press, 2009.

McLean, Jeanne P. *Leading from the Center: The Emerging Role of the Chief Academic Office in Theological Schools*. Atlanta: Scholars, 1999.

Mutch, Barbara Horkoff. "Leading as an Act of Academic Hospitality." In *C(H)AOS Theory: Reflections of Chief Academic Officers in Theological Education*, edited by Kathleen D. Billman and Bruce C. Birch, 188–97. Grand Rapids: Eerdmans, 2011.

Palmer, Parker J., and Arthur Zajonc. *The Heart of Higher Education: A Call to Renewal*. San Francisco: Jossey-Bass, 2010.

CHAPTER 12

Radical Hospitality

Queering Admissions and Student Services

KATHERINE H. SMITH
and AMY E. STEELE

HOSPITALITY TENDS TO BE a universal religious value inviting institutions and individuals to loosen their grip around the limits and boundaries of community. In "The Academy and Hospitality," John B. Bennett, Provost Emeritus of Quinnipiac University, claims that "a key virtue for the academy is hospitality—the extension of self in order to welcome the other by sharing and receiving intellectual resources and insights."[1] He goes on to say that, "Hospitality is often taken to mean a bland congeniality. As theologian Henri Nouwen notes, for many if not most of us, hospitality suggests 'tea parties, bland conversations, and a general atmosphere of coziness.'" Bennett and Nouwen point toward the purpose in our naming this work *radical hospitality*, that is, to signal sites, in addition to the classroom where possibilities for meaningful 'sharing and receiving' can become an eschatological vision of engagement across difference, an ethical aim of theological education. Queering admissions and student services, we argue, requires an intellectual and social hospitality that is both honest and vulnerable, welcoming and teachable. It is both a wise administrative practice and a profoundly theological act, urging us toward the possibility of a realized eschatology here and now.

---

1. Bennett, "Academy and Hospitality," 23–35.

This chapter attends specifically to the experience of white students and students of color who identify as Lesbian, Gay, Bisexual, Trans*, and Queer (LGBTQ+) in our theological schools.[2] We begin by characterizing the notion of hospitality and note it as a form of innovation for institutions who are challenged to re-discover its communities and their needs. We also examine the language of "queer" as a contested space, seeking to reclaim the term from its historically derogatory uses, underscoring its doubly-relevant call to offer genuine welcome to all God's children and to open ourselves to practices that may be new, different, and emergent. Using our own setting as a laboratory, we reflect on possibilities for wise practice while acknowledging that all of us are called to continual renewal and transformation. We seek to pay particular attention to the range of theological and ecclesial commitments that guide and inform the work of ATS-affiliated institutions, offering resources for those interested in strengthening their current practices around LGBTQ+ students in diverse and complex settings and developing institutional partners to explore and implement this work. This includes a series of questions and recommendations for individuals and teams invested in organizational growth and change.

THE PERSONAL IS POLITICAL

Black feminist Audre Lorde's phrase the "personal is political" is a helpful starting point for those whose embodiment falls within and beyond the queer continuum. For Lorde, observing "the implications of our lives" has to do with "scrutinizing" how our humanity impacts the way in which we work, the values of that work, and the relationships that comprise our work.[3] For the authors of this essay, that kind of personal scrutinizing is central to how we determine equity in our work and vital in our commitment to radical hospitality as an ethical norm and a professional virtue. It begins by understanding our proximity to power and the constructive ways in which we use privilege.

2. This chapter emerges from workshops led at previous gatherings of the Student Personnel Administrators Network (SPAN, 2017) and at the Wild Goose Festival (2018). We want to recognize particularly the contributions of Damien Domenack, a Master of Divinity student at Vanderbilt Divinity School and Admissions Fellow (2018–19), who helped to craft and co-facilitate the session at Wild Goose (with Amy Steele) and has expanded our imagination and work on this topic. Phillis I. Sheppard recommended several outstanding resources for the SPAN presentation and helped us understand how to name our location within this work.

3. Lorde, *Burst of Light*, 13–14.

Both of us come to this work through our experiences with students, close friends, colleagues, and family. We have witnessed the joy, pain, longing, and hope that surfaces in spaces where multiple sexual identities are welcomed or marginalized, sometimes simultaneously. In our professional roles, we are among those who symbolically and administratively stand at the institutional gates, tasked with inviting in and creating space for the myriad voices that broaden and enliven our shared life. Yet neither of us directly inhabit the identities we are centering here.

Katherine enters the conversation after more than a decade of administration in ATS institutions, both ones in which LGBTQ+ voices are centered and those in which denominational and theological commitments limit channels for LGBTQ+ conversation and engagement. She is daily reminded, as one who does not identify on the LGBTQ+ spectrum, of the great danger and destructiveness in appropriating identities or presuming others' experience. This concern rightly causes anxiety for many ATS professionals who provide support for students and requires, on a personal and professional level, continually questioning and reimagining the scripts that have informed one's own social location. As a straight, white, cisgender pastor in the Presbyterian Church (USA), Katherine's experience of theological education is challenged, enlarged, and enlivened by interlocutors whose experiences have been very different. This chapter is one way to begin exploring the challenges and implications of using one's position and privilege as an institutional advocate.

Amy enters the conversation after almost two decades in administration and ordained ministry (Baptist and Methodist churches primarily) and after completing a doctorate in religion. As an administrator, teacher, and pastor who is a black, heterosexual, cisgender woman, she daily considers what it means to navigate her own identity while making space for others. She, too, is careful about presumptions, appropriations, speaking for, rather than with those who embody LGBTQ+ identities. What she has learned, most acutely from especially transgender students who fight for their right to be seen and heard as they understand themselves to be, is that radical hospitality has to do with seeing *the person and hearing their narrative*. So much of the way we are taught to navigate the world rests upon understanding the world in binary categories (male/female, black/white). These categories, while providing us some meaning, often circumnavigate our ability to truly see the revelation of personhood that shows up as a kaleidoscope of gender, racial/ethnic, and sexual identity.

While some might dismiss this conversation as progressive politics and blind acceptance of a liberal agenda in higher education, we understand radical hospitality as the incarnational gospel. We connect this invitation to the one Jesus embodies and extends as a sign of grace, redemption, and hope. For those struggling to understand dynamic presentations of human genders and sexualities and to those more advanced in their studies, this is a challenge to meet human need with an incarnational grace, to understand radical hospitality as the blurred vision of a new heaven and a new earth barely discernible in the present and yet emerging before our eyes.

INCARNATIONAL THEOLOGY AS LIVED PRACTICE

It is our contention that radical hospitality for LGBTQ+ students is both incarnational—insofar as it attests that God is made known to us in and through human flesh—and teleological, pointing us toward a fuller and more realized vision of God's beloved community. Parker Palmer helps us here. He argues that a cold, detached, purely objective relationship to learning is not helpful, but rather 'objectivism along with an inward capacity for relatedness is the key.'[4] What is useful for the academy, especially for the work of student personnel professionals, is an invitation to listen, to engage, to respond to the emergent needs of students whom we have invited to come learn and prepare for the future of religious leadership. This radical hospitality urges toward relationships with new people, places, and concepts that might disrupt our comfortable understanding in pursuit of a wider good and a more sustainable future for us all.

By queering admissions and student services we are intentionally resisting notions that *all* of our students and therefore *all* of our analysis and consideration of them follow a white heteronormative template. Instead we are suggesting that queer identity and its facets of personhood complicated by race and ethnicity, class, the experience of being a first-generation graduate student, etc., warrant us risking new conversations, research, and practices so that all students *feel* and *contribute* to a sense of radical welcome and affirmation at our institutions. We use queer interchangeably with LGBTQ+ in this chapter, aware that sometimes queer has "come to denote not only an emerging politics but also a new cohort of academics working in programs primarily in the humanities centered around social and cultural criticism."[5]

Practicing radical hospitality is a way of living into the full incarnational realities of our students and colleagues and thus ourselves. We discover human and spiritual potential not yet realized when we intentionally allow 'queer' students to disrupt our prior notions. Or, put more positively,

4. Palmer, "Community," 20–25.

5. Cohen, "Punks, Bulldaggers, and Welfare Queens," 22.

we are becoming more "cognizant of our students' multi-subjectivities, the array of identities that encompass race, ethnicity, gender, sexuality, religious/spirituality, and class. Stratifying identities potentially fragments our students' multifaceted selves in ways that undermine our desire to enlighten and empower."[6] Our awareness challenges heteronormative assumptions and expectations, resisting notions that *all* of our students/audiences and therefore all of our analysis and consideration should follow a white heteronormative template. We know and embrace that queer identity and its facets of personhood complicated by race, ethnicity, class, mental health, family background, etc. warrant us risking new conversation, research, and practices so that all students feel and contribute to a sense of radical hospitality.

RADICAL HOSPITALITY AS A LEADERSHIP CHALLENGE

Radical hospitality for LGBTQ+ students in our theological schools involves, as Ron Heifetz and Marty Linsky term it, both technical problems and adaptive challenges.[7] Technical problems can be solved with information and practices already in hand and are typically easier to implement on the ground. Adaptive challenges require new learning, innovation, and new patterns of behavior. Some of the questions addressed here may be resolved in the space of a committee meeting or conversation with staff colleagues or senior administrators. Others get at the heart of institutional identity, deeply-held beliefs, and ecclesial commitments that will require different approaches and timelines. Our ability to engage adaptive challenges will determine the course of our institution(s).

We all start from different places. For some, the theological language around hospitality for the LGBTQ+ community is already deeply embedded in the DNA of the institution. For others, history, theology, and context have limited engagement on these issues to discussions of compliance and equal opportunity. For all of us, a deeper reflection of our institutional ethos requires disrupting entrenched norms and power structures in ways that can cause discomfort and challenge the status quo. We move, as Sharon Daloz Parks describes it, "from a familiar but inadequate equilibrium—through disequilibrium—to a more adequate equilibrium."[8]

As with most things, we are confined by our limits. Every ATS-affiliated institution manages a unique and complex set of connections, opportunities,

6. Clark, "Are We Family?," 269.

7. Heifetz and Linsky, *Leadership on the Line.*

8. Parks, *Leadership Can Be Taught,* 9.

and constraints. An internal audit can help institutions identify the limits of their hospitality, which may not always be obvious. Naming limits and assumptions are helpful assessment measures that keep institutions honest to the emerging truth they experience through their students. By way of example, our current institution does not provide housing; however, our institutional checklist of questions that affect our hospitality includes factors related to housing. In thinking about and naming our limits, we can, with some sense of integrity, provide students with information that allows them to make the best possible choices. Other questions include inquiries about: (1) representation—how are the people we wish to welcome represented in our promotional materials? How does the faculty, staff, and administration reflect a commitment to radical welcome; (2) power—do those who hold power represent a broad spectrum of humanity? How do we check for heteronormative paternalism that sometimes maintains the very structures it wishes to challenge; and (3) dialogue—do we have conversations with LGBTQ+ students and alumni? Is there openness to explore the concerns and challenges they have or have had?

While institutions enter a conversation on radical hospitality at different places, there are common assumptions that can hinder the efficacy of its language and practices:

- Institutions that care about difference often assume they know/are aware of all the difference that exists in their community (or at least the difference that matters). We are often not aware of the nuances, and why they matter, so without really trying, we operate with an "essentialist identity politics," which often "reinforces hegemonic power structures [norms] rather than dismantling them."[9] This may at times look like assuming what "women identifying students" need or what all the black students need. We have better practices when we note differences among women, cisgender and transgender, American and immigrant, first generation graduate school, etc.

- Institutions sometimes assume that blanket statements about human dignity and the institution's values toward humanity are received as anti-racism, anti-sexism, or gender-inclusive; but unless these things are explicitly stated and backed up by tangible policy and action, they are often not heard by those they wish to welcome. Unless institutional commitments around such issues are engrained in the culture, they will likely be unrecognized.[10]

9. Johnson and Henderson, *Black Queer Studies*, 4.

10. We are particularly indebted here to the work of Domenack, for naming this critical element of institutional culture.

- Institutions often assume that because folks are teaching and preaching radical ideas that they are also practicing them and advocating for these practices in community.

- Institutions do not often gauge or address how radical welcome and its practices unnecessarily falls on the shoulders of people of color, and that this particular kind of 'disruptive' work bears additional existential weight on the minds, bodies, and spirits of these administrators, faculty, and students creating issues of workload and compensation.[11]

- Institutions are often unaware of the 'destabilizing' effects of this work and how to attend to a community that constantly feels under the threat of deconstruction.

Part of the adaptive challenge is to allow our students to teach us ways in which "hospitality is yet to be discovered."[12] We borrow here the language of Michaela Frischherz in her thesis, "The Possibility of Queer Hospitality" using theory from Jacques Derrida and Luce Irigaray. Frischherz writes that, "hospitality as 'yet to be discovered' is certainly a risk; however, this undetermined and vague terrain, where language is new and difficult to understand, might be the precise site where risks plays out advantageously. Much like queer, hospitality can never be delimited in advance precisely because we do not know when, where, or what the Other may hold."[13] Our students, so often the driving force for institutional change, have been teaching us that in some ways, hospitality is yet to be discovered because "we do not know when, where, or what the Other may hold" or need.

REIMAGINING INSTITUTIONAL PRACTICES

With this awareness in mind, we now clarify some of the experimental strategies we have used to move our community toward more radical welcome and engage some of these assumptions and missteps and address them in constructive ways. We know that student services do not exist in a silo, and we depend heavily on staff and faculty colleagues, as well as students who lead by example, urging us forward and challenging our norms and

---

11. The recent scholarship of Richard J. Reddick, Associate Professor in Educational Leadership and Policy at the University of Texas at Austin, is particularly notable for exploring the experiences of black faculty and faculty of color at predominantly white institutions.

12. Frischherz, "Possibility of Queer Hospitality," 11.

13. Frischherz, "Possibility of Queer Hospitality," 11.

expectations.[14] As in all things, we do not always recognize our own blind spots. Finding a community of voices—within or beyond your institution—who can ask different questions and open up perspectives and possibilities beyond what we've already considered is essential to breaking out of heteronormative hegemony.

One way in which Vanderbilt Divinity School has codified its values is through our Purposes and Commitments statement, which guides and informs the curriculum, student life, and recruitment practices. The school is held accountable to this document through a Living the Commitments document, co-written by students, faculty, and staff and periodically updated to reflect an evolving understanding of our shared life and lived practice. In recent years, for example, this has included greater attention to language supporting trans* identified students, those living with disabilities, and a deeper reflection on the intersectional nature of our identities.

With our values and commitments intact, we begin to think strategically about LGBTQ+ hospitality in our recruiting, admissions and financial aid, student life, worship, and all the places where our roles as student services professionals impact the lives of our students. We affirm the following underlying practices in radical hospitality:

- Welcoming and affirming all humanity as the kaleidoscope of God;

- Engaging, challenging, making space for disagreement, constructive critique, and prophetic practice;

- Attending to the intellectual, emotional, spiritual, and professional lives of the community;

- Assessing regularly and improving upon practice, statements, and common understandings of what it means to be a theologically invested community.

We set benchmarks for who we hope to become as a community and how we plan to get there. For example, we set aside a half day during New Student Orientation to talk about how we engage our expectations around community life and Living the Commitments. In conversation with the

14. In this work, we are particularly indebted to our colleagues in the Carpenter Program in Religion, Gender, and Sexuality at Vanderbilt Divinity School, who for more than twenty years have been leaders in fostering conversation about these topics within and beyond the walls of the school. Staff colleagues, including Lyndsey Godwin, have been critical supports for LGBTQ+ students and have called in our community toward greater hospitality and creative imagination. Current professors AJ Levine, Ellen Armour, Bonnie Miller-McLemore, Emilie M. Townes, Phillis I. Sheppard, Annalisa Azzoni, and so many others have been integral in shaping how we both talk and live into these ideals.

faculty and student services staff, we launched in fall 2018 a mandatory first-year course that seeks to thread the Commitments through our class-room experiences and our common life.[15] We extend special invitations to worship and liturgical leadership to those whose experience, they report, often find themselves on the margins of the community.[16] We respond in a timely and pastorally sensitive way to listen deeply and improve upon what we know and tweak our practices.

The following list offers suggestions for institutional reflection and practice.[17] If your institution isn't able to attend to all of these questions right now, we encourage you to consider which ones you *can* engage and start there.

A CHECKLIST TO FACILITATE INSTITUTIONAL CONVERSATIONS

Institutional Policies & Partners

- In what ways does our institution articulate hospitality in its state-ments and policies? Where might we deepen our statements into bet-ter practices? Who was at the table to write them?

- Does our institutional mission statement adequately and honestly cap-ture and reflect our priorities and commitments around hospitality?

- In what ways are marginalized voices empowered to speak (question, disagree, challenge)? In what ways to do we engage these voices (com-pliment, acknowledge, agree, challenge)?

- Name the places of contention in your institution. Are the challenges theological? practical? financial? denominational? technical? adaptive?

15. As the frontispiece of the Vanderbilt Divinity School curriculum, the first-year course is intentionally joined with the second (Field Education) and third (Senior Sem-inar) stages of the MDiv degree, and with the Project 360 statement for the MTS degree, which is intended to link a student's academic plan of study and vocational objectives.

16. A few of the ways in which Vanderbilt Divinity School specifically seeks to honor the experiences of LGBTQ+ members of our community in worship are through the annual Trans Day of Remembrance, services led by our LGBTQ+ student organiza-tion (GABLE), and a GABLE stole ritual during Commencement Worship.

17. While academic services are beyond the scope of this chapter, we acknowledge that this list is only a starting point for much larger conversations that touch on *all* areas of the student experience. Faculty hiring, targeted curricula and concentration options, diversifying syllabi, and exposing students to a wide variety of thinkers and experiences will be essential and complementing considerations to the student life factors named here.

- Are faculty and staff familiar with terminology related to gender and sexuality (e.g., asexual, gender fluid, non-binary, etc.) and do they have adequate opportunities and support to seek further education as needed?

- Are sexuality and gender identity expressly protected in your institution's equal opportunity and affirmative action statements?

- Does your institution provide an environment in which gender and sexuality can be discussed openly?

- Are anonymous, safe, and accessible channels of reporting available for incidents or concerns affecting LGBTQ+ persons on your campus?

- For embedded institutions: does the school maintain strong relationships and open lines of communication with centers for LGBTQ+ life, student health/well-being, and psychological counseling? Who are your internal and external conversation partners on these topics?

- For independent seminaries: what denominational resources, local organizations and affiliated institutions, and other external resources (e.g., Association of Theological Schools, Forum for Theological Education), are available to you that might help to deepen and enrich current conversations and practices?

- What might new or existing Field Education partners have to teach us or guide us in this work? What has been helpful to them in moving toward these kinds of innovations? What has been unhelpful?

Recruitment

- Are those who recruit for your institution—staff, students, alumni—familiar with the theolog(ies), polity, and practices that currently govern your institution's stance on LGBTQ+ issues? What additional training might be needed? Are these statements public?

- What policies guide, limit, or invite deeper engagement in your office with LGBTQ+ students? Are student perspectives on the recruitment experience sought after at regular intervals, and are they taken seriously by administration?

- Who are the most visible faces of your institution? Do they have the tools and training to make visitors and guests across the LGBTQ+ spectrum feel heard and welcomed?

- Do your current recruitment practices include spaces, events, and or-ganizations where LGBTQ+ persons are well-represented?

- Do marketing materials reflect the actual student experience and de-mographics of your institution or are they aspirational? Are print and digital media authentic to the school and its population?

Admissions

- Is gender a required field on your application for admission? If so, what language is used?[18]

- If an applicant self-discloses their sexuality on an application, what protocols govern how that disclosure is discussed or handled by those with access to the materials?

- Do essay questions and other application elements provide opportu-nity for students to engage the institution's particular theological com-mitments through the lens of their experience? For example, we have asked students to read the Living the Commitments statement and to explain what is compelling to them and why.

Financial Aid

- Do the LGBTQ+ students in your institution have access to the same financial resources (denominational support, institutional scholar-ships, etc.) as other members of the student community? If not, how does the school recognize or address economic disadvantage for this and other vulnerable populations?

- Is your institution aware of possible differences in average debt loads associated with LGBTQ+ students? Have you explored agencies and resources that have funded and/or offered internships and additional funding for LGBTQ+ students?

---

18. As an institution that receives Title IV funding, Vanderbilt is required to report gender identity in concordance with current federal language. Though we are unable to broaden the available categories, framing the language provides an important signal for applicants.

Worship

- Does your institution encourage the use of inclusive voices and inclusive language in worship for God and human beings? To the best of your ability does the community practice using non-binary and expansive language for the sacred in music, preaching, and liturgy?

- Who is planning? Does your institution encourage and recruit a wide variety of representation on the worship committee? Are those persons empowered to speak and create services that do not diminish their real experiences?

- What resources are you using to develop liturgy? Have you curated a variety of hymnals or genres of music from which to choose?

- Are you moving beyond heteronormative resources that imagine a continuum of human relationship, family configurations, gendered experiences?

- Do you invite a broad, but responsible use of scripture and other sacred writings that support the goodness of God's creation and acts of love, justice, and mercy found in LGBTQ+ stories and theological musings?

- Are LGBTQ+ students encouraged to share their gifts and talents with the community in regular weekly worship? Are they asked to preach, when appropriate? (Note: we require students to have had at least one preaching class, before preaching in chapel).

- Are there intentioned processes for planning special days of communal celebration related to gender and sexuality? (e.g., Trans Day of Remembrance Service, a service that commemorates the lives of Trans* persons who have been murdered or Trans Day of Celebration, a service that commemorates those who are living and thriving as Transgender).

- Are theology, ethics, homiletics, and/or liturgics faculty, for example, willing to offer workshops on language, being, selection of scripture and music, which honors all humanity?

- What assessments have the worship planning committee developed to assess its work?

Student Life

- What are LGBTQ+ students saying about their sense of connection to the community? Are there graduated approaches the institution can take for first-year students, second-year, etc. to help students feel a greater sense of belonging and connectivity?

- What benefits are provided for Trans* identifying students through your affiliated student health insurance plan? How is this information communicated to Trans* students?

- Where do your students tend to seek out medical care? If located on or near campus, have you discussed their office practices and policies for care across the sexual spectrum and for multiple gender identities? For example, are Trans* identified students able to check in and be called by their preferred name and pronouns? Is regular primary care available that meets the needs of diverse populations?

- If students are seeking medical care, are there "buddies" (e.g., Trans Buddy Program[19]) that can assist them in getting the resources they need?

- What resources are available in your local community for LGBTQ+ students? Is a community resource list easily accessible to students?

- Are there support groups on campus? If not, how might your institution encourage these students to start support groups? (e.g., Queer Students of Color, LGBTQ+ Theologians/Seminarians, LatinX Seminarians, etc.)

- Does your institution permit students to select their preferred name for use on class rosters and digital learning platforms?

- Are preferred pronouns regularly requested and utilized in and beyond the classroom, and modeled by those in leadership? (e.g., "My name is Dean Steele, and I use she/her/hers pronouns") Are there communal partners who can help describe and implement these changes as educational opportunity?

- According to the CDC, a positive school climate has been associated with decreased depression, suicidal feelings, and substance use among LGBTQ+ students.[20] Are campus mental health resources for students and training for staff available at your institution? If not, is your institution willing to invest in these resources?

19. See "Program for LGBTQ Health."
20. See "Lesbian, Gay, Bisexual, and Transgender Health."

- What processes and procedures are in place for students with addiction issues? Does the institution respond to substance abuse as a disciplinary matter only? Are there accountability measures that mandate substance abuse treatment and proof of completion as a requirement for return to the program?

- If there are episodes of violence toward LGBTQ+ students on campus, are campus or local police officers trained to understand the unique threats to trans* students and black and brown queer students, in particular, and respond in ways that these students need to feel safe and protected? Are there any trained staff willing to advocate and/or help transact a police report with appropriate pronouns, names, etc.

- Are there opportunities for LGBTQ+ students to invite to campus guest lecturers, who represent them and model intellectual curiosity and sound theological scholarship? Are there faculty advisors who might assist them in the process?

- Are there resources that theological librarians can assist LGBTQ+ students with on research papers that query religion, gender, and sexuality?

- Can the institution provide listening forums to create a culture of understanding for students to discuss their identity and the ways in which they struggle and celebrate who they are?

- To encourage whole body-mind-spirit wellness does your institution invest in opportunities for students to honor the body with movement and meditative practices like Tai Chi, embodied prayer, yoga, etc.?

- Are there resources (like film, novels, short stories, poetry, visual art, comedy, etc.) you can use to encourage community-wide discussion around understanding human difference? Is there a team of people comprised of students, faculty, and staff willing to develop these opportunities?

Housing

- What accommodations are provided for on-campus housing or recommendations for off-campus housing for LGBTQ+ students?[21]

21. For a reference template, see "Lesbian, Gay, Bisexual, Transgender, Queer, & Intersex Life," a webpage built by Vanderbilt's K. C. Potter Center for LGBTQ+ Life.

- Are all-gender restrooms and shower facilities available for students who may not feel comfortable sharing restrooms labeled only "male" or "female"?

- How is housing assigned or chosen? What are the avenues by which students can raise confidential concerns or questions related to their housing environment?

- What housing accommodations are provided for LGBTQ+ students on immersion trips or in global learning programs? Can we normalize these questions in applications for these kinds of opportunities? Have you assessed the risk for LGBTQ+ students traveling abroad?

Assessment

- What are some of the signs and symbols that have made students and visitors feel (un)welcome at your institution?

- Do our current assessment practices adequately capture the voices of students who may not be in the majority at your institution?

- How do you currently measure institutional effectiveness around hospitality and inclusion?

- Are there routine evaluative measures to understand communal reluctance to change around policies addressing LGBTQ+ student concerns? How would you categorize those? Are these roadblocks theological, practical, financial, etc.?

- Is there institutional history around addressing LGBTQ+ concerns? Are there constructive ways to acknowledge that history as a part of the institutional narrative?

- Where do you hope to be in five, ten, or twenty years on these conversations? What local, national, international resources might you partner with in some way to help move the institution in its practices? Where will you meet reluctance or downright refusal to implement change? Can you articulate these concerns and address them while maintaining your commitment to change?

FINAL THOUGHTS

In developing achievement markers and assessment loops, each of our institutions must remember to ask: Whose voices will speak to our institutional effectiveness in these objectives? How do we measure progress? What timeline is realistic and appropriate to ensure that we are moving with deliberate but thoughtful speed? What—and who—are we still missing? How do we live into the challenges of human community and administrative practices? As you and your colleagues undertake these important conversations, we hope you will uncover new invitations to listen, to engage, and to respond in ways that prove life-giving to you as a student services professional, as well as to all of those whom you serve. May we together offer hospitality to all God's children and discover with joy how our institutions move closer to the kin-dom God desires for us.

BIBLIOGRAPHY

Bennett, John B. "The Academy and Hospitality." *CrossCurrents* 50.1–2 (2000) 23–35.

Clark, Keith. "Are We Family? Pedagogy and the Race for Queerness." In *Black Queer Studies: A Critical Anthology*, edited by E. Patrick Johnson and Mae G. Henderson, 266–75. Durham: Duke University Press, 2005.

Cohen, Cathy J. "Punks, Bulldaggers, and Welfare Queens: The Radical Potential of Queer Politics." In *Black Queer Studies: A Critical Anthology*, edited by E. Patrick Johnson and Mae G. Henderson, 21–51. Durham: Duke University Press, 2005.

Frischherz, Michaela. "The Possibility of Queer Hospitality: Reading Public Sexual Sites." MA thesis, Universiteit van Amsterdam, 2009.

Heifetz, Ronald A., and Marty Linsky. *Leadership on the Line: Staying Alive through the Dangers of Leading*. Boston: Harvard Business Review Press, 2002.

Johnson, E. Patrick, and Mae G. Henderson, eds. *Black Queer Studies: A Critical Anthology*. Durham: Duke University Press, 2005.

"Lesbian, Gay, Bisexual, and Transgender Health." Centers for Disease Control and Prevention. Online. https://www.cdc.gov/lgbthealth/youth.htm.

"Lesbian, Gay, Bisexual, Transgender, Queer, & Intersex Life." Vanderbilt University. Online. https://www.vanderbilt.edu/lgbtqi/resources/housing-in-nashville.

Lorde, Audre. *A Burst of Light and Other Essays*. Ithaca, NY: Firebrand, 1988.

Palmer, Parker. "Community, Conflict, and Ways of Knowing." *Change* 19.5 (1987) 20–25.

Parks, Sharon Daloz. *Leadership Can Be Taught: A Bold Approach for a Complex World*. Boston: Harvard Business School Press, 2005.

"Program for LGBTQ Health." Vanderbilt University Medical Center. Online. https://www.vumc.org/lgbtq/trans-buddy-program.

CHAPTER 13

[Degree] Planning Ahead

Transforming the Student Experience through Academic Advising

Jo Ann Sharkey Reinowski

TODAY'S SEMINARY STUDENTS OFTEN face challenges as they endeavor to successfully complete their theological education. Students are taking longer to graduate, incurring more debt, and feeling less sure about where they will go and how they will serve after graduation. "Non-traditional" students are now the norm as seminaries experience an increase in enrollment of older students, students working full-time, and students attending seminary online. Defining what it means to be a traditional or non-traditional student in theological education is a challenge due to the increasing diversity evident in theological school enrollment. Fewer students are attending seminary directly after their undergraduate degree. More students are working full-time while they attend seminary[1] and attending seminary later in life,[2] often after having worked in ministry or other fields for decades prior to enrollment.

The manner in which theological education is provided and the students who access theological education have transformed during the past

1. According to table 11 in ATS, "Total School Profile: Graduating Student Questionnaire," 51.9 percent of all students worked more than 20 hours a week in the 2017–2018 graduating class and 55.2 percent in the 2018–2019 graduating class.

2. While the 26–30 age range category is still the largest group of students graduating from seminary, the second largest group is the 56 years and older category (see table 4 in ATS, "Total School Profile: Graduating Student Questionnaire").

two decades. Due to the changing demographics within the average seminary student body as well as the changing delivery methods of theological education, the manner in which schools provide academic advising and academic services must adapt and update. How does academic advising help seminary students navigate the challenges that hinder the successful and timely completion of their degrees? What does a robust academic services office look like in today's theological education landscape?

WHY IS ACADEMIC ADVISING IMPORTANT?

The central role of an academic services office is to provide academic advising and academic resources for students. Academic advising helps seminary students navigate the complicated and often changing landscape of theological education. Academic services should contribute to increased student satisfaction, student retention, and degree completion.

In his influential 1972 article, "A Developmental View of Academic Advising as Teaching," Burns B. Crookston, a former academic dean and student affairs authority, advocated for the developmental role of academic advising. Crookston states, "Developmental counseling or advising is concerned not only with a specific personal or vocational decision, but also with facilitating the student's rational processes, environmental and interpersonal interactions, behavioral awareness, and problem-solving skills. Not only are these advising functions but . . . teaching functions as well."[3]

Heidi Koring further elaborates: "Advising teaches skills like decision-making and critical thinking, as well as content like curriculum and academic regulations."[4] Just as students must learn to successfully execute a well-researched paper to excel in seminary, students must also learn how to navigate the academic policies of their school.

In his chapter in *Academic Advising: A Comprehensive Handbook*, Don G. Creamer writes: "Academic advising is an educational activity that depends on valid explanations of complex student behaviors and institutional conditions to assist college students in making and executing educational and life plans."[5] In the context of theological education, academic advising

3. Crookston defines advising as "a teaching function based on a negotiated agreement between student and teacher in which varying degrees of learning by both parties to the transaction are the product." (Crookston, "Developmental View," 17). See Crookston, "Developmental View," 12–17.

4. Koring, "Advising and Teaching."

5. Don G. Creamer served as the former American College Personnel Association (ACPA) president. He is a former college administrator and professor and author of numerous books and articles about higher education. See Creamer, "Use of Theory," 18.

goes beyond simply advising students about what classes they should take and when.[6] The advisor is not only responsible for helping students address their educational decisions but their life, vocational and spiritual decisions as well.

Seminary students are following a call to ministry and pursuing vocational ministry. Students must know how their academic choices impact their professional ministry. A student's calling should be taken into consideration when academic advising is provided within the theological education context.

TRADITIONAL METHODS OF ACADEMIC ADVISING

Traditional academic advising methods include include two basic models: prescriptive and developmental.[7] In the prescriptive approach, the advisor is the authority; he or she is most knowledgeable and generally instructs the student what to do—what classes to take and when. The advisor ensures that students understand registration procedures and academic requirements.[8] The prescriptive model is often the easiest and most necessary approach when dealing with a large group of students. According to the organizational researcher, Adelina Broadbridge, prescriptive advising "leaves most of the control in the hands of advisors, which allows them to remain uninvolved in the relationship, viewing it as mostly an administrative function primarily concerned with short-term goals (such as class registration)."[9]

The second traditional method of advising is developmental which describes a two-way relationship between the student and the advisor.[10] The advisor advises the student and together they establish educational and professional goals. However, the student is ultimately responsible for their own decisions.[11] Cathleen Smith calls developmental advising "a student-centered process." It "acknowledges the individuality of students, helps them integrate life, career, and educational goals, connects curricular

6. Academic advising has been defined by Terry O'Banion as a process that includes the following dimensions: "(1) Exploration of life goals, (2) exploration of vocational goals, (3) program choice, (4) course choice, and (5) scheduling choice." O'Banion goes on to say that, "ideally, the college would provide the student with a variety of experiences in each of these dimensions" (O'Banion, "Academic Advising Model," 10).

7. Developmental and prescriptive advising terminology accredited to Crookston, "Developmental View."

8. Montag et al., "In Their Own Words," 27.

9. Broadbridge, "Academic Advising."

10. Broadbridge, "Academic Advising."

11. Broadbridge, "Academic Advising."

and co-curricular aspects of their educational experience, and provides opportunities to practice decision-making and problem-solving skills."[12]

Academic advisors began looking for a way to acknowledge and advance the traditional methods of advising, which resulted in the praxis method. The praxis method has been described as a "hybrid of prescriptive and developmental advising through which advisors give students expert advice on course selection, but also engage them in discussions about their declared major."[13]

While traditional models of advising still work in traditional seminary settings, the average seminary student is no longer traditional. New and innovative models of academic advising must be adopted for our diverse seminary landscape. The following stories are a snapshot of the students enrolled in seminary today; they demonstrate why innovative and creative methods of academic advising are necessary in theological education.

THEOLOGICAL EDUCATION STUDENTS AT A GLANCE

Brenda is a fifty-five-year-old veteran. After a career of military service, she received the GI Bill and is now following the call to ministry that she has always felt. She received her undergraduate degree while she was in the military, completing her bachelor's degree by attending several schools located where she served as well as attending online universities. Brenda thrives in a structured environment where the expectations of her degree and all details related to her schooling are clearly stated. Brenda, like many older students, is attending seminary after ending her professional career. Brenda is similar to one-fifth of all students who are enrolled in seminary; she is in the fifty-years old and older age bracket.[14]

Lawrence is a forty-seven-year-old who has been serving in church ministry for over twenty years. He is looking for a deeper theological education to supplement his ministry experience. He does not have an undergraduate degree but he has been provisionally accepted to seminary.[15]

12. Smith, "Essential Functions of Academic Advising," 56.

13. Montag et al., "In Their Own Words," 27.

14. Seminaries are facing a changing demographic when it comes to the typical seminary student. There are less 20-somethings and 40-somethings attending seminary, while there are more students in their 30s and their 50s going back to school. In their March 2016 article, Chris Meinzer and Tom Tanner wrote about the enrollment trends in theological education. See Meinzer and Tanner, "What a Difference a Decade Makes."

15. Standard A.4.2 on MDiv admission states: "As many as 15 percent of the students in the MDiv degree program may be admitted without possession of the baccalaureate

Lawrence still pastors a church and he is interested in attending a seminary that acknowledges his many years of experience and active role in ministry leadership which is why he selected a school that offers competency-based education. Lawrence has an elderly mother who lives with his family, and he and his wife are her primary care givers. Lawrence also has two adult children, one who is attending college; Lawrence depends on loans to fund his and his college-aged child's education. Lawrence, like many adult learners, may also fill the role of spouse, parent, caregiver to an older parent, full-time or part-time minister, employee or volunteer in addition to being a student.[16]

Advisors must help adult students understand what their actual capabilities are in light of their new reality. This includes encouraging students to consider their responsibilities outside of the classroom as they determine their class load and to help them strategize about what classes they take and when. Successful academic advising with adult students works better when advisors understand the multitude of roles adult students are managing.

Timothy is a twenty-three-year-old student. He completed his bachelor's degree the semester prior to enrolling in seminary. Timothy graduated from a small, private Christian school where he received personal attention from the faculty and staff, especially from his academic advisor. Timothy considers himself to be a millennial[17] and thrives on one-on-one attention. He will visit his academic advisor every few weeks "just to check in." He desires for his degree to cater to him in a personal way, allowing flexibility for him to pursue his calling in unique ways.[18]

---

degree or its educational equivalent. An institution admitting persons without a baccalaureate degree or its educational equivalent shall demonstrate that its process and criteria for evaluating academic ability are educationally appropriate and rigorous" (ATS "Degree Program Standards," 6).

16. Cheryl J. Polson, in her article, "Adult Graduate Students Challenge Institutions to Change," discusses several trends in graduate school education and difficulties faced by adult students. See Polson, "Adult Graduate Students," 63.

17. Just as we see a rise in older students attending seminary, we also witness growth in another generation of seminary students—millennials. The Pew Research Group defines millennials as the generation of people born between 1981 and 1997. See Dimock, "Defining Generations."

18. In their book, *Millennials Rising*, Neil Howe and William Strauss describe key characteristics of millennials, including a sense of specialness and a desire for individual attention. They are often protected, and have been protected, throughout their academic career, which leads them to rely on others for support and attentiveness. Whereas the millennial generation can be characterized by dedicated and hardworking students, they are also a generation of students who demand a great amount of personal attention.

Timothy, like many millennials, responds best to personal attention.[19] This means that academic advisors may not be able to operate with a "once size fits all" model for their students. However, advisors must create suitable boundaries and expectations that will allow their millennial students to have appropriate expectations and to thrive within the institution.

Jamie is a thirty-year-old who works full-time as an administrator for a school district. She lives two hours from a seminary that offers both residential and online classes. Although Jamie would like to be a residential student, this is not possible due to her work responsibilities and her commute time. She will commute to campus during the summer and for intensive courses, but she will primarily complete her degree by taking online courses. Jamie may rarely visit campus, yet she needs access to the library, academic support services, and advising just like any other student would need.

Jamie's example represents one of the major changing trends in the way seminaries deliver theological education. Whereas twenty years ago, the majority of seminary students learned in residential programs, online education is on the rise. According to a March 2017 article written by Tom Tanner, "Twenty years ago, no ATS member school offered any courses online. Ten years ago, only a fourth of our schools offered any courses online, and less than a tenth of them had any substantive online programs. None offered any degrees completely online. Today, nearly two-thirds of our 273-member schools have online offerings. More than half have substantive online offerings, and more than a fourth offer entire degrees completely online."[20] The rapid growth in online programs offered in theological education demonstrates the need for a flexible and responsive academic services program.

Each of these stories represent a snapshot of the diverse students in theological education today. How do we provide resources for a student body that is characterized by multiple generations, learning styles, degree programs, and educational models?

19. In a study conducted over five universities, advisors from those schools drew conclusions about how best to advise millennials. They published their findings in an article called, "In Their Own Words: Best Practices for Advising Millennial Students about Majors." This study found that their millennial participants expressed a sense of specialness as well as conventional motivation, optimism, and a need to feel protected. The findings suggest that academic advisors should acknowledge and at times accommodate these millennial characteristics when working with students. See Montag et al., "In Their Own Words."

20. Tanner, "Online Learning at ATS Schools," 1.

HOW IS ACADEMIC ADVISING EFFECTIVE IN OUR CURRENT LANDSCAPE OF THEOLOGICAL EDUCATION?

Attention has been drawn to the numerous challenges that face students in theological education today. How do seminaries move from identifying the challenges to creating successful models for academic services? How do academic services personnel provide helpful and effective academic advising resources for students? As one considers the changing trends in theological education, what should students expect a seminary to provide by way of academic advising and academic services? What should be expected of the student to do on their own behalf when it comes to successfully completing their degree?

Academic advising occurs in a variety of locations within the seminary—it may be provided by faculty, academic advisors, registrars, administrative staff, a website or even unofficially provided in a student-to-student context as seminarians often seek advice from those who have gone before them. Ideally, a seminary would house an office of academic services which refers to a person, group of personnel, or even the website/online tools that provide academic advising, degree program information, graduation planning, as well as tools and strategies that enable students to navigate their educational experience. An academic services office should have some familiarity with the vocations that its seminary students are pursuing and any education requirements that accompany those vocations. An embedded seminary may have access to a university-wide academic services office which offers accommodations and resources for students with disabilities, veterans, adult learners, first generation, and non-traditional students. In stand-alone seminaries, academic services personnel should be prepared to provide the needed resources for all students.

In order to assist students as they navigate their seminary journey, academic services personnel must start early in the students' academic careers as expectations are set. Teaching students that they must be the initiator in their own academic success is key. When a school provides the student with the tools they need for academic success, it enables that student to take responsibility to successfully complete their degree program.

The seminary student's very first encounter at their school establishes a pattern for how they expect to be treated throughout their entire academic career. If the academic advisor can impart a sense of empowerment, independence, and responsibility in the prospective or incoming student during their first seminary experience, expectations are set regarding how the student should behave and how they can expect the seminary to behave in response. Academic services must be a part of the student experience throughout their entire graduate program. Providing a robust new student orientation and yearly mentoring and advising can give the student a healthy understanding of their degree requirements and the seminary's guidelines.

At new student orientation, students should be made aware of the resources that are available to them, both electronically and on-site. Students may tour the academic services office as well as any office on campus that provides resources for them. Students with disabilities should be made aware of the accommodations their school will provide. Many students will not immediately self-identify that they need learning accommodations, but if the academic services office makes it known that accommodations are available, students will feel more comfortable seeking out the assistance they need. If certain accommodations are being provided by different personnel, such as a designated office that serves veterans, invite experts from those offices to speak to incoming students during their first semester.

As academic advisors shape the expectations of their students, they should empower students to take responsibility and accept the consequences of their academic decisions. When a student faces a problem, academic services cannot immediately solve it for them or prescribe the steps to take. Instead, the student and the advisor should meet and establish the objectives the student wants to reach, and the advisor empowers the student to take the required steps. The advisor supports and encourages the students yet enables the students to problem solve for themselves. This practice enables the students and the academic services office to maintain a balanced relationship that will contribute to the overall successful academic experience of all students.

A key characteristic required of all who work in academic services is listening. Although many administrators who work in higher education may feel that they must first impart their expertise, a successful academic advisor in theological education will listen and ask the right questions. Students in theological education are working out their calling while in seminary. Advisors serve as partners in their discernment process, inviting the student to be open to the possibilities that their calling will bring. It is imperative that the advisor not dictate what their path will look like, as each individual must discern their path for themselves.

ONLINE RESOURCES

As more seminaries offer online education, extension campuses, and alternative routes to degree completion,[21] school administrators and faculty are often working with students that they have never met in person. Depending upon the manner in which most students access their education, schools should determine whether their academic services office will be a physical office or a virtual office (in the form of an online academic advising website). If the majority of students are accessing their information online, are the academic resources available in an online format that is easy to find and guides students appropriately? Is the academic services website relevant, up-to-date, and communicating the message that is most important for students to hear? Because most students first visit a school's website to learn more about the school and many students continue accessing the website after they have been accepted and start a program, it is recommended that a school provide online resources even if they have a physical office on campus.

In her October 2016 article, "Accessible, effective: How online theological education is shifting the formation model," Eliza Smith Brown draws attention to the hesitancy of many ATS schools surrounding how to duplicate successfully the academic, spiritual, and human formation that occurs in a classroom with dedicated seminary faculty when we are limited to working with our students through an online medium.[22] In essence, how do we truly form and influence our students when we never have the chance to meet, face-to-face? Academic services offices must be innovative and effective within the online context. Creating academic resources and tools that students can access in the same manner that they access their online education allows for students to take the initiative for their own academic success.

Online resources provide a reference point for perspective students. If a seminary provides academic services online, perspective students can access important degree planning information as well as gain a better understanding of the school's expectation for them. Prospective students should

21. Educational Standard ES.1.6.2 states: "Schools offer programs of theological education using several different educational practices: courses offered on the main campus of the school granting the degree, at an approved branch campus or extension site, by approved programs of distance learning, and as needed, by faculty-guided individual instruction. In all cases, faculty shall have regular and substantive interaction with students throughout courses and regularly be available to students to mentor, advise, and counsel. Because correspondence education lacks regular and substantive interaction between faculty and students, no Commission-approved courses can be offered by correspondence education" (ATS, "Educational Standard," 14).

22. Brown, "Accessible, Effective."

be directed to review academic advising information so that they gain a clear understanding of the requirements they must meet to graduate from that school.

Online academic advising resources should include degree plans, class schedules, and suggestions on course load planning. It should also include instructions related to registration, advanced standing, and transfer credit. Students should have a clear pathway that gives them instructions on how to register for their first class to how to graduate.

OTHER TOOLS

A seminary may offer tools such as a degree completion plan which allows the academic advisor to work with the student to outline each class that student will take from now until graduation. By using a degree completion plan, students are responsible for understanding the requirements of their degree program yet they are able to work with an advisor who oversees that their plan is feasible and correct. Some theological schools offer an online advising system, such as a degree audit generator. These tools are especially helpful for students to access prior to registration each semester to ensure they are registering for the correct classes.

It is recommended that seminaries offer advising meetings each semester or annually. At advising meetings, advisors will inform students about any changes to the curriculum, updates to degree requirements, and upcoming course schedules. Advising meetings can also provide an opportunity for faculty to meet with students and advise about course selection, degree options, and vocational goals.[23]

At the start of a student's academic career, advisors use mostly directive advising with students. Advisors offer advice and structure and regulations to incoming students. Students are taught that they must learn how to be successful within the established institution. However, the same level of advising doesn't work and perhaps isn't necessary for students who have successfully navigated their degree program and are close to graduating.

Academic advisors can increase their monitoring of students within their last year. This is often the time when students need the most encouragement as well as accountability. Many factors can deter students from

---

23. General Institutional Standard 5.3.3 offers these guidelines on advising: "Faculty should participate in practices and procedures that contribute to students' learning, including opportunities for regular advising and interaction with students and attentiveness to the learning needs of diverse student populations" (ATS, "General Institutional Standards," 15).

graduating and the advisor stands in one of the most important positions to help seminary students succeed in completing their degree.

STUDENT RETENTION AND COMPLETION RATES

Theological schools spend a tremendous amount of money, time, and energy in recruiting students. Is the same effort exhausted to keep current students enrolled? With appropriate resources applied to an academic services office, academic services can be a vital tool in student satisfaction, student retention, and degree completion.

Consistently evidenced throughout graduate programs, various factors contribute to student attrition. The burden of financing a graduate degree can lead students to take breaks or withdraw from their program completely. Lack of understanding of the time and work involved in completing a graduate degree can also lead to student drop-out. These are areas where academic advisors can positively influence their student bodies. Giving students realistic expectations about the changes they will need to make in their lives in order to successfully complete their graduate degree is key. Budgets must be adjusted to allow for the increased financial burden of graduate school. Personal schedules, employment, family responsibilities, and volunteer work must be adjusted for students to allow the appropriate amount of time their degree requires. Advisors must speak into their students' lives at the very beginning of their program, and hopefully before.

In her article, "Tending the flock: Is retention the answer to enrollment declines?" Eliza Smith Brown discusses the problem of student retention within seminaries. MA degrees that are designed to be completed in 2 years are taking students 3.8 years. MDiv degrees, designed to be completed in 3 years, are taking students on average 4.2 years.[24]

Brown continues on, stating that, "a number of circumstances likely contribute to the retention challenge. Extended completion times certainly offer greater opportunities for interruption. . . . An estimated average of approximately 20 percent of students are lost along the way. Looking at the full range of ATS schools, some lose nearly 50 percent, while others lose practically none; longer completion times add to the growing problem of student debt that, in turn, comes full circle to contribute to the attrition rate."[25]

Brown notes multiple reasons why seminary students fail to complete their degrees, including more "seeker" students who attend seminary without a clear calling to ministry as well as students who intend to stay at

24. Brown, "Tending the Flock," 1.
25. Brown, "Tending the Flock," 1.

seminary for a short season of life and never intended to complete the program or pursue full-time ministry. There are also those students who face "unexpected life changes, including health problems, financial setbacks, family issues, work conflicts, or general time pressure."[26] In addition, Brown identifies the group of students who realize they are not equipped to face the academic rigors of theological education, which is an area where academic services can often provide the biggest support and contribute to increased retention and completion rates. For the students who want to successfully complete their degree but seem to have inordinate challenges to overcome, academic advising can help those students discern their next steps.

CONCLUSION

Academic advising is a vital component to student satisfaction, student success, and degree completion. Academic advisors are burdened with the growing demand to meet the needs of their diverse student bodies. As seminaries experience a growing population of non-traditional students, including the "second career" students to the fresh out of college millennials, seminaries must create innovative and effective academic advising resources for all students.

Academic services administrators fill a variety of roles. On any given day, these titles describe their profession: academic advisor, counselor, vocational coach, advice-giver, listener, encourager, role model, and rule enforcer. Often, academic services becomes a catch-all office where anything related to the academic success of the student, outside of their actual class time, is handled. Academic advising enables seminary students to navigate the challenges that often stand in the way of their graduation. Essentially, the work of academic services can influence and improve completion rates within theological education.

As theological education becomes more innovative, so must the manner in which schools provide academic services also innovate and progress. A robust and comprehensive academic services office is the key to providing instructions for degree planning, support for students who are struggling to succeed, and a pathway to graduation.

26. Brown, "Tending the Flock," 2.

BIBLIOGRAPHY

Association of Theological Schools (ATS). "Degree Program Standards." Online. http://www.ats.edu/uploads/accrediting/documents/degree-program-standards.pdf.

―――. "Educational Standard." Online. https://www.ats.edu/uploads/accrediting/documents/educational-standard.pdf.

―――. "General Institutional Standards." Online. https://www.ats.edu/accrediting/standards-and-notations.

―――. "Total School Profile: Entering Student Questionnaire 2017–2018." Online. https://www.ats.edu/resources/student-data/total-school-profile-reports.

―――. "Total School Profile: Graduating Student Questionnaire 2017–2018." Online. https://www.ats.edu/resources/student-data/total-school-profile-reports.

―――. "Total School Profile: Graduating Student Questionnaire 2018–2019." Online. https://www.ats.edu/resources/student-data/total-school-profile-reports.

Broadbridge, Adelina "Academic Advising—Traditional or Developmental Approaches?: Student Perspectives." *British Journal of Guidance & Counselling* 24.1 (1996) 97–111.

Brown, Eliza Smith. "Accessible, Effective: How Online Theological Education Is Shifting the Formation Model." *Colloquy Online* (October 2016). https://www.ats.edu/uploads/resources/publications-presentations/colloquy-online/formation-online.pdf.

―――. "Tending the Flock: Is Retention the Answer to Enrollment Declines?" *Association of Theological Schools* (May 2014). Online. http://www.ats.edu/uploads/resources/publications-presentations/documents/tending-the-flock.pdf.

Creamer, D. G. "Use of Theory in Academic Advising." In *Academic Advising: A Comprehensive Handbook*, edited by Virginia N. Gordon, et al., 18–34. San Francisco: Jossey-Bass. 2000.

Crookston, Burns B. "A Developmental View of Academic Advising as Teaching." *Journal of College Student Personnel* 13 (1972) 12–17.

Dimock, Michael. "Defining Generations: Where Millennials End and Post-Millennials Begin." *Pew Research Center*, March 1, 2018. Online. http://www.pewresearch.org/fact-tank/2018/03/01/defining-generations-where-millennials-end-and-post-millennials-begin.

Howe, Neil, and William Strauss. *Millennials Rising: The Next Great Generation*. New York: Vintage, 2000.

Koring, Heidi, et al. "Advising and Teaching: Synergistic Praxis for Student and Faculty Development." *The Mentor: An Academic Advising Journal* 6 (2004). Online. https://journals.psu.edu/mentor/article/view/61666/61313.

Meinzer, Chris, and Tom Tanner. "What a Difference a Decade Makes: As Seminaries Reverse a 10-year Enrollment Decline, What Does the Future Hold?" *Colloquy Online* (March 2016). https://www.ats.edu/uploads/resources/publications-presentations/colloquy-online/what-a-difference.pdf.

Montag, Tamara, et al. "In Their Own Words: Best Practices for Advising Millennial Students about Majors." *NACADA Journal* 32.2 (2012). Online. http://www.nacada.ksu.edu/Portals/0/Regional_Divisions/region5/documents/Common%20Reading%20for%20Region%205.pdf.

O'Banion, Terry. "An Academic Advising Model." *NACADA Journal* 12.2 (1994). Online. https://www.nacadajournal.org/doi/abs/10.12930/0271-9517-14.2.10.

Polson, Cheryl J. "Adult Graduate Students Challenge Institutions to Change." *New Directions for Student Services* 102 (2003). Online. https://onlinelibrary.wiley.com/doi/pdf/10.1002/ss.90.

Smith, Cathleen L., and Janine M. Allen. "Essential Functions of Academic Advising: What Students Want and Get." *NACADA Journal* 26.1 (2006) 56–66.

Tanner, Tom. "Online Learning at ATS Schools: Part 1—Looking Back at Our Past." *Colloquy Online* (March 2017). http://www.ats.edu/uploads/resources/publications-presentations/colloquy-online/online-learning-part-1.pdf.

CHAPTER 14

In Service of Character Formation

REID A. KISLING

THE LANDSCAPE OF HIGHER education is changing, shifting from what may be considered traditional notions of student growth to more focused outcomes which students must attain as they complete their educational programs. The shift for those of us in student development in theological education is no different. Leaders in student development have been calling for this change with an emphasis on student learning rather than common perspectives of development.[1] But what does this mean as we seek to contribute to student learning and even join with faculty at our institutions in the creation of curricula to this end?

DEVELOPING STUDENTS

As noted above, traditional notions of student development included the idea of staff facilitating the growth of students by providing a supportive environment in which that growth could occur. However, these notions of growth were rarely defined and often nebulous. More recently, perspectives on student development have shifted such that they mirror terminology that faculty use in the curriculum; ideas of learning outcomes pertaining to student formation and development are more common in the profession. While this move seems to have happened in secular education contexts (particularly when considering the "student affairs" profession and

1. See Blimling and Whitt, *Good Practice in Student Affairs.*

supporting associations), this still appears to be relatively rare within theological education.

Learning Outcomes

Yet, what are learning outcomes and how might we use them? For many of us in theological education, the concepts of learning outcomes may not be part of our typical vocabulary so a brief overview is in order. You may be more familiar with the idea of course objectives that are part of a syllabus for courses at your institution. These objectives are a form of an outcome statement, emphasizing what a student who completes the course will be able to know, do, or feel (noting three recognized domains of learning). However, at many institutions of higher education, these course objectives may be identified for individual courses but rarely seem to be linked together into more holistic program outcomes in which the course objectives build toward overall competencies that students should be able to achieve by the time they complete the educational program in which they are enrolled.

There have been a number of different outcomes frameworks developed over time, each emphasizing different things. Many of these have been operationalized at the undergraduate level including such notions as liberal education, degree qualifications within bachelor's level programs, and even career-readiness outcomes. While emphasizing a different audience, each of these frameworks can be helpful to those of us in theological education as we craft outcome and competency statements that are useful in directing our activities in student development.[2]

Limitations of Learning Outcomes

One of the challenges, however, of utilizing learning outcomes is that they have some inherent limitations. One of those limitations is the tendency for us to see student growth and development in only functional terms. In other words, we can start to see student development based solely on what a student will "do" rather than who the student is "becoming." If you have attempted to craft affective student outcomes (those emphasizing what students may "feel") you may recognize the challenge. Perhaps one reason is the emphasis on function rather than relationship. For those of us in theological education, the emphasis on relationship through the identity

---

2. A helpful discussion of several different outcome frameworks and how to use them is found in Presence, "Student Learning Outcomes."

of humanity as being made in the image of God (Gen 1:26) may be easier to grasp and implement and may help us with balanced notions of student learning outcomes that include relational growth and development for our students.

Relational Realism

Wan, working in the field of anthropology (and thereby describing both interpersonal interactions and development), developed a paradigm that emphasizes this concept of relationship.[3] This Relational Realism Paradigm is pertinent to those of us in theological education as we seek to help students grow not only interpersonally and intrapersonally (self-awareness) but also spiritually in their relationship with God. Indeed, the paradigm emphasizes our proper vertical alignment with God enables us to become properly aligned horizontally with other people.[4] This speaks to what the Apostle John notes about the importance of relationship in our love for God and for other people (1 John 1:5–7; 2:9–11). What does this have to do with student development and formation?

(TRANS)FORMATION

The concept of "formation" in theological education is fundamental as manifested in the degree program standards for theological schools. Yet, these same standards don't specify the manner in which this formation is to occur, only that it should occur and institutions must give attention to how it does.[5] Neither do these standards address the manner in which schools must deliver student services except in support of institutional mission. Yet, student services are the very means through which student development staff interact with students.

It is apparent that it is possible to accomplish the task of serving students in very different ways. In fact, as a leader in student development at my own institution, I regularly discuss the idea of transformational versus

3. See especially chapter 2 in Wan and Hedinger, *Relational Missionary Training*. This chapter defines the "Relational Realism Paradigm."

4. Though primarily focused on one's relationship with God rather than with others, a model of *relational spirituality* that incorporates relational realities can be found in Sandage and Shults, "Relational Spirituality and Transformation," 261–69. This model is addressed further below when considerations for assessment of spiritual formation are noted.

5. See ATS, "Degree Program Standards."

transactional services. This terminology is seen regularly in leadership literature that often juxtaposes transactional leadership (sometimes even referred to as management) with transformational leadership (in which both leader and follower are both changed for the better as a result of the interaction).[6] I have found this distinction helpful in leading staff into an understanding that our interactions with students are far more than just "accomplishing a business function" and more about supporting their formation as ministers.

Identity

Ultimately, when we talk about the concept of formation within theological schools, we are talking about the formation of a ministerial/pastoral/priestly/academic "identity" in our students. We as student development staff need to realize that the formation of such an identity occurs through more than just the interactions in the classroom between faculty and other students.

Identity formation is far more than simply helping students form a moral and ethical understanding of their actions though this is often the focus of our efforts.[7] There are various perspectives on identity formation in education and many of our educational models are built on these conceptual frameworks.[8] Identity includes mental models of who a person is compared to "others" and in relation to the world around them. This identity is formed (and re-formed) throughout our lifetimes and is influenced through various events yet our own experience is often interpreted through our existing perspectives. As such, growth often requires "perspective transformation."[9] In many ways, perspective transformation is synonymous to character growth as it affects the way we see both ourselves and the world around us and our action, whether moral or immoral, emanates from our character.[10]

6. See Burns, *Leadership*.

7. See Holmes, *Shaping Character*.

8. See Erikson, *Identity*.

9. For more information about perspective transformation, see Kegan, *Evolving Self*; "What 'Form' Transforms?," 35–69.

10. For more information about the model connecting beliefs to behavior, see Ajzen and Fishbein, *Understanding Attitudes and Predicting Social Behavior*. For the extended model based on Ajzen and Fishbein that shows the connection between character and moral behavior, see Kisling, "Character for Leadership," 25.

Character

Many of our institutions use the term "character" to describe the type of (trans)formation we are seeking in our students that goes beyond cognitive (thinking/beliefs) or conative (skills/behaviors) areas of our curricula. Though we use the term we may at the same time be unable to define the components of solid, mature character that lead to effective personal relationships (and ministry effectiveness). One challenge with the notion of character development in our students is that of definition. We know that there exist attributes or traits by which we identify someone or something. There are popular definitions, such as "character is what you do when no one is looking." However, these perspectives leave us grasping for more as we attempt to better understand what is required to develop a solid character that can stand the test of time.

It is through our foundational character, whether good or bad, that we develop a value system that helps us make ethical or unethical, moral or immoral decisions about what actions to take in any given situation.[11] Therefore, defining and understanding the components of well-developed and mature character are necessary to promote good actions as well as further our own growth and development. But what exactly is character?

WHAT IS CHARACTER?

As noted, when we use the word "character" we typically mean those attributes by which we identify someone or something. If we are to consider what the Bible says about the characteristics by which we should be identified we would do well to first look at the character of God himself because humanity was created in the image of God: "Let us make mankind in our image, in our likeness" (Gen 1:26). Therefore, our highest aspiration should be to mirror God's character as we were created to do. In fact, God has clearly identified what our primary responsibility is: "He has showed you, O man, what is good. And what does the LORD require of you? To *act justly* and to *love mercy* and to *walk humbly* with your God" (Mic 6:8, emphasis added). These qualities—justice, mercy, and humility—are the fundamental qualities necessary to accomplish the greatest commandments—to "love the Lord your God with all your heart and with all your soul and with all your mind" and "love your neighbor as yourself" (Matt 22:37, 38). If these are the primary attributes to which we should aspire, how are they developed in us?

11. Kisling, "Character for Leadership," 25.

The Old Testament likewise discusses character through the attribute of "wisdom." Solomon states in the introduction to the Book of Proverbs that discipline or instruction in wisdom is his goal. In fact the word used for "discipline" (Hebrew—*musar*; used over thirty times) carries with it the notion of restraining an object or animal. Abstractly, it includes the sense of formation—something that is being molded from one form into another. God disciplines us for our growth and development in godliness; spiritual formation and character are inextricably linked.

In the New Testament, the Apostle Paul considers character development when he writes about how suffering produces character (Rom 5:3–5). Suffering provides an opportunity to develop a long-term perspective that is not rooted in our temporal surroundings. Continual changes in this long-term focus develop character that lasts. Essentially, Paul describes the spiritual formation process—the process of being transformed from our temporal perspective to an eternal one. But what is good character and what does it look like in the lives of our students? Let's start by understanding how character has been defined.

Popular Discussions of Character

Probably the most significant popular treatment of the topic of character is the book by Gail Sheehy[12] in which he evaluated the character of the candidates for the 1988 United States Presidential election and concluded that their character profoundly impacted the manner and propensity with which they lead. Leadership and business literature address the concept in various ways. As one author notes,

> Character—the inner world of motives and values that shapes our actions—is the ultimate determiner of the nature of our leadership. It empowers our capacities while keeping them in check. It distinguishes those who steward power well from those who abuse power. Character weaves such values as integrity, honesty, and selfless service into the fabric of our lives, organizations, and cultures.[13]

School-based programs have been created to develop the character in young people necessary for good citizenship. According to the Character Education Partnership, "good character involves understanding, caring

---

12. See Sheehy, *Character*.

13. Thrall et al., *Ascent of a Leader*, 1–2.

about, and acting upon core values."[14] In like fashion, most such programs consider character to be the development of core ethical values in students. For example, the *Character Counts!* program established by the Josephson Institute of Ethics seeks to engender the values of trustworthiness, respect, responsibility, fairness, caring, and citizenship in the students who participate in the program.[15]

Psychological Definitions

Psychologically, character is an aspect of personality *distinct from temperament*, meaning that personality is the combination of both temperament and character.[16] Character is "consistency in behavior across time" but is "more than just a sense of self."[17] It also includes the ability to inhibit or adjust impulsive behaviors. In addition, personal beliefs and values are often included in the character components of personality. There have been significant attempts to identify and classify character.[18] However, the terms "personality" and "character" are still used interchangeably in many cases.

The "Psychobiological Model of Temperament and Character,"[19] in contrast to other treatments, addresses three primary character traits—self-directedness, cooperativeness, and self-transcendence—in addition to temperament. These character traits comprise means of relating to oneself, other individuals, and the surrounding world, respectively.

In this model of character each specific trait contains "bundles" of secondary traits that comprise the overall characteristic. For the character trait of *self-directedness*, these sub-traits include responsibility, purposefulness, resourcefulness, self-acceptance, and good habits.[20] These traits correlate to numerous other self-regulatory traits, some of which have also been applied to educational contexts.[21]

The character trait of *cooperativeness* includes the sub-traits of tolerance, empathy, helpfulness, compassion, and ethical interaction with

---

14. Character Education Partnership, "11 Principles."

15. Character Counts, "Six Pillars of Character."

16. APA, *DSM-5*; Sperry, "Leadership Dynamics," 268–80.

17. Leonard, "Many Faces of Character," 240.

18. Peterson and Seligman, *Character Strengths and Virtues*.

19. Clonginger et al., "Psychobiological Model," 975–90.

20. Clonginger et al., *Temperament and Character Inventory*, 24–25.

21. McCall, "Identifying Leadership Potential," 49–63; Bandura, *Self-Efficacy*; Duckworth et al., "Grit," 1087–1101.

others.[22] Cooperativeness is one's ability to interact appropriately with others—the essence of the Golden Rule—"do to others what you would have them do to you" (Matt 7:12).[23]

Self-transcendence refers to one's perspective on his or her relationship to the rest of creation. Such a perspective goes beyond interpersonal interaction to include the manner in which a person views his or her place in the universe. While this may seem like a purely secular orientation to spirituality it contains some components that are a necessary part of true Christian spirituality. Self-transcendence includes the sub-traits of creative self-forgetfulness, transpersonal identification, and spiritual acceptance.[24]

While self-directedness is paramount in the three character traits presented here,[25] cooperativeness is also an essential component of mature character. Too often personally driven leaders "drive over" other people to accomplish their own goals. We are all aware of our own tendency to be either task or relationship-oriented (temperament). Here, there is some link to the notion of transaction versus transformational student services mentioned above as each tends to be oriented toward task and relationship, respectively. Yet, even though we each have automatic responses in given situations our character demands that we consider both our goals and the people around us before we initiate action. Mature character requires both personal responsibility and the humble understanding of our need for other people.

Therefore, mature Christian character requires balance between appropriate self-direction and discipline, the ability to interact with others, and the ability to embrace the mystery of life that goes beyond what we can see with our eyes. This mature character—the interaction of all three traits in concert with one another—looks like humanity's primary responsibility noted above—"To *act justly* and to *love mercy* and to *walk humbly* with your God" (Mic 6:8).[26]

22. Cloninger et al., *Temperament and Character Inventory*, 26–27.

23. There is a relationship of this trait to the use of power and various aspects of emotional intelligence. For more information, see McClelland, *Power*; "Two Faces of Power," 29–45; Goleman, *Emotional Intelligence*.

24. Cloninger et al., *Temperament and Character Inventory*. We may find related to this trait those concepts of flow and even spirituality. For more information, see Csikszentmihalyi, *Flow*; Frankl, "Self-Transcendence as a Human Phenomenon," 97–106; Slater et al., "Measuring Religion and Spirituality."

25. The TCI authors note that the lack of self-directedness *always* manifested as a personality disorder in assessment in clinical populations.

26. For a more complete development of these character traits, their connection to biblical maturity, and their applications to spiritual formation and growth, see Kisling, "Character for Leadership," 175–210.

HOW DOES CHARACTER DEVELOP?

If we accept the thesis that character formation is part of our responsibility within student development, how do we approach our task? A difficulty lies in the fact that, even though it is possible to experience a transformation of character, "most people are not exposed to the types of life-changing influences that stimulate such transformations, and, further, if exposed, they tend not to change—that is, people are motivated toward consistency in character, not change or development."[27]

However, most psychologists would agree that, "people develop character over time, primarily through socialization."[28] If this is true, we have a desperate need for true community in which we can grow and be nurtured. This community must be one where the members practice "speaking the truth in love" (Eph 4:15). The Apostle Paul notes that the way we are to accomplish this is by following the command—"Submit to one another out of reverence for Christ" (Eph 5:21). We must belong to a community where each person can both know others and be known.

Theological education is designed to function as dialectic in the formation process—dialectic as an examination of the assumptions that form the basis for a particular belief system.[29] In fact, the educational process known as Transformative Learning Theory[30] has much the same goal in mind—perspective transformation. This process requires an event that triggers the evaluation of one's understanding of "the way that the world works," often referred to as one's worldview.

At the core of the process is the consideration of what has been called *operational* versus *professed* theology. The goal of theological education is to "narrow the gap" between these two belief systems that can only occur through a fundamental reflection on and evaluation of our identities apart from transformed Christian character. Different church traditions have seen fit to formalize this relationship between spiritual director and follower. This is also the emphasis at our institutions within the formal theological reflection process that happens within the traditional curriculum. Yet, it can also occur through interactions with students in our offices. Yes, it can occur in the context of internship or small group, but it can also happen when discussing limitations on borrowing loan funds to finance education, responding to a failing grade, discussing issues of power in the classroom, or while

27. Hogan and Sinclair, "For Love or Money?," 257–58.
28. Hogan and Sinclair, "For Love or Money?," 260.
29. Tracy, "Can Virtue Be Taught?"
30. Mezirow, *Transformative Dimensions of Adult Learning.*

planning courses for a future semester. The difference between transactional services (those in which we focus on accomplishing the task before us) and transformational services (in which we take a relational opportunity to impact a students' perspectives on themselves and others) is often as simple as intentionality. In my own experience, reframing the services that we provide as those through which we are attempting to affect the outcomes of students and their ministerial identity is that intentional framework.

At this point, it may be helpful to note that outward manifestations of "growth" don't necessarily indicate progress in spiritual formation, and there may be external evidence of virtue that isn't connected to a developing relationship with God. "In other words, there are naturalistic ways to form acquired virtue that run independently of growth in one's relationship with God."[31] There may be maturation in character according to the model presented above that doesn't include the spiritual development that we also seek in theological education, and this is a confounding issue in our own assessment of formation of seminarians. Yet, based on the notion of relational realism also noted above, we would say that development in a relationship with God is also requisite to a fully-formed person and to the concept of developing Christian character. In addition, it is also due to a relationship with God (and supportive others) that can actually create an environment in which transformation can occur (and may be similar to what Sandage and Shults call a "crucible" as they propose the concept of *relational spirituality*).[32]

ASSESSING CHARACTER DEVELOPMENT THROUGH LEARNING OUTCOMES

Even if we intentionally reframe our services in terms of learning outcomes and there is apparent growth in our students, how can we tell if we are being effective? In the academic enterprise of our institutions, assessment is expected to be regular and systemic. Yet, faculty can struggle with the assessment of "soft skills" across the curriculum. The advent of competency-based theological education (CBTE) may offer some tools in the assessment of these skills as it necessitates definition of the competencies the institution seeks to develop in its students.[33] Perhaps, as student development professionals, we need to engage with faculty discussing the development of student competencies to ensure that those aspects of development that

31. Porter et al., "Measuring the Spiritual," 19.

32. Sandage and Shults, "Relational Spirituality and Transformation," 265.

33. McGillivray, "Mentor's Dilemma."

we oversee within our institutions are incorporated into the competency frameworks that we may implement. As CBTE matures, there will be opportunities for us to partner with faculty at our institutions, perhaps even proposing language that is consistent with that which we already use in the student development profession, to help shape our students for effective ministry for the future.

THE NEED FOR COURAGE

As you read this, you may say to yourself, "This is fine and good but how does it actually work?" In my experience, engaging with students in such a way as to influence their own character formation requires courage on our part as student development leaders. This is particularly the case as students go through "crucibles" that are often the greatest opportunities for influence in these characteristics since they provide the context for identity (trans) formation as has been noted above. Yet, this is also the "messiness" of life and requires that we engage with students pastorally and that often necessitates that we actively choose to move toward students in these times. This is when we have opportunity to come alongside students and relationally engage with them about the implications of their challenges and help them reframe their circumstances from both a practical and theological perspective. Sometimes these circumstances are the result of their own need for character growth such that they make better decisions in the future; some are the result of ways in which others have failed them or even the representation of a fallen world (such as in the case of personal sickness or injury to no fault of themselves). In all cases, we can help students "make meaning" from their experiences while experiencing the transformation of theological education applied in their own lives and identities.

In conclusion, the development of character in our students is our ultimate outcome; our desire being for our students to mirror the character of God as just, merciful, and humble people who minister with others in mind. This development requires a long-term perspective in a loving community focused on the maturity of all its members. This process, while challenging, also produces joy that comes from loving God "with all your heart and with all your soul and with all your mind" and loving "your neighbor as yourself" (Matt 22:37, 38). Such mature character is necessary to create ministerial leaders who, through the power of God working in them, transform lives, transform families, transform communities, transform societies, and transform the world.

BIBLIOGRAPHY

Ajzen, Icek, and Martin Fishbein. *Understanding Attitudes and Predicting Social Behavior*. Upper Saddle River, NJ: Prentice-Hall, 1980.

American Psychiatric Association (APA). *Diagnostic and Statistical Manual of Mental Disorders (DSM)*. 5th ed. Arlington, VA: American Psychiatric Association, 2013.

Association of Theological Schools (ATS). "Degree Program Standards." Online. http://www.ats.edu/uploads/accrediting/documents/degree-program-standards.pdf.

Bandura, Albert. *Self-Efficacy: The Exercise of Control*. New York: W. H. Freeman, 1997.

Blimling, Gregory S., and Elizabeth J. Whitt. *Good Practice in Student Affairs: Principles to Foster Student Learning*. San Francisco: Jossey-Bass, 1999.

Burns, James M. *Leadership*. New York: Harper & Row, 1978.

Character Counts. "The Six Pillars of Character." Online. https://charactercounts.org/program-overview/six-pillars.

Character Education Partnership. "The 11 Principles of Effective Character Education." Online. http://character.org/wp-content/uploads/11-Principle-2018-comp.pdf.

Clonginger, C. Robert, et al. "A Psychobiological Model of Temperament and Character." *Archives of General Psychiatry* 50 (1993) 975–90.

Clonginger, C. Robert, et al. *The Temperament and Character Inventory (TCI): A Guide to Its Development and Use*. St. Louis, MO: Center for Psychobiology of Personality, Washington University, 1994.

Csikszentmihalyi, Mihaly. *Flow: The Psychology of Optimal Experience*. New York: Harper & Row, 1990.

Duckworth, Angela L., et al. "Grit: Perseverance and Passion for Long-Term Goals." *Journal of Personality and Social Psychology* 92.6 (2007) 1087–1101.

Erikson, Erik H. *Identity: Youth and Crisis*. New York: Norton, 1994.

Frankl, Viktor E. "Self-Transcendence as a Human Phenomenon." *Journal of Humanistic Psychology* 6.2 (1966) 97–106.

Goleman, Daniel. *Emotional Intelligence: Why It Can Matter More than IQ*. New York: Bantam, 1995.

Hogan, Robert, and Robert Sinclair. "For Love or Money? Character Dynamics in Consultation." *Consulting Psychology Journal: Practice and Research* 49.4 (1997) 256–67.

Holmes, Arthur Frank. *Shaping Character: Moral Education in the Christian College*. Grand Rapids: Eerdmans, 1991.

Kegan, Robert. *The Evolving Self: Problem and Process in Human Development*. Cambridge: Harvard University Press, 1982.

———. "What 'Form' Transforms? A Constructive-Developmental Approach to Transformative Learning." In *Learning as Transformation: Critical Perspectives on a Theory in Progress*, edited by Jack Mezirow, et al., 35–69. San Francisco: Jossey-Bass, 2000.

Kisling, Reid. "Character for Leadership." In *Foundations of Spiritual Formation: A Community Approach to Becoming Like Christ*, edited by Paul Pettit, 175–210. Grand Rapids: Kregel, 2008.

———. "Character for Leadership: The Role of Personal Characteristics in Personal Leadership Behaviors." PhD diss., Regent University, 2007.

Leonard, H. Skipton. "The Many Faces of Character." *Consulting Psychology Journal: Practice and Research* 49.4 (1997) 235–45.

McCall, Morgan. "Identifying Leadership Potential in Future International Executives: Developing a Concept." *Consulting Psychology Journal: Practice and Research* 46.1 (1994) 49–63.

McClelland, David C. *Power: The Inner Experience*. Oxford: Irvington, 1975.

———. "The Two Faces of Power." *Journal of International Affairs* 24.1 (1970) 29–45.

McGillivray, Ruth. "The Mentor's Dilemma: Tips for Assessing 'Soft' Competencies in Competency-Based Theological Education (CBTE)." *Colloquy Online* (Summer 2018). https://www.ats.edu/uploads/resources/publications-presentations/colloquy-online/the-mentor%27s-dilemma.pdf.

Mezirow, Jack. *Transformative Dimensions of Adult Learning*. San Francisco: Jossey-Bass, 1991.

Peterson, Christopher, and Martin Seligman. *Character Strengths and Virtues: A Handbook and Classification*. Washington, DC: American Psychological Association; New York: Oxford University Press, 2004.

Porter, Steven L., et al. "Measuring the Spiritual, Character, and Moral Formation of Seminarians: In Search of a Meta-Theory of Spiritual Change." *Journal of Spiritual Formation and Soul Care* 12.1 (2019) 5–24.

Piaget, Jean. *The Psychology of Intelligence*. New York: Routledge, 2001.

Presence. "Student Learning Outcomes & Co-Curricular Experiences: The Complete Guide to Planning and Building a Co-curricular Framework for Your Campus." Online. http://www.presence.io/wp-content/uploads/2018/05/Presence-ExperientialLearningEbook-Final.pdf.

Sandage, Steven J., and F. LeRon Shults. "Relational Spirituality and Transformation: A Relational Integration Model." *Journal of Psychology and Christianity* 26.3 (2007) 261–69.

Seligman, Martin E. P., and Mihaly Csikszentmihalyi. "Positive Psychology: An Introduction." *The American Psychologist* 55.1 (2000) 5.

Sheehy, Gail. *Character: America's Search for Leadership*. Rev. ed. New York: Bantam, 1990.

Slater, Will, et al. "Measuring Religion and Spirituality: Where Are We and Where Are We Going?" *Journal of Psychology & Theology* 29.1 (2001) 4–21.

Sperry, Len. "Leadership Dynamics: Character and Character Structure in Executives." *Consulting Psychology Journal: Practice and Research* 49.4 (1997) 268–80.

Thrall, Bill, et al. *The Ascent of a Leader: How Ordinary Relationships Develop Extraordinary Character and Influence*. San Francisco: Jossey-Bass, 1999.

Tracy, David. "Can Virtue Be Taught? Education, Character and the Soul." In *Theological Perspectives on Christian Formation: A Reader on Theology & Christian Education*, edited by Jeff Astley, et al., 33–52. Grand Rapids: Eerdmans, 1996.

Wan, Enoch, and Mark Hedinger. *Relational Missionary Training: Theology, Theory & Practice*. Skyforest, CA: Urban Loft, 2017.

CHAPTER 15

A Lamp unto Their Feet

Guiding Questions to Assist Graduate Theological Students in Vocational Discernment and Career Planning

LILLIAN HALLSTRAND LAMMERS

"I DON'T KNOW WHAT I want to do when I graduate." This troublesome statement is not entirely unfamiliar to faculty and staff working at theological schools. Students choose to pursue graduate theological education for a myriad of reasons, which may not include a clear sense of vocational direction or career plans. Rather, a sense of being "called" or "led" to pursue this type of education may translate into an educational journey in which the work of vocational discernment and career planning is minimized as students claim to be following along a divinely-inspired path. In working with students to engage in a process of vocational exploration and planning for future careers, student personnel administrations at theological institutions can assist in illuminating how passions, skills, interests, and experiences will translate into employment following completion of degree programs, thereby offering a lamp unto the feet of those walking the path of preparation for careers in ministry.

In examining how vocational discernment and career planning take shape at theological institutions, it is helpful to look at the shifts in trends that inform this work because the landscape of theological education is rapidly changing. At the time of their founding, most theological schools espoused their explicit purpose of preparing ministers to fill the pulpits in parish and congregational settings. Even though the understanding of what constitutes ministry has expanded beyond the brick and mortar of church walls, this is still understood to be the primary purpose of these schools today. While many serving in theological education give lip service to the diversity of professions that can be pursued with the degrees offered, as recently as 2007 a research report on theological education and vocation prepared by the Auburn Center for the Study of Theological Education noted, "The primary social function of North American theological schools—most agree—is to prepare religious professionals for ministry, most often as ordained clergy."[1] Current trends and data suggest that many students seeking theological education are doing so with different vocational plans in mind. As a result of this dissonance, theological school professionals may find themselves unprepared to aid students in connecting the dots in how their coursework and experiences translate into employment.

As ministry settings change and evolve and theological education becomes more versatile in the career marketplace, institutions must accompany and support students in their process of vocational discernment during their degree programs. This need poses a challenge for many institutions that have not been equipped to do this work in the past. The number of ATS member institutions that currently employ an individual with formal responsibilities in assisting students in vocational discernment and planning, sometimes referred to as "placement" or "career services" is very small. Additionally, in the Graduating Student Questionnaire administered by ATS, the category for "Career and Vocational Counseling" is routinely one of the lowest rated services across all ATS schools. Year after year, a very small percentage of graduating students indicated using their institution's placement service, many citing that they either were unaware this service was offered, chose not to use the service, or are seeking work not directly related to their theological degree. This data demonstrates the need for theological schools to give particular attention to improving the vocational counseling and career services offered to graduating students, and to ensure that this counseling is helpful to students pursuing both traditional and nontraditional forms of ministry.

The data illustrating a lack of robust vocational counseling and career services at theological schools is troublesome for several reasons. First, with the rising cost of education, the importance of helping students to secure gainful and meaningful employment quickly following graduation will help them to be in a position to meet the financial realities they face, including

---

1. Wheeler et al., *How Are We Doing?*, 2.

educational loan repayment. In 2017 alone, over 20 percent of entering students indicated they already possessed educational debt exceeding $30,000.[2] Additionally, over 20 percent of 2018 graduates report having incurred over $40,000 of educational debt in pursuit of their theological degree.[3] These financial realities underline the importance of graduates securing gainful employment upon graduation. Second, theological schools certainly wish to make the case that students investing the time and resources into securing a graduate degree will be able to successfully gain employment that is in line with their passions and skills, even if that work is outside of the traditional definitions of ministry. With enrollment challenges across theological education, graduate employment statistics are an important metric for demonstrating the value of a graduate theological degree.

This chapter will offer an organized framework of eighteen guiding questions, divided into four "clusters," along with an accompanying timeline that administrators can tailor to their institutional setting. The questions are intended to move students through thinking about vocational direction broadly, narrowing focus down to a handful of careers, and offering practical steps for preparing students for their job search as they approach graduation. A common question that arises within institutions seeking to improve these programmatic offerings is, "Who is best suited to do this work with our students?" As each graduate theological school has a different institutional structure, varying levels of staffing resources, and also utilizes different modalities and technologies for curriculum delivery, there is no one-size-fits-all response to this question. Institutional leadership should examine where this work may already be informally happening within their schools, perhaps with professionals tasked with coordinating field education and/or internship experiences, or with individuals in student life or dean of students offices who are already engaging in counseling work with students navigating and interpreting their experiences and discoveries within their degree programs. This work may already informally be a component of faculty-student advising, and these questions could be built into that advisory and mentoring relationship. Further, institutions should explore whether the need for this work is compelling enough for these responsibilities in vocational discernment and career planning to be officially recognized as the full-time or part-time role of a member of their administrative staff, as many theological schools have done in recent years.

2. ATS, "Total School Profile: Entering Student Questionnaire."

3. ATS, "Total School Profile: Graduating Student Questionnaire."

UNPACKING THE CONCEPT OF VOCATION

Before exploring the guiding questions and suggested timeline for vocational discernment work, it is helpful to examine what "vocation" means today. This term has multiple meanings both within the Judeo-Christian tradition as well as in the secular realm. Derived from the Latin word *vocare*, meaning, "to call," religious communities have long understood this term to mean the work to which one is summoned by the divine. The earliest and still most basic understanding of this term within the Judeo-Christian community is that vocation is a summons by God to a particular task. God instructing Moses on Mt. Sinai was a means of God instructing him on vocation. Jesus' invitation to his disciples to drop everything and follow him was likewise a summons to a new way of life, or a new vocation. There are plenty of scriptural cases in both the Hebrew Bible and the New Testament where God calls individuals to a single action or to a new way of life. While these scriptural references offer a helpful foundation for theological students, this understanding of vocation is rather oversimplified and long removed from the present understanding of this concept and the strong link this term now has to the concept of career or profession.

Reformer Martin Luther offered among the greatest contributions to the Christian notion of vocation, many of which are still helpful for theological students today. As a firm believer in the equal status of clergy and laity, Luther believed that clergy were summoned by the community based on their God-given gifts and talents, and not because they possess a special relationship to God. As Gary Badcock notes in his book *The Way of Life: A Theology of Christian Vocation*, the key for Luther is that vocation, "is a theological word, which applies only to the believer; the unbeliever has an earthly office but does not embrace it in faith as calling."[4] As such, Luther emphasized how vocation can be located in any form of work, and that any job, no matter how large or small, could be seen as vocation because vocation was less about the work being performed, and more about the worker and the meaning that is ascribed to the work being done. This understanding is helpful for the growing number of current students who understand their calling to be toward a form of ministry that does not fall into a traditional category of ministerial or ordained positions that have traditionally been sought by theological school graduates.

As students at any theological school may represent a wide array of beliefs and theological positions, it is helpful to understand the concept of vocation as both a religious term as well as a secular term. While the roots

4. Badcock, *Way of Life*, 37.

of the term are in the theological community, "vocation" has come to have significant meaning and use in the secular world as well. The secular community has adopted this term to reference work that constitutes a role that has more meaning and significance than merely a "job," or something that one does simply for the purposes of financial compensation and not because they feel any sense of connection to the work being performed. Both in sacred and the secular contexts, the concept of vocation represents the search for employment that provides fulfillment and is aligned with one's values.

For religious communities, the terms "vocation" and "calling" suggest that there exists some external divine entity that is doing the calling that directs an individual toward a particular type of work. For the secular community, the same concept is utilized, although the act of summoning is attributed to something other than the divine. Bryan Dik and Ryan Duffy researched the effect of a sense of calling and vocation in work. Using a more secularized understanding of vocation that was not necessarily tied to religiosity, they developed a definition of calling as "a transcendent summons, experienced as originating beyond the self, to approach a particular life role in a manner oriented toward demonstrating or deriving a sense of purpose or meaningfulness and that holds other-oriented values and goals as primary sources of motivation."[5] Another secularized definition of calling offered by A. R. Elangovan and Craig Pinder defines calling as "a course of action in pursuit of pro-social intentions embodying the convergence of an individual's sense of what he or she would like to do, should do, and does."[6] Both of these definitions demonstrate that one of the hallmarks of the secular understanding of vocation is a sense of service to others, or selflessness, which are concepts that will also resonate with persons of faith. Interjecting these secular definitions into vocational work at theological schools is useful as it allows persons from all faith traditions and religious persuasions to insert their own particular beliefs into the definitions, while persons who may struggle with naming a tradition as their own can adopt a broader understanding.

VOCATIONAL DISCERNMENT FOR MINISTRY

Discerning a call to a vocation in the ministry is a sacred and time-honored tradition. This discernment process is paramount because, as John Neafsey notes, vocation has the potential to touch and encompass every level and dimension of our lives, including family lives, love lives, creative interests,

5. Dik and Duffy, "Calling and Vocation at Work," 424–50.

6. Elangovan et al., "Callings and Organizational Behavior," 428–40.

and politics.[7] Yet, many theological students have been falling through the cracks when it comes to finding supportive individuals and communities to help facilitate this work. As previously noted, theological schools have often been ill-equipped to do this work, and denominational bodies have likewise lacked engagement with students that are not actively pursuing ordained ministry. In her article entitled "Annunciations in Most Lives: Vocational Discernment and the Work of the Church," Kathleen H. Staudt notes how the process of ministry discernment has long been oversimplified. By prioritizing those whose call is distinctly toward ordained ministry, she points out that we have created a sense of second-class citizenship in theological education for those whose call is understood to be toward a lay or non-ordained form of ministry. While many pay lip service to other forms of ministry, Staudt points out that the question of discernment in ministry almost always begins with a question of ordination, to which there are only two answers: yes or no. If one discerns that their calling to ministry does not include ordination, the church then has very little interest in supporting the further development of this vocational discernment.[8]

One of the advantages of theological schools seeking to fill this void in vocational discernment with current students is that they already possess two of the most crucial components of this work: faculty and staff with a current understanding of professions in ministry and a community of individuals seeking to engage in discernment together. While individual counseling and mentoring are vital to the work of discernment, the importance of community cannot be understated. In seeking to establish a vocational discernment model for ministry, both the individual and the community are important in clarifying and developing this response to their unique summons. Individuals are most often not able to fully understand and clarify their call toward a ministerial profession alone because as Staudt reminds us, "Few persons, lay or ordained, hear a call from God that includes a detailed job description."[9] Rather, as Neafsey notes, authentic vocational discernment seeks a balance between inward listening to our own hearts and outward, socially-engaged listening with our hearts to the realities of the world.[10] As an inward practice, Neafsey notes the importance of learning to listen, often through such spiritual practices as prayer and meditation.[11] However, he similarly notes that in listening for the voice of vocation, we

7. Neafsey, *Sacred Voice Is Calling*, 3.

8. Staudt, "Annunciations in Most Lives," 130–43.

9. Staudt, "Annunciations in Most Lives," 136.

10. Neafsey, *Sacred Voice*, 1.

11. Neafsey, *Sacred Voice*, 10–12.

inevitably encounter a conflicting mix of voices both within ourselves and within our world that attempt to beckon us in multiple different directions. It is at this point that the Christian community becomes vital to assisting in the process of vocational discernment. As such, theological institutions would be wise to provide occasions for communities of students engaged in vocational discernment to explore the guiding questions offered in this chapter together, offering the gift of listening to one another, asking clarifying questions, and seeking wisdom together through thoughtful dialogue.

GUIDING QUESTIONS FOR VOCATIONAL DISCERNMENT AND CAREER PLANNING

Listed below are eighteen guiding questions that are divided into four "clusters," representing four important occasions within the graduate degree program for students to do important work in their process of clarifying their vocation and pursuing employment opportunities. As with any process, the questions are intended to move students through different stages of thinking through their notions of vocation and working on translating those into a career. Because theological education is such a transformative experience for students, it is not uncommon for students to move through the first one or two clusters, and then have an experience that causes them to need to revisit and revise questions that have already been worked through earlier. Students should be reminded that this does not represent failure, as the process is seldom simple and linear when engaging in ministry work, which often involves some trial and error in clarifying how natural gifts, skills, and interests connect to the work being done.

Students should be reminded that the work of vocational discernment and career planning require active participation and is not something that merely happens by attending to this work only on the four occasions noted here. Rather, it is helpful for students to think about this work as an additional course that they are always enrolled in throughout their time in school. Regularly checking in on the questions offered in the most recent cluster will encourage students to continue to attend to the questions posed and to do any accompanying "assignments" before the next cluster of questions are posed. To keep students attentive to this work, theological school professionals can create mechanisms to serve as reminders such as creating opportunities to continue to explore the questions in community, building the questions into academic advising, and offering workshops or activities that relate to discerning vocation and professional preparation. If students are attentive to working through the four clusters of guiding questions and are given both individual and communal support from their institution, students should find themselves prepared to seek employment at the conclusion of their programs.

CLUSTER 1: GUIDING QUESTIONS UPON ENTERING THEOLOGICAL EDUCATION

Guiding Questions:

1. *What are you most passionate about?*

2. *What are the jobs and/or experiences that have made you come alive?*

3. *What motivations brought you to pursue your particular graduate theological degree program?*

Taking stock and engaging in deep reflection at the very beginning of a student's graduate theological education is an important tool for later exploring how passions, skills, interests, and notions of calling evolve and shift throughout the degree program. This type of education represents a time of rapid transformation and transition for these individuals and as such, the guiding questions at the very start of the degree program offer a sense of a starting place or foundation from which concepts of vocation will further develop.

There are several opportunities to introduce these foundational questions early in the degree program. For example, these questions could be incorporated into new student orientation programming or a first-year experience seminar or course. These programs are universal at theological schools, although their design, delivery method, and duration may differ. At many schools, these programs may also provide an opportunity for students to meet in groups to share and explore these foundational questions that encourage the student's ability to articulate their reasons for pursuing their particular degree program and how those reasons relate to their stated passions and prior significant experiences.

CLUSTER 2: INITIAL ASSESSMENT AT THE CONCLUSION OF YEAR ONE

Guiding Questions:

1. *How have your notions of call and vocation been changed, strengthened, or expanded after your first year of theological education?*

2. *What do you believe to be your strongest gifts, skills, and talents?*

3. *What have others remarked are your best gifts and abilities?*

4. *What are those activities you really enjoy, but feel are areas where you could use some further growth and development?*

5. *What spiritual practices (prayer, meditation, journaling, etc.) have you incorporated into your discernment process?*

The conclusion of the first year of study presents an opportune time for students to do an initial assessment of their skills, gifts, and talents, and to do some reflection of how a year of theological education has strengthened, shifted, or transformed their initial notions of vocation from when they began their programs. An added benefit of assessing the student's skill set at this particular juncture is that it can provide helpful information when discerning field education and internship placements and the skills to be honed and refined through these types of experiences. Finally, this second occasion for asking guiding questions is a good moment to remind students to incorporate their preferred spiritual practices into their process of vocational discernment—prayer, meditation, holy listening, clearness committees, journaling, etc. These practices provide students with an opportunity to listen to their own inner wisdom and to listen for the voice of the divine as they further discern how vocation is unfolding throughout their education journey.

CLUSTER 3: BEGINNING THE FINAL YEAR OF STUDY

Guiding Questions:

1. *What types of positions will you be eligible for upon completion of your theological degree?*

2. *Which of the professional opportunities you have explored feels like the best fit for you when considering your vocational calling, experiences, and natural gifts?*

3. *Are there additional requirements or steps that can be taken that will make you more competitive for these types of professional positions following graduation?*

4. *Have you located some organizations and/ or institutions that you would be interested in working with, and if so, have you engaged in conversation with individuals at those locations to learn more about employment opportunities?*

Whether students are in a two-year or three-year course of study, the beginning of the final year is an important time to help students to begin thinking concretely about how notions of vocation translate into professional careers that they should be exploring. The guiding questions for this stage in the degree program ask students to move from a place of broadly naming vocational interests and skills while cultivating possibilities for professions to narrowing down to actual career fields and professional positions that they may explore in depth and prepare to pursue. These questions encourage students to examine what positions they are qualified to apply for with the completion of theological degree, and whether there are any additional steps to be taken to prepare for a desired profession. For example, a student that has discerned an interest in pursuing a position in the field of chaplaincy may discover that the completion of Clinical Pastoral Education will best position them as an applicant for chaplain positions. Students may also determine that the final year of study offers an opportunity to gain some professional experience most closely aligned with the career path that they wish to pursue, either through internships, part-time work, or other possibilities.

At this point, students should be advised to narrow down their list of vocational possibilities to a handful of professional positions, perhaps two or three, that can be explored deeply. Another consideration is whether the student will be conducting job searches that are geographically bound to a city or region, or whether they will be open to pursuing opportunities in multiple locations. If a student's search is centered on a city or small region, it is helpful to encourage them to be open to a larger number of professional positions than if they were able to relocate to where the ideal position may be found. Finally, the final question in this cluster encourages students to begin networking before they are actively applying for positions. Theological schools are in a position to be supportive of these networking efforts through connecting students with various alumni and professionals in the community that have personal and professional ties to the institution.

CLUSTER 4: BEGINNING THE FINAL SEMESTER

Guiding Questions:

1. *Which of the professions you have explored do you have the most confidence in pursuing?*

2. *Considering your professional opportunities following graduation, which feels like the best fit for the lifestyle that you envision and require (i.e., salary, work hours, travel, professional setting, etc.)?*

3. *Are your application materials such as resume/ CV and cover letter updated and ready to be sent out to prospective employers?*

4. *Are you regularly looking at websites to view available positions?*

5. *Do you feel confident in your interviewing skills, or would you benefit from some practice or mock interview sessions? Why or why not?*

6. *Have you determined the salary that you would require in order to manage your expenses?*

The beginning of the final semester of study is the best opportunity to connect with students about their job search strategy and application materials. By this point, students should have a sense of two or three types of professional positions that they have researched and are interested in pursuing. The questions in this cluster ask the student to articulate the specific positions they intend to pursue, their strategy for applying for these positions, and whether or not their application materials and interviewing skills are updated and polished. Additionally, students should be reminded to consider their compensation needs in relation to their cost of living and any student debt incurred that will need to be repaid.

As a best practice, theological institutions should have resources and at least one individual tasked with assisting students in writing curriculum vitae and/or resumes and cover letters, and to help students to refine their interviewing skills. If there is not someone at the school able to be tasked with this important work, the school should have connections with professionals in the community who can support students with these items. Many theological students will require assistance creating or updating their application materials and refining how they articulate the value of their theological degree for the particular positions being sought.

SUMMARY GUIDANCE

When offering vocational discernment and career planning support for students, theological schools must also acknowledge that not all individuals are considered equal in the eyes of the Christian community. Some students are also members of populations for whom professional ministerial opportunities toward which they feel led are not an option for them to pursue. Two of the most historically marginalized groups in ministry are women and those who identify as lesbian, gay, bisexual, transgender, or queer (LGBTQ). The disadvantaged position these individuals have historically held within the Christian tradition and ministerial professions means that vocational discernment may be a slightly different process that is in part based on the availability of employment opportunities that will not conflict with their identities.

Both faculty and staff at theological schools are aware that many students lack an understanding of the importance of doing the work of vocational discernment and career planning throughout their degree program. In fact, those students who are most in need of assistance for this work seldom seek out help from the institutional resources offered. Rather, students often choose to focus on their academic studies and other co-curricular experiences and fail to make time for the important work described in this chapter. As such, these guiding questions may need to be required and embedded within the regular offerings of the school in order to ensure students will engage with them at the times noted.

It can be argued that the value of a theological education has never been greater considering the wide array of professional opportunities that exist for graduates. At the same time, this same diversity of career possibilities means that vocational discernment for current theological students has never been more complex. Institutions must partner with students in this work in order to ensure that graduates are strongly-positioned to find employment quickly and to secure positions that are well-aligned with their natural gifts and skills and a sense of divine purpose. Through a combination of individual counseling and mentoring and discerning in community, students can gain confidence in understanding their unique calling to the professions of ministry. The future of theological education depends on this partnership, and requires an institutional commitment to supporting vocational discernment and career planning efforts throughout the educational program of students.

BIBLIOGRAPHY

Association of Theological Schools (ATS). "Total School Profile: Entering Student Questionnaire 2017–2018." Online. http://www.ats.edu/uploads/resources/student-data/documents/total-school-profiles/esq-total-school-profile-2017–2018.pdf.

————. "Total School Profile: Graduating Student Questionnaire 2017–2018." Online. http://www.ats.edu/uploads/resources/student-data/documents/total-school-profiles/esq-total-school-profile-2017–2018.pdf.

Badcock, Gary D. *The Way of Life: A Theology of Christian Vocation*. Grand Rapids: Eerdmans, 1998.

Dik, Bryan J., and Ryan D. Duffy. "Calling and Vocation at Work: Definitions and Prospects for Research and Practice." *The Counseling Psychologist* 37 (2009) 424–50.

Elangovan, A. R., et al. "Callings and Organizational Behavior." *Journal of Vocational Behavior* 76 (2010) 428–40.

Neafsey, John. *A Sacred Voice Is Calling: Personal Vocation and Social Conscience*. Maryknoll, NY: Orbis, 2006.

Staudt, Kathleen Henderson. "Annunciations in Most Lives: Vocational Discernment and the Work of the Church." *Sewanee Theological Review* 43.2 (2000) 130–43.

Wheeler, Barbara G., et al. *How Are We Doing? The Effectiveness of Theological Schools as Measured by the Vocations and Views of Graduates*. Auburn Studies 13. New York: Auburn Theological Seminary, 2007.

CHAPTER 16

Transforming Economic Challenges and Student Financial Well-Being

KRISTEN P. BENTLEY,
CHARISSE L. GILLETT,
and WINDY KIDD

ACCORDING TO RESEARCH ON the well-lived pastoral life in the *Flourishing in Ministry* Project conducted by Matt Bloom, financial well-being is an important dimension of overall well-being in ministry. Bloom reports, "As one pastor explained it, finances represent a 'theological challenge' for pastors. Their calling was to serve God and the church, so on one hand they believe that finances should in no way influence their work or life. On the other hand, financial needs and problems are very real in their lives."[1] As students enroll in seminary and prepare for ministry, they also face very real financial needs and problems. Some of the economic challenges students face are due to the cost of theological education itself as well as the kinds of resources they have to pay for seminary; some of the challenges also relate to the way students think and behave regarding money within the twenty-first-century North American consumer-oriented culture.

Providing support for students to make well-informed, thoughtful decisions about how to finance their theological education and strengthen their financial well-being is important work for student services professionals. It attends to both institutional and student interests. Developing a support

---

1. Bloom, "Well-Lived Pastoral Life," 3.

system includes helping students make decisions concerning student loans, smoothing the pathway for them to manage financial challenges while enrolled (whether they borrow or not), and encouraging habits and attitudes that will serve them well in ministry. The economic challenges students face are varied and complex; they call for collaborative work. In this chapter we touch on various avenues that financial aid officers and other educational leaders may take to help theological students find paths that allow them to pursue educational goals without sacrificing financial well-being.

FACTORS CONTRIBUTING TO STUDENT INDEBTEDNESS

The factors contributing to indebtedness among seminary students are complex. The problem is not limited to the expenses associated with theological education or the borrowing decisions seminary students make while pursuing theological education. It is complicated by the amount of educational debt students carry with them from previous education, the responsibilities they may have as family members, and the personal assets and resources available to them during seminary. More complications emerge from the powerful influences of a consumer-oriented, debt-friendly, cultural environment where it is tempting to borrow and relatively easy to obtain student loans. Student loans require no collateral, but they also cannot be discharged in bankruptcy. Further, some students may not have fully taken into consideration the real cost of repayment once they graduate and begin serving in ministry. They may not have estimated how much they will earn once employed or how much loan repayment will impact their future income. The problem of student debt for those pursuing theological education has complexities that are systemic in nature; in 2005 it was rightfully called a "gathering storm."[2]

Students preparing for congregational ministry are also directly affected by the economic challenges congregations face when seeking to fund ministry and provide adequate compensation and benefits for those they employ as ministers. Low compensation packages for ministers as well as inadequate financial literacy and management skills among congregations and ministers decrease the probability of vital and sustainable congregational ministry.

The challenges students face are intertwined with changes in support for theological education within the larger context. The past decades have shown changing patterns of philanthropic and denominational support for

2. Ruger et al., *Gathering Storm*, 1.

theological education.[3] Once there was a pervasive sense that paying for seminary was an investment made by the church in its own future ministerial leadership, and resources were available to do that. Theological schools received broad support from congregations and denominations. Scholarships and other forms of support were available for many students training to become ministers. However, the situation shifted over the past few decades; it no longer reflects that reality.

In addition, it seems at the same time costs associated with theological education have risen and resources within congregations and denominations have fallen, the understanding of who is responsible for paying for seminary has changed. In the current context, there is now a sense that theological education is primarily an investment made by students in the context of their professional advancement. Not only is paying for seminary seen as individual students' responsibility, but even churches and denominations that want to invest may not have the means to make much of a dent in the cost of a seminary education. However this came about, the result is that today's theological students have fewer resources of financial support than once was available.

FINANCIAL COUNSELING AND STUDENT LOAN DECISIONS

Schools can help students face these varied economic challenges by offering financial counseling. At one time, best practices helped students find the maximum loan eligibility available. However, it has become clear burdensome student debt impacts the lives of graduates for many years later. Student loan decisions need to be well-informed and loans undertaken with careful thought. When institutions provide financial counseling that helps students make responsible decisions about borrowing (in addition to the required FAFSA counseling), student financial is both meeting the needs of individual students and ensuring that receiving the aid also is a "part of the student's learning experience."[4]

Financial counseling can help students look at their financial circumstances and make thoughtful decisions about loans so that they find ways to borrow less, if possible. Students entering the borrowing process through the Federal Financial Aid program are required to complete financial counseling, which is often conducted through an online module[5] when filling out

3. Ruger and Meinzer, *Through Toil & Tribulation*, 14–17.

4. Dannells, "Financial Aid," 57.

5. Anderson, "Student Loan Counseling."

the FAFSA. The required counseling process ensures they understand the financial loan process, but it does not spur them to ask, "Should I borrow this $___ amount?" Offering additional counseling sessions that include targeted conversations with specific action steps help students make incremental changes; they can be an important part of helping students finance their education and also move toward financial well-being. Schools can help support students' decisions by providing a process with financial planning resources that support targeted conversations and prompt action. Some of these resources include:

- Student household budgets, worksheets, or other interactive tools that ask students to look at their current income and expenditures. When students recognize their actual financial situation they are enabled to figure out how to live as a student.

- *Exemplars* or stories of what other students have done that help students envision alternatives and motivate them to take action. When students hear stories of others who have successfully completed theological school with less financial stress and only manageable debt, they can envision how they might do the same.[6]

- Post-graduation budgets, worksheets, or other interactive tools that ask students to estimate their post-graduation income and expenses, including the cost of loan repayment. When students think long-term and consider what future compensation and loan repayment might look like after seminary, they make well-informed decisions.

- Student loan payment calculators (widely available on the Internet at this time) that allow students to quickly calculate how much their monthly loan payments would be as they think about how much they should borrow.

- Up-to-date information about varied sources of financial support that offers students guidance in pursuing alternatives to student loans. While fewer resources are available for today's students than in the past, many congregations, denominations, and other institutions and organizations still have scholarships and grants available to theological students, especially those who are preparing for congregational ministry.

---

6. Stories and examples that reflect the diversity of people and perspectives within theological schools increase the likelihood that students find something that resonates with their own experience.

Financial planning resources such as these help students slow down, take time to analyze their needs, explore their options, and resist the impulse to reach first for student loans.

FINANCIAL COUNSELING OUTCOMES

Lexington Theological Seminary (LTS) has conducted one-on-one financial counseling since 2015 with students preparing to borrow through the Federal Financial Aid program. The director of financial aid conducts counseling that is informed by the students' engagement with three financial-planning resources—an interactive student household budget; the video "Student Loans and Seminary Costs: How to Keep from Mortgaging your Future" produced by Auburn Theological Seminary,[7] and an interactive post-graduation budget. All are fully accessible on the LTS website alongside a description of the counseling process. It is up to the students to initiate conversations about borrowing when they are admitted; the director of financial aid does not assume students are interested in taking out loans.[8] The financial counseling process begins with students' initial contact with the director of financial aid, followed by a one-on-one conversation and explanation of the counseling process, independent engagement by students with the financial planning resources, and a one-on-one conversation prior to students requesting student loans.

The experience at LTS reflects that of many other schools and indicates that financial counseling can provide the kind of guidance for students that leads to improved outcomes (though not predictable) for both students and institutions. The LTS director of financial aid has been encouraged—both the average amount of student debt of graduates who borrow and the percentage of graduates who have borrowed have declined. The average amount of federal aid debt of those LTS graduates who borrow has decreased from $32,457 in 2014 to $22,788 in 2018. This is shown in the chart below.

---

7. Auburn Seminary, "Student Loans and Seminary Costs," presents the stories of actual students and decisions they make about borrowing while in seminary. Three stories narrate how students made it through seminary and funded their education without burdensome debt while the fourth story delivers a warning about the burden of heavy debt for a student's life and ministry after graduation.

8. In the 2017–18 academic year, LTS processed just under $50,000 in federal student loans with only 15 percent of eligible students taking out student loans. That same year, the average loan amount for LTS students was $3,682.

Average Student Debt of LTS Graduates Who Borrow, 2014-2018

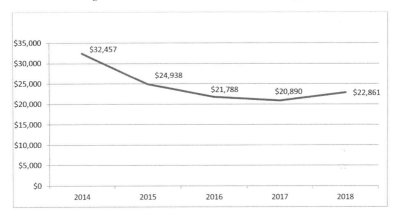

In the same time span, the percentage of graduating students who have taken out federal student loans also has declined from 42.86 percent in 2014 to 17.8 percent in 2018. This is shown in the chart below.

Percent of LTS Graduates Who Borrow, 2014-2018

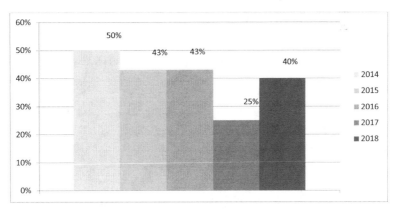

The director of financial aid and other LTS administrators believe the financial counseling process put in place in 2015 has contributed to the improved data regarding student loans. However, they also attribute the improvement to other changes at LTS that reduce the cost of theological education and help students successfully fund their education and manage their finances during enrollment. A particularly important policy decision at LTS was to recalculate the "cost of living" in connection with the "cost of attendance" for student loans when LTS adopted its new educational model. In the new model, students only come to the Lexington campus for face-to-face coursework during January and June Intensives. Therefore, the "cost of living" is only included in "cost of attendance" when students are enrolled in Intensives. This policy shift impacts the way students calculate expenses related to LTS enrollment.

COUNSELING SCENARIOS WITH STUDENTS WHO PLAN TO BORROW

The financial counseling experience at LTS has shown that students who engage in the counseling process do so at varying levels. Some see it as an obstacle to borrowing; others approach the process as an opportunity to learn. For instance, in 2015, three newly enrolled students participated in the financial counseling process at LTS and responded in three very different ways.

- Student 1: This student who was entering the MDiv program completed all the steps in the counseling process, including engagement with the three resources, with minimal involvement. This student quickly completed all the steps and did not indicate it was helpful in any way or that it impacted decisions about borrowing. This student borrowed the maximum amount available.

- Student 2: This student began the counseling process with plans to borrow a large amount to finance enrollment in the MDiv program. This student went through the counseling process and engaged fully with the resources. Afterwards, this student even sent an unsolicited email to the director of financial aid, expressing gratitude for a "thoughtful and responsible approach to financing graduate education." As a result of the counseling process, this student decided to borrow at a minimal level, taking out a loan for only enough to partially cover tuition expenses.

- Student 3: This student entered the counseling process with plans to borrow a large amount to pay for expenses associated with enrolling in the MDiv program. While working on the post-graduation budget, the student concluded the plans to borrow were unaffordable. As a result, this student altered academic plans, enrolled with a smaller course load, and decided not to borrow.[9]

9. In 2015, this student shifted plans from enrollment in the MDiv program (76 credit hours) to the Certificate of Pastoral Ministry program (24 credit hours). The Certificate programs at LTS offer options for many students preparing for ministry who do not wish to pursue the MDiv degree. Experience at LTS indicates the Certificate of

Although financial counseling encourages students to slow down and analyze their financial circumstances, it does not guarantee students will make responsible decisions nor does it lead to predictable outcomes.

It would be beneficial to reflect on the third student scenario described above. Financial counseling needs to attend to both institutional and student interests to be truly effective. This third scenario highlights the reality that some students who go through a financial counseling process may decide they cannot pursue their plans for enrollment. It shows student and institutional interests do not always run in a parallel direction. However, as Miller, Early, and Ruger state, "If graduates trained in theological institutions are unable to pursue their calling because of educational debt, then schools have failed to steward the institutions' resources or accomplish their mission."[10] Practices that lead to the enrollment of students unprepared for the financial challenges of theological education serve neither institutional or student interests. Such students are more likely to drop out of seminary, default on loans, and/or enter ministry with serious financial obligations that damage the possibility of well-being in ministry. For students such as the third one described above, a financial counseling process impels them to attend to problems before they have obligated themselves to educational expenses and/or loans and thus increases the likelihood of their eventual successful graduation. Seminaries providing such support for students show a level of care can lead to strengthened relationships of trust between students and institutions.

POLICIES AND PRACTICES SUPPORTING STUDENT MANAGEMENT OF EDUCATIONAL EXPENSES

Whether students borrow or not, it is challenging for them to meet the obligations of their education. Financial counseling alone cannot smooth the path for them nor can it solve students' problems associated with paying for seminary. Institutional leaders who wish to help students manage the cost of theological education are wise to critically assess established policies and practices in order to better support students and mitigate problems that arise. Seminary policies and practices provide a structure (for good or ill) that often delineate the paths students take to finance their education.

Pastoral Ministry program also serves as a "stepping stone" for some students into the MDiv program. In the graduating class of 2019, 60 percent of the Certificate of Pastoral Ministry graduates are continuing their enrollment and entering the MDiv program.

10. Miller et al., *Taming the Tempest*, 3.

Some of the challenges students face are routine, such as managing their cash flow; others emerge seasonally or in times of crisis. Schools can establish policies that offer students options so they can meet expenses and make a way through. Such policies include tuition payment plans that allow students to make monthly payments, "no interest" payment plans that allow them to spread out tuition payments when needed, and student emergency loans for smaller amounts in order to help students when they encounter sudden financial obstacles.

Other helpful policies in place at some schools are those that help students maintain, or obtain, sources of income that help fund their education. A recent survey of seminary graduates shows students receive financial support from a variety of sources to pay for their education, including scholarships and grants, employment income, spouses' employment income, savings, family support, as well as by raising funds for their education.[11] Income from employment is important for many students, some of whom also report they are bi-vocational ministers while students. Many seminaries are aware that students' employment income, as well as that of others in their household, are important financial resources for students, and some schools have initiated institutional changes to better accommodate students who are employed.

Employment friendly policies provide flexibility that allow students to fit coursework around their schedules at work. Some schools are offering courses on weekends or in evenings and some distance courses. Some also are reviewing the way they structure academic schedules, academic requirements, and how coursework is delivered, possibly allowing them to remain where they live and work while enrolled, thereby avoiding the cost in time and money of relocating for seminary.[12] Although these types of institutional changes may not be options for some schools, when leaders collect data about student debt and student demographics and use it to assess established policies and practices, it can help them to form strategies that could reduce barriers for students who are employed while going to seminary.

Some factors are outside the control of seminary leaders, including changes in investment markets, changes in patterns of student enrollment, and declining denominational support for theological education.[13] Current realities for theological schools include variables that can make decision-making difficult. This means theological schools need to stay current with

11. ATS, "Total School Profile."

12. Ruger and Meinzer, *Through Toil & Tribulation*, 5–8.

13. Ruger and Meinzer, *Through Toil & Tribulation*, 14–17.

internal and external factors that impact their capacity to address financial challenges and effectively engage their mission.

RESOURCES FOR STUDENT FINANCIAL WELL-BEING IN MINISTRY

Developing a support system for students' financial well-being moves beyond helping students make thoughtful decisions about loans and/or managing how to pay for seminary. It also involves helping students form and strengthen habits concerning money that will serve them well in ministry. It involves creating a climate where financial responsibility is taken seriously and where the development of financial literacy skills, such as planning and budgeting, is valued and where students reflect upon the meaning of money in their lives and ministry.

Some schools are now offering required course in their academic curriculum (as well as electives) that address financial literacy and stewardship. This practice is an effective way to help students develop a strong sense of the meaning and practice of stewardship within the church and to strengthen their own habits and skills concerning money. Adding courses such as these to the academic curriculum (especially when they are required) by seminaries communicates the importance of financial well-being to students.

Through involvement in the Lilly Endowment Inc. Initiative, the *Economic Challenges Facing Future Ministers*, coordinated by the Association of Theological Schools, a number of schools developed and shared resources and tools that they are using to assist students with improving financial literacy and financial management skills.

Provision of resources can also help students deepen their own understanding of the role of money in their lives. As Nathan Dungan states, "when it comes to developing healthy money habits, words are just as important as actions. Words provide the context for all the money choices we make, and they can help us see why and how we make those choices."[14] Even lunch table conversations and book discussions may stir thought-provoking exchanges regarding the challenges that students, ministers, and congregations face when it comes to economic challenges and financial well-being. For students preparing for ministry, their own personal financial well-being is tantamount, as is the way they model and nurture financial well-being within their ministry.

14. Dungan, *Money Sanity Solutions*, 2.

CONCLUSION

This chapter began with a statement that finances represent a theological challenge for ministers while also emphasizing the importance of financial well-being to overall well-being in ministry.[15] Helping seminary students with the theological challenge of finances and supporting them to find paths toward financial well-being is important work. Seminary financial practices and policies can make a transformative difference, even in the midst of complex economic challenges for theological students.

BIBLIOGRAPHY

Anderson, Somer, and J. D. Solomon. "Student Loan Counseling: Time for a Refresh." *University Business*, March 21, 2019. Online. http://universitybusiness.com/student-loan-counseling-time-for-a-refresh.

Association of Theological Schools (ATS). "Total School Profile: Graduating Student Questionnaire 2016–2017." Online. http://www.ats.edu/uploads/resources/student-data/documents/total-school-profiles/gsq-total-school-profile-2016–2017.pdf.

Auburn Seminary. "Student Loans and Seminary Costs: How to Keep from Mortgaging Your Future." December 29, 2011. Vimeo video, 29:55. https://vimeo.com/34319045.

Bloom, Matt. "The Well-Lived Pastoral Life: Summary of Results from the Initial Study." *Flourishing in Ministry Project* (Summer 2010). Online. https://www.ats.edu/uploads/resources/current-initiatives/economic-challenges-facing-future-ministers/financial-issues-research/bloom-well-being.pdf.

Dannells, Michael. "Financial Aid." In *College Student Personnel Services*, edited by William Packwood, 51–101. Springfield, IL: Charles C. Thomas.

Dungan, Nathan, *Money Sanity Solutions*, Minneapolis: Shave Save Spend, 2010.

Miller, Sharon L., et al. *Taming the Tempest: A Team Approach to Reducing and Managing Student Debt*. Auburn Studies 10. New York: Auburn Theological Seminary, 2014.

Ruger, Anthony, and Chris Meinzer. *Through Toil & Tribulation: Financing Theological Education, 2001–2011*. Auburn Studies 18. New York: Auburn Theological Seminary, 2014.

Ruger, Anthony, et al. *The Gathering Storm: The Educational Debt of Theological Students*. Auburn Studies 12. New York: Auburn Theological Seminary, 2005.

15. Bloom, "Well-Lived Pastoral Life," 3.

Afterword
Diversities. Lead. Change.

FRANK M. YAMADA
Executive Director
The Association of Theological Schools
and the Commission on Accrediting

THE THREE WORDS IN my subtitle for this afterword—diversities, lead, change—point to important themes that emerge frequently in gatherings among the Association of Theological Schools (ATS). As well, like many contemporary marketing slogans, these three distinct words make up a larger sentence that rings true for the work of student personnel administrators. Diversities lead change. It is a well-established in higher education that diverse institutions are more effective institutions. Moreover, diverse institutions are, in my experience, also able to lean more adaptively into the changing environments that schools are facing in the twenty-first century. The current volume represents the diverse perspectives of leaders who are responding to the changing landscape of theological education. In this way, the volume already makes a substantial contribution to those who are interested in the best practices and adaptive work needed to transform theological schools in this period of significant change.

ATS, as a graduate school member organization and accrediting body, represents a diversity of diversities. ATS schools are diverse in terms of their ecclesial families, the membership being comprised of North American schools from the three major ecclesial families of Christianity—Evangelical Protestant, Mainline Protestant, and Roman Catholic and Orthodox. ATS student bodies are also growing dramatically in their diversity. Ten years ago, African American, Latino/a, and Asian North

American students made up just over a third and white, Euro-American students about two-thirds of the overall student population in theological schools. In 2018, racial/ethnic students comprise about 43 percent of ATS students. Demographers have projected that, by the year 2040, the United States population will not have a racial/ethnic majority. If that is the case, ATS schools, at their current pace, will have 2040 demographic realities among their students decades earlier than the broader population in North America. ATS schools are also diverse in their size, organizational models, and educational delivery. In fact, in a recent publication, Dan Aleshire, the former executive director of ATS, was attributed with the idea that theological education is "not moving from one model of theological education to another, but from one model to *many* others."[1]

The writers of these essays—in the schools where they serve, in their theological traditions, in their demographics, and in the various roles that they occupy—display the diversity that characterizes ATS member schools. The Association gathers administrative and faculty leaders for professional development every year. Among the administrators, by far, the most diverse group is the Student Personnel Administrators' Network or SPAN. The authors of this volume are leaders at their respective school, and leaders among their peers within SPAN. They are a diverse set of leaders, and they lead in their diversities.

In higher education, no one area or department has gone through as much significant change as the area commonly known as student services. Staff positions include enrollment management, recruiting, admissions, financial aid, student support, student employment services, community life, and in theological schools, student formation and development. To compile a set of essays to resource this important group of educational professionals is a substantial accomplishment given the diverse nature of this field. Most importantly, it is among this group of administrators, where the heart of a school's mission, its students, is worked out. Thus, these essays represent where diversity is changing the most, and is, therefore, a critical entry point into how theological schools are changing and addressing the changing landscape of North American religion.

Within this central point of a school's educational mission—its work with students—this group of administrators are able to provide a unique perspective on leadership in theological education. Because they serve students, they lead from the ground up. Because their departments serve a variety of functions within a student's life cycle, SPAN leaders are collaborative by nature. Because their work supports the educational journey of students,

1. Smith et al., "Special Issue," 9.

they are able to see the larger picture while also paying attention to the fine details. This overdue volume is packed with wisdom that adds substantially to the literature on leadership in higher education generally and theological education specifically. I am grateful to the contributors not only for outlining contemporary issues related to the work of student services but for being leaders in the transformation of student affairs in theological education and within their institutions. This volume represents the collective wisdom that results when diversities lead change, when leaders work at the center of mission, even when the structures of that mission are uncertain and dynamic. Toni Morrison, the Nobel laureate author and poet, who died days before this afterward was written, sums up best the form of leadership required in theological education "for such a time as this" (Esth 4:14):

> Don't make choices based only on your security and your safety. Nothing is safe. That is not to say that anything ever was, or that anything worth achieving ever should be. Things of value seldom are. It is not safe to have a child. It is not safe to challenge the status quo. It is not safe to choose work that has not been done before. Or to do old work in a new way. There will always be someone there to stop you.
>
> But in pursuing your highest ambitions, don't let your personal safety diminish the safety of your stepsister. In wielding the power that is deservedly yours, don't permit it to enslave your stepsisters. Let your might and your power emanate from that place in you that is nurturing and caring.[2]

BIBLIOGRAPHY

Morrison, Toni. "Cinderella's Stepsisters." Commencement address delivered at Barnard College, May 1979.
Smith, Ted A., et al. "A Special Issue with Essays from Theological Education Between the Times." *Theological Education* 51.2 (2018) 9.

2. Morrison, "Cinderella's Stepsisters."

Contributors

C. Mark Batten, former Assistant Dean of Admissions and Strategic Communications at Wake Forest University School of Divinity.

Kristen P. Bentley, Project Director for Conversations on Stewardship & Finances at Lexington Theological Seminary.

Donna Foley, former Associate Dean of Students at Franciscan School of Theology at the University of San Diego.

Charisse L. Gillett, EdD, President at Lexington Theological Seminary.

Shelly E. Hart, Director of Academic Administration and Registrar at Candler School of Theology, Emory University.

Shonda R. Jones, EdD, Senior Associate Dean, Strategic Initiatives and Integrative Learning, and Assistant Teaching Professor in Intercultural Theological Education at Wake Forest University School of Divinity.

Anastasia E. B. Kidd, DMin, Director of Enrollment at Boston University School of Theology.

Windy Kidd, Registrar and Director of Financial Aid at Lexington Theological Seminary.

Reid A. Kisling, PhD, Vice-President of Student Development/Chief Information and Effectiveness Officer at Western Seminary.

Lillian Hallstrand Lammers, DMin, Director of Stewardship and Vocational Planning at Vanderbilt Divinity School.

Pamela R. Lightsey, PhD, Vice President for Academic and Student Affairs and Associate Professor of Constructive Theology at Meadville Lombard Theological School.

Alexandria Hofmann Macias, Director of Seminary Academic Programming at North Park Theological Seminary.

Vince McGlothin-Eller, former Director of Academic Studies and Registrar at Garrett-Evangelical Theological Seminary.

Graham McKeague, PhD, Dean of Human Services and Associate Professor of Educational Leadership at Cornerstone University.

Adam J. Poluzzi, PhD, Assistant Vice Provost for Graduate Enrollment Management at Boston College and former Associate Dean of Enrollment Management in the School of Theology and Ministry at Boston College.

Jo Ann Sharkey Reinowski, Director of Academic Services at George W. Truett Theological Seminary, Baylor University.

Katherine H. Smith, Associate Dean for Strategic Initiatives at Duke Divinity School and former Assistant Dean for Admissions, Vocation, and Stewardship at Vanderbilt Divinity School.

Joanne Solis-Walker, PhD, Partner & Theological Education Consultant at CaminoRoad and former Assistant Dean of Global Theological Education at Wesley Seminary at Indiana Wesleyan University.

Amy E. Steele, PhD, Assistant Dean for Student Affairs and Community Life at Vanderbilt Divinity School.

Ashley Nichols VanBemmelen, Director of Admissions at Grand Rapids Theological Seminary, Cornerstone University.

Yvette D. Wilson-Barnes, JD, EdD, Associate Dean of Student Affairs at CUNY School of Law and former Associate Dean of Student Affairs at Union Theological Seminary.

Frank M. Yamada, Executive Director of the Association of Theological Schools and the Commission on Accrediting.